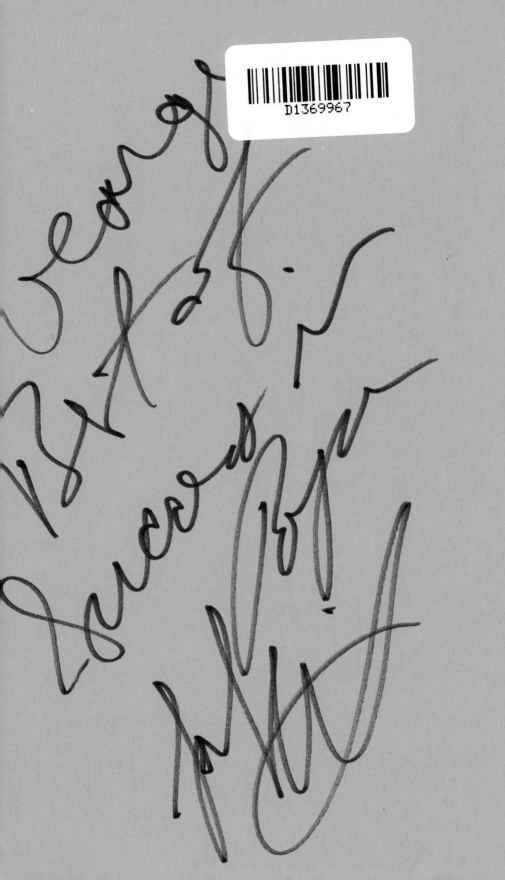

THE
STEFANCHIK
METHOD

The STEFANCHIK METHOD

Earn $10,000 a Month for the Rest of Your Life—in Your Spare Time

John Stefanchik

William Morrow and Company, Inc.
New York

It is the policy of William Morrow and Company, Inc., and its imprints and affiliates, recognizing the importance of preserving what has been written, to print the books we publish on acid-free paper, and we exert our best efforts to that end.

Library of Congress Cataloging-in-Publication Data

Stefanchik, John.
    The Stefanchik method : earn $10,000 a month for the rest of your
life—in your spare time / John Stefanchik.
        p. cm.
    Includes index.
    ISBN 0-688-12741-X
    1. Discounted mortgages—United States.   2. Deeds of trust—United
States.   3. Secondary mortgage market—United States.   I. Title.
    HG5095.S73   1994
    332.63'244—dc20   93-46111
                                                                        CIP

Printed in the United States of America

First Edition

1   2   3   4   5   6   7   8   9   10

BOOK DESIGN BY CIRCA 86, INC.

I would like to dedicate this book to some very special people in my life.

To my parents who always gave me the very best they could.

To Ricki for her friendship, devotion, and ability to stick it out with me through all the tough times.

To Heidi who came into to my life and opened up a new dimension for me—a family. She has stood by my side to be a special friend as well as a wonderful wife.

"The faster you make my system work, the faster you'll get to wealth and financial freedom. There are very few programs that are a sure bet to financial security and financial independence. I know that this is one of them.

"It has taken me a long time to realize how powerful this program is. My primary message in this book is to urge you to get involved with paper.

"Do it *now!*"

—John Stefanchik

Contents

THE
STEFANCHIK
METHOD

Introduction

I buy paper.

I'm not talking about wallpaper, computer paper, toilet paper, or recycled paper.

I buy a very special kind of paper.

I buy paper that has mortgage, trust deed, real estate contract, and contract for deed written on it.

That is how I make my living.

That's how you, too, can make your living.

It's a very good living.

Paper is a financial term referring to the legal documents committing and/or formalizing a loan secured by property. Paper confers on its owner the right to collect the amount of the loan in payments at intervals over the period of time stated in the note. If payments are not made, the loan documents give the holder the right to take the property that secures the loan (foreclose), and keep it or sell it to get his or her cash back. The property can be anything of value that someone has chosen to lend money on.

The only kinds of paper I buy are personally held mortgage notes or trust deeds with some kind of real estate as collateral.

I'm not talking about paper secured by cars, cameras, furniture, appliances, or small personal possessions. I am not talking about real estate mortgages or trust deeds held by banks, S&Ls, or other financial institutions. That's an entirely different market.

The collateral for a personally held mortgage or trust deed can be a single-family home, an apartment building, commercial property, or even a piece of land. If it's secured by real estate, I'm interested in buying it.

Being interested in buying does not, of course, mean *actually* buying. I buy only when I can get paper at a discount that guarantees me a profit. I buy only when the property fits criteria that make the paper a safe investment.

When you understand the opportunities available in buying and selling paper, you'll be interested in purchasing and flipping (reselling) this kind of paper, too.

Paper is an excellent way to make money, part-time or full-time, using little if any of your own money. If you have your own funds, you can choose to use them or not. Buying and selling paper is a purely entrepreneurial opportunity. In *The Stefanchik Method* I'll show you how to create a way of making money by identifying and working a small niche in a major business.

The Stefanchik Method of buying paper is exactly the kind of business that creates major profits by working a small niche. It's an entrepreneurial endeavor that takes advantage of a niche in the vast business of buying and selling mortgages and trust deeds, focusing on personally held mortgages instead of the mortgages and trust deeds of banks and S&Ls.

Who is an entrepreneur? Can you be one?

An entrepreneur is someone who does not *wait* for something to happen; he or she takes the actions that *make* something happen. If you take action, you can make things happen. If you wait for things to happen, they won't. And, if you're willing to take actions that make things happen, you're an entrepreneur.

How Do I Make Profits on Paper?

When I buy paper, I don't pay the face value of the mortgage note. Buying for less than the face value is called buying at a discount. You may have encountered a term like "discounted mortgages" and wondered what it meant.

This is it.

If you can't buy at a discount, there's no profit and no reason to buy. The Stefanchik Method is about how to find and buy discounted paper.

You can invest in paper from an office or out of your own home, even from your kitchen table, so long as you have the desire to change your life.

The Stefanchik Method offers a clear plan that has worked for many people who have followed it step by step. Because it is a precise strategy, it eliminates the hassles of "What do I do next?" Lack of an answer to that question has prevented many people from achieving success in many fields.

The major obstacle to your success—where to find the money to purchase the paper—is taken care of for you by my company, S.E.S. Funding Corporation, or other sources like it. We will buy the paper you find provided that it meets our standards.

You, however, must provide two key elements of success that neither I nor anyone else can give you in a book: the effort to do it and the desire to change your life forever. You must focus these key elements of success into a plan of action that works for you. That's what the Stefanchik Method is all about.

In this book I will give you a blueprint to use and the tools to begin. It's up to you to understand the plan, to use these tools constructively to build your successful future. And you can.

Why Is Paper a Good Investment?

In my business I do a lot of traveling. Every time I'm on a plane, the person sitting next to me invariably asks what business I'm in. I almost hesitate to answer because I'm certain they won't know what I'm talking about, but I usually go for it anyway.

I turn to them, and say, "I buy and sell personally held paper on the secondary market."

Their response is almost always the same: "*What?*"

When I tell them what it is, they almost always look mystified and say, "Why? What makes it a good investment?"

Then I spend the rest of the flight trying to explain what I do. I wrote this book to answer the question, "What?" and to explain why.

The next time I'm traveling and someone asks me what I do for a living, I'll turn to them with a smile, hand them *The Stefanchik Method*, and ask them to read it.

I'd guess that about 99.9 percent of the people in this country have no idea what it means to buy and sell paper, or even that it is possible to do so. Perhaps I should be grateful, because that leaves the market wide open for me and you.

Actually, I'm not worried by competition at all. There's plenty of paper available for everyone who wants to get involved with it. I've heard an estimate that there's more than 400 billion dollars' worth of personally held paper out there. That's just an estimate, because paper is constantly being created, bearing interest, bought and sold, and paid off.

There is no better time than now to get involved in paper. There are so many reasons that I could spend far too much time just on this one subject, but let me outline a few.

First, the present bank and S&L situation and the slow real estate market in many parts of the nation are contributing to explosive growth in the paper market.

Why? Because the banks are running scared from primary lending—not refinancing—because of the enormous number of delinquencies and foreclosures they had to deal with in the '80s and early '90s. That has caused many ordinary people difficulty in getting home loans, which has led to a resurgence of seller financing. The slow market has meant that many sellers, who have often waited too long for their homes to sell, are far more willing to carry a mortgage note than they were even a few years ago. These sellers don't really want the note they accepted. They took it only so they could sell their homes. Many would rather have cash, even if it isn't the full value of the note.

Second, because few people know of the opportunity this creates, competition for the paper is minimal.

Third, the opportunities for buying discounted paper are not really dependent on the economic conditions I've just described. When interest rates are low, people want to buy paper in the expectation that the property owners will refinance the property, thus paying the note off early. But if interest rates are high, sellers of property hold paper because it becomes very difficult for the average person to qualify for bank financing. There is always an ample supply of paper to buy.

Fourth (and I could go on and on), sellers of property often find it easier to hold paper themselves than to have the buyer qualify for a new loan. This kind of arrangement is especially true in high-priced areas of the country, where a 20 percent cash down payment is out of reach for many people.

The Best-Kept Secret Really Isn't a Secret

Buying and selling paper is the best-kept secret on public record, not because anyone has hatched some evil plot to keep the knowledge from the public, but because the public doesn't know it exists. It isn't the kind of thing that makes newspaper headlines or attracts the attention of talk-show hosts.

Public and financial industry employees who work with mortgages and trust deeds every day, even those who buy and sell the loans of major institutions, often don't realize the money that can be made buying and selling *personally* held mortgages and trust deeds, or where or how to find them.

And yet, as you read this book, you'll see that a great majority of leads for the paper I buy are on public record.

Anybody can go look them up, but so few people know they can take advantage of them that it's just as though it were kept secret.

Ask your friends if they know about buying and selling personally held mortgages. All, or almost all of them, like the people I meet on airplanes, will tell you they don't know what you're talking about.

Most people assume it involves lending money, working for a bank, or that you need some advanced degree in high finance to even think of doing such a thing. Working with paper doesn't take any of this. All it takes is some knowledge and the motivation to go out, do some work, and make money.

Let me tell you this right up front. The business of buying and selling paper is very, very lucrative if you know what you're doing.

I've been buying and selling paper for a number of years. I know what the mistakes are and how to avoid them. More important, I know how to make a lot of money in the paper business.

And don't kid yourself; this *is* a business. You need to plan it and run it like one. But it's not like any business you've ever seen before.

This book will give you a firm foundation to start you on your way to owning and operating a paper business. It will help you secure your financial future.

Let's start learning, and get into it!

CHAPTER 1

Problem-Solving the Paper Way

If you're like many readers, you've read this far thinking, "Of course John Stefanchik makes it sound easy—he does it every day. But *I've* never done it!"

Yes, I do buy paper every day, and for me it's easy—as it will be for you when you've learned the Stefanchik Method and done a number of deals. But don't forget: At one time I'd never done it, either.

When I started I didn't have anyone to tell me how or to warn me about the pitfalls and problems I might encounter. I had to learn it all myself, through experience, by trial and error.

I didn't have any family background or special talent or training to help me get started. All I had was what you have. Like you, I wanted to enhance my financial future. Like you, I wanted to change my life. Like you, I was not afraid to take action to do so.

I grew up in New York City, in the South Bronx, and spent almost all my adolescent years there. I didn't know a thing about investing; I hardly heard anything about it at all. My family never invested in anything. My father worked for the U.S. Postal Service and my mother at a variety of secretarial jobs. We weren't dead poor, but we sure weren't affluent, either.

My parents did all they could to provide for my brother and myself, but there was never enough disposable income left at the end of the month to even think about investing. I never heard my parents talk about the stock and bond markets.

We never owned our own home because there were no single-family homes in my part of the South Bronx. The only people who owned property were landlords. I never even heard the term "mortgage" mentioned. Only the wealthy owned property or invested in stocks or bonds.

Even the *idea* of investing was absent from my childhood. I can never change that. Nothing suggested that I could become some kind of financial whiz kid, or even that I might ever want to.

I was a good student, however, and went on to college and then to graduate school.

After graduation I went out into the real world feeling awfully good that I'd prepared myself to be more successful than my parents. I soon realized that everything I'd been taught had prepared me to work for someone else.

I'm not saying this is bad. Like a lot of kids just out of college, I just wasn't sure it was what I wanted to do. But I knew I needed a job, so I got one.

I eventually worked for a Fortune 100 company in Westchester County, New York. As jobs go it was a good one. I was making a salary of $30,000 a year and had all the benefits that go along with working for a big company.

At that time it was a really good job, and I felt fortunate to have it. I was especially happy about the great benefits, which are something most major corporations offer as a bonus for working for them. They give you benefits instead of more cash. They point out that you aren't taxed on your benefit package, so it's worth even more than the cash equivalent. They beef up the benefits package and give you the hard sell about how it will make your life secure so you can be a happy and productive employee.

The benefits package usually includes medical coverage and a retirement account. The costs for these are tax-deductible to the company. They can give you a dollar's worth of benefits discounted by the percentage of tax they'd pay on that money if they didn't give you the benefits. That's a simple substitute for paying you more cash now. They'll point out, if you ask, that if you had to pay for those benefits out of direct salary, you'd be paying after-tax dollars, so both you and the company come out ahead. They, of course, pay higher taxes than you, so they get the larger benefit.

It wasn't long before I decided I wanted to make more money, so I went to my manager and asked for a raise.

He said something that I'm sure he thought was profound. He told me, "John, if you want to make more money, you can work longer hours."

Since I was on a salary, I couldn't understand how this would work. When you're on salary you make a certain amount, in my case $30,000, for one year's work. You're expected to work forty hours a week. If you work less, the company gets unhappy about your performance. If you work more, you still get your fixed salary, but you become a "valued employee."

If I increased the number of hours I worked, I'd only decrease what I was actually paid per hour.

My boss went on to say that when it was time for my annual review, if I had worked harder and longer and been more productive than some of the other employees, I could expect a raise of 5 percent, maybe even 10 percent.

Well, gee, that sounded great. Work more, make more. That's what the American Way is supposed to be about. You're rewarded according to how hard you work.

Then I realized that some of the upper-management people were putting in almost eighty hours a week. That revealed the flaw in the system. Yes, they were making a lot more money than I, but if they made $60,000 a year working twice as many hours, had they gained anything? Not to mention having no time to enjoy the money they were making?

If I accepted my boss's recommendation, I'd work more hours, get paid less (per hour), and hope that the raise would justify what I was doing. In other words, I would work more *now* and get paid more *later*. I didn't know it then, but that was an early lesson in the time value of money.

You can see that this was just great for the company. They motivated me to work harder, based on the promise of a good raise, but they didn't have to pay me to do it. They got the benefit of my extra work for free. They didn't say, "Okay, John, if you work more hours now, we'll advance you some of the raise."

What would happen if I didn't get a raise? Maybe the company had a bad year and nobody got a raise. Maybe somebody thought I wasn't working hard enough. Maybe they thought someone else was working harder. Maybe someone played office politics better than

I. There were no guarantees. I couldn't sue the company to get my money.

All that happened was that they got more work out of me for the same money—their benefit, not mine. My company's policy reminded me of the IRS and tax "refunds."

Most people brag about how large a refund they got back on their taxes each year. They're so happy they didn't have to pay anything that they never stop to think that the government has had the use of their money for a year without paying a cent of interest for it! Suppose you got a $2,000 refund. If bank interest was 5 percent, the government just made an extra $100 on your taxes!

What a joke the government has played on you! You made them an interest-free loan and they took their own sweet time in giving it back to you, right? And still, everyone is so grateful to get that refund check!

That's exactly the way my company, and many, perhaps most others, get more work for less pay out of their most dedicated employees.

I realized I had a problem. I needed to do something about it or my life would be just like my parents' life was. Although I'd be living a few steps up the economic ladder, I'd be just as limited. At least, I told myself, I've got this great retirement plan. If I work hard now, I'll be able to retire and enjoy life later.

Then I received my individualized statement of my current status in the company's generous retirement plan. I hadn't really paid much attention to previous statements, because retirement was a long way off. I knew the benefits were great, so I didn't sweat the details.

This time I looked.

And I read the fine print.

I was shocked.

If I retired at age 65, I'd get $1,600 a month!

That actually wasn't bad, as pension plans went at the time—but it was a *lot* less than I was making!

I didn't need scientific math to know what inflation would do to that amount over the next thirty-five years or so.

And if that wasn't bad enough, there was the fine print: a whopping disclaimer that said, very simply, "assuming everything remains constant." When have you heard of anything in life remaining constant?

I could assume I'd get promotions, pay increases, bonuses, and so on, but again I didn't need more than grade-school math to figure out that I'd have to be unusually successful within the company to end up with better than the equivalent, at the time I retired, of the $1,600 they were talking about. I could see the very real possibility that in three decades my pension would be worth *less.*

I didn't know much, then, about the time value of money, but I sure knew that the place I wanted to be was not $30,000 a year now and $1,600 a month (if I was lucky) thirty-five years from now.

Did that scare me?

You bet it did! Right there at my desk, I learned the true meaning of "cold sweat."

I started to think of some of the other things that could happen.

I could get fired.

The company could close. (This, too, was before the massive corporate layoffs of the last few years.)

I might become ill and lose the means not only of making money, but of continuing to build my pension.

And so on. Our minds do real well at coming up with doomsday-disaster scenarios if we give them half a chance.

I don't think I'd ever been quite as scared in my life as I was at that moment. It was like everything I'd taken for granted had been destroyed; like there'd been an earthquake or tornado, and nothing was left standing around me.

Put yourself in my position and try to imagine what it felt like to be that scared, and imagine what you'd have done if you were sitting at my desk that day.

Before reading on, take a minute, lean back in your chair, close your eyes, and think about what you'd have done. Ask yourself if there have been any moments like that in your life, and what you did about them.

Well, if I knew I had a problem before I read that statement, now I had a real motivation to do something about it. The only question was what I could do to solve the problem.

I began searching for something that could make me extra money part-time. I wasn't about to dump my job. After all, it was secure and I enjoyed it.

My schooling gave me a lot of knowledge about a lot of things, but very little about making money. The problem with our school system is that you graduate with a degree in something or other and know you need to work for someone to make money. You become tied to the job. You live by the cash flow that the job provides. There's little left at the end of each month. You never have enough money to even think about investing in anything.

The question I was asking myself came down to: How can I start making more money part-time when I have no money? How can I start investing in anything without money?

Nothing Down, So Nothing to Lose?

Then I came across one of the books, so popular in the '80s, that explained how to buy real estate with no money down.

That sounded great. It was just what I needed. All you had to do was use one creative technique or another and you could put together a real estate deal without using a dime of your own money.

I knew I qualified for this type of investing. I didn't have any money to invest!

I did have a strong desire to make money and I had a great partner. Ricki Eskenazi, a friend who worked at the same company, was also interested in no-money-down investing. We created a partnership, J&R Associates (the initials stood for John and Ricki).

Ricki and I took turns convincing each other we knew what we were doing and that we could be successful.

We began doing just what the book said. It wasn't hard. We did it over and over. We bought a lot of real estate in a very short period of time. We were very aggressive and became pretty proud of ourselves.

We purchased a variety of properties in three states using a number of creative real estate techniques with little, if any, of our own money. We put in long hours, working evenings, weekends, and holidays. We gained so much momentum that we didn't even realize how many extra hours we were putting in. We thought we had it made; our friends patted us on the back and told us how great we were doing, which does wonders for one's ego.

There's one thing the "nothing-down" books rarely bother to tell you, and the one we read didn't mention it at all: You have to have assured positive cash flow or you can lose your shirt.

It wasn't long before the ugly side of no-money-down deals reared its malevolent head. Quickly, I found myself with a large negative cash flow each month. I had never experienced debt or anticipated it.

When I began investing, I had a zero cash flow. That's when the money going out each month is the same as the money you make from your job each month. Positive cash flow means more money is coming in than going out, and negative means you're spending more than you're bringing in.

Now, what do you think happened when I went out there and bought a whole lot of property in a short time? I wound up with a brand-new problem called negative cash flow. I'd started with no money, and effectively invested myself to less than no money!

Now *that's* what I call a real financial problem!

Ricki and I had more money going out in expenses, because of our real estate purchases, than we had coming in from rents.

Now I had a problem.

I was still working at my job, but all the job did was allow me to pay the bills I had before I started investing. I didn't have any money to cover the monthly negative cash flow of my real estate investments.

If I'd really understood what I was doing, I might have been able to arrange the deals so I would have been in a better position, but I didn't know how to do that then, nor had I even known that I ought to. Instead of making me money, all my hours of work meant that I was being financially buried by my investments. My negative cash flow was even worse than working extra hours for the company, hoping I'd get paid someday.

I'm sharing this story with you for two reasons.

First, I want you to understand that by blindly investing in nothing-down real estate I really created a nightmare for myself. I had to cover that monthly negative cash flow. Each month I had to get money from someplace to pay my bills. I was slowly sinking into financial quicksand. I owed an ever-increasing amount of money each month.

Isn't that a great way to get started on the road to fame and fortune?

Second, I want you to know I had a real desire to succeed. I wanted this program to work so badly that I was willing to do whatever it took to be successful.

Looking at the monster I'd created, I was reminded of the comment attributed to George McGovern after his massive loss to Richard Nixon in the '72 presidential election: "I wanted to run for president in the worst way—and I sure did!"

McGovern didn't get a second chance to do it right. I knew that if I was to have a second chance, even to merely get out of the financial hole I'd dug for myself, it was up to me.

While it was easy to recognize that I'd created a problem for myself, I also knew there had to be a way out of it. I was convinced that if I could just get some cash I could solve my problems.

My experience in real estate gave me a heightened awareness that there were many ways to make money I'd never known or even thought of. Just as no-money-down creative real estate techniques were new to me, I knew there had to be plenty of ways to make money that I didn't know about.

I set out on a search for ways to generate cash. And this time I was determined to pay much closer attention to the risks of negative cash flow!

Paper to the Rescue

I can't remember whether I read about paper somewhere or heard about it from someone else, but one day I found out that you can buy a mortgage at one price and resell it at a higher price.

I went out and did some research. I wasn't going to go into paper blindly, the way I had with no-money-down real estate. Obviously, I didn't know everything there was to know about paper when I started, but I knew enough to start making cash. That cash bailed me out of the real estate hole I had dug for myself.

That's a nice success story, right?

It sounds simple when I put it in a few words, but it wasn't that easy. It took time and effort to learn the things I'll teach you. The technique for generating cash is simple, but your understanding of all the details involved in buying and selling paper will be the source of your success. Like anything that can give you financial rewards, you need to know what you're doing. You need to know the problems so you can deal with them when they arise. You need to know the indicators of success so you can follow the path they point to.

Cash is what buying and selling paper is all about. Cash is what everyone wants more of. Cash can solve your financial problems. Cash can buy you a better, more secure life-style, but cash is just the beginning of the benefits paper can provide.

Over the years I've had people come up to me and say how surprised they were to discover that paper produced even more financial benefits than they expected. People have bought and sold paper with only one goal in mind—to make cash—and then discovered other benefits as well.

In the next chapter, I'll tell you how paper investing works, and give you ten reasons why it's such a great deal.

Paper Basics

Buying and selling personally held mortgages and trust deeds is fundamentally a simple procedure.

The neat thing about it is that its details are simple, too. They only appear confusing or complicated when you try to absorb them all at once. We'll take it a step at a time.

Let's begin with the simple existence of paper.

As I've said, most people who hold personal mortgages or trust deeds secured by real estate didn't make those loans because they wanted to be in the lending business. If you go to paper holders with an offer to buy their mortgage, the cash you offer will look awfully good to them.

The catch is that you can't pay full face value for the paper. That will cause many people to decide they'd rather keep their paper and continue to get income from it.

It will *not*, however cause *every* mortgage holder to refuse to sell. You and I are seeking out those who for whatever reason no longer want their mortgage, or who have a pressing need for cash.

There are so many privately held mortgages and trust deeds out there that even a fraction of a percent of the total would provide a nice living for everyone who wants to invest in them.

Finding Paper

There are many ways to find paper.

All mortgages and trust deeds are recorded at the county recorder's office at your county courthouse. They are public record; you can go there and look them up. Any mortgage or trust deed that is shown to be held by an individual name rather than a bank, S&L, or some other financial corporate entity is a potential for purchase. In some parts of the nation, as many as 40 percent of the mortgages may be held by private individuals.

Make a list of all you find, then write each person a letter expressing interest in buying their mortgage.

The second way to find mortgages is to advertise. A small classified ad, run regularly, can produce good results. A mailing to attorneys, accountants, and tax preparers will usually bring inquiries on behalf of clients who hold paper and need cash.

Personal networking is another way to learn of mortgages that comes after you become known as a mortgage buyer. People will begin to refer their friends and clients to you. You can begin this process when you first seek mortgages by letting friends, business associates, and fellow church or club members know what you're doing. Word of mouth and reputation can create a lot of business. But it takes time to establish a good reputation.

Buying Paper

You may have read the Introduction and wondered how in the world you could ask someone to sell a mortgage for less than its face value.

Once you have found someone with a mortgage you want to buy, you enter a process of explanation of the time value of money and negotiation.

You have to explain why you can't pay face value. Then you either agree that they won't sell for a discount or you negotiate an acceptable price.

Buying Paper Without Cash

If you have your own funds to buy mortgages, that's great, but most of you don't. You're reading this book because you want to make enough money to create that kind of wealth.

The best way to begin is the same way I did: Find a mortgage you can buy at a discount, then find an investor who will pay more than you've offered. You pocket the difference. This is called *flipping* the paper. That is, you buy it for instant resale. The term is also used in real estate when you buy a property, fix it up, and sell it at once for a profit, and when you tie up a property with *(your name) and/or assignee* as the buyer. You can then flip the contract to another buyer at a higher price by assigning the contract.

If that sounds a little risky—like, what if you can't find someone who wants the mortgage?—you're right. I made the mistake, on my first paper deal, of offering to buy the paper first and then finding the investor. I was fortunate to locate an investor who paid me $6,000 more than I'd offered the mortgage holder.

If I'd offered the wrong price, I might have found myself stuck trying to cover a $6,000 gap between what I'd offered and the best I could get from an investor. And I didn't have $6,000 to lose!

That's why, in the Stefanchik Method, you never make a firm commitment to buy a mortgage until you have the funding in place to buy the mortgage and make a profit.

Ricki and I have created a company, S.E.S Funding Corporation, which specializes in purchasing paper from buyers just like you. Many companies and individuals invest in this manner. S.E.S Funding, and others like us, pay you for finding paper.

I recommend that you make no price offer before obtaining a commitment to purchase from an investor or S.E.S. Funding. In your negotiations with the note holder, determine that they will sell for a discount, then tell them you will figure a price based on the information they gave you, locate an investor, and offer the note holder less than the investor offers you.

If the Note Is Paid Off Early   ·

The average person moves about once every seven years. That means most mortgages are paid off early. Is this bad or good?

It's good. In fact, it's great. It's wonderful.

Suppose you bought a thirty-year $80,000 mortgage, discounted to $50,000, with monthly payments of $775. That would mean the total payments (360 months times $775) would be $279,000. Quite a return on a $50,000 investment, right?

Yes, but don't forget the effects of inflation, which are a part of the time value of money, which you'll be reading about a lot in this book.

Suppose you bought that note with twenty-nine years remaining. You'd be buying $269,700 worth of payments, spread over that rather long period.

Now what happens if you buy the note and a year later it's paid off?

You've already collected twelve payments ($9,300). At payoff you get the remaining balance of the loan. After two years that's about 99 percent of the original balance, or $79,200. For your $50,000 investment, you make a direct profit of $29,200, plus the $9,300 you collected in payments. You made $38,500, eroded only by one year of inflation and other time-value factors. If you assume inflation was 3.5 percent, your money is worth $37,152.50 in terms of the value of your original investment dollars. This is simplified, of course. Other factors than mere inflation can affect the value of money over time. But it basically shows how profitable an early payoff can be.

Now you have almost $40,000 in profit to reinvest.

If the loan was paid off after the typical seven years, you'd have received six years of payments ($55,800) and you'd have about 95.5 percent of the original balance remaining, or about $76,400. At S.E.S Funding Corporation, we even had one deal where the timing was such that the person was selling the house even as we made the deal to buy the mortgage. We were so-so about the deal, not sure at all that we were going to buy the mortgage. The appraiser called us and said, "I'm really sorry about the picture I'm sending with my appraisal. It was difficult to get a good angle on the property without that big sign in front of the house getting in the way."

So we asked, "What sign?"

And he said, "I'm in a hurry, I'll show you, let me know when I Federal Express you the pictures."

So Federal Express delivered the pictures and we took a look at them. The "big sign" he was referring to said, FOR SALE.

Now, a "for sale" sign doesn't guarantee that the property is about to be sold, but it certainly makes it likely.

But why would the note holder sell the note if the property was about to be sold, which would give them a full payoff, not the discounted price of selling the note?

Well, think about it. The note holder sold the property some time ago. The note holder could have moved out of town, to the other side of town, or wherever, and now wants to sell the cash flow, not the property. The holder may not know that the property is for sale. The person paying on the note is under no obligation to tell the note holder anything until there is an actual, accepted purchase offer and agreement to sell. At that point, the deal goes to the title company, which notifies all note holders.

The person selling you the mortgage may not know the house is for sale. You are under no obligation to disclose the fact. The note holder has a legal responsibility to learn about anything that might affect the security of the note, including sale of the property. If the note holder didn't bother, you don't have to tell him.

Seeing the For Sale sign in the photo turned that deal from so-so to desirable. We bought the note, and the property sold shortly afterward. We were paid off early.

Building Your Paper Business

Six thousand dollars does not a fortune make.

True, it was a really nice profit for the work I'd done, at a time when I really needed the money, but what do you think would have happened if I'd congratulated myself and stopped there? Would I be wealthy? Would I be writing this book?

No, and no.

The secret to wealth, and to success in anything, is repetition. You must keep repeating your success.

To succeed in paper, after you've congratulated yourself and celebrated the success of your first deal, you must go right back out and do it again, and again, and again. When you've done it often enough, you'll have the cash to buy paper yourself without having to bring in outside investors.

The Steps to Paper Success

1. Make a commitment to yourself that you will make the Stefanchik Method work for you
2. Search for and locate profitable paper
3. Determine that the mortgage holder will sell at a discount
4. Find an investor who will buy the note
5. Offer the note holder less than the investor offered you
6. You earn the difference between the two prices
7. Repeat the process

Follow these steps and you will succeed.

Why Is Paper a Good Deal?

Paper has a high yield.
High yield means you can get a very high return on your investment. High yield makes paper very attractive to people who understand what paper is. The good news is that once you understand paper yields, your financial life will never be the same. The bad news is that very few people understand paper yields. You can't pick up *The Wall Street Journal* and find out how the paper market is doing. (Maybe that really isn't bad news after all.)

Paper is real estate secured.
Real estate is the collateral for the paper I deal in. I know the value of the collateral before I make the deal. Up until a few years ago, this is the way banks secured all their loans. When they got away from using real estate as collateral, they got into trouble. One of the major reasons why real estate is the best form of collateral is because it isn't going anywhere. I have never seen a piece of real estate pick itself up and move down the street.

Paper provides you with a monthly paycheck.
When you buy paper, you set yourself up with a positive cash flow. When your collective monthly cash flow is large enough, you can quit your job and live off your paper profits. Once you start working paper, you'll find this will not take long.

Paper returns both principal and interest.
Collecting interest offers wonderful new ways to budget your finances. By the end of this book you'll understand how to live on part of the interest and reinvest the rest of the interest and the principal. You are provided with a powerful way to always have enough spendable money as well as enough cash available for investment. You can make enough money to both increase your standard of living and increase your investment capital.

If someone doesn't make payments on the paper you hold, you can foreclose and take over the property.
There's no other investment you can so certainly recover if it goes bad. What happens if you invest in stock and it goes bad? If you call your broker and ask for your money back, he or she will just laugh (perhaps privately) and tell you better luck next time. Foreclosure is one of paper's most powerful tools.

When someone pays you off early, your yield increases because you get your money quicker.
This phenomenon is due to the time value of money, which I'll explain in detail later.

You can split up the asset.
Paper is an asset. It's much more flexible than any other investment. You can buy or sell parts of a note. If you don't want to buy the entire note you can buy only a *partial*. You can be very creative with paper.

Paper is liquid.
Paper has a positive cash flow, which makes it very easy to resell if you need to. There's always a good market for good paper. There's even a market for *bad* paper! Your care in buying only good paper

will keep you out of a position where you have to sell bad paper, but it's good to know that if one of your paper investments goes sour, you can sell it and minimize any loss.

You can get into the paper business with any amount of money, from zero on up.
Remember, I got into paper with no money. I had *less* than no money, because I had a negative cash flow! You're not limited by a certain minimum or maximum dollar amount. You set your own investment levels.

The leads to buy paper are a matter of public record.
You don't have to be a detective to find them. They're right out there in the open for you to find and use to create your profit.

As you get into paper, you'll discover more and more benefits. Those listed here are the basics. They should give you a good feel for the advantages paper offers as a sound investment.

In the next two chapters I'll discuss the three entities that form the foundation of the theory of paper success and safety and how they relate to the practical, real world. In the following chapter, I'll give you the tools for planning and goal-setting, without which all the theory and practice in the world won't get you anywhere.

CHAPTER 3

The Stefanchik Method: The Three-Entity Approach to Wealth

The unique assurance of success in paper the Stefanchik Method has to offer comes from the interaction of three entities.

Many of you may be wondering what I mean by an "entity," and why we need three of them. You probably aren't sure just what this means.

I could have called my system a "three-part" or a "three-step" approach, but these terms aren't quite accurate.

Each entity in my system is real, has a distinct existence, and is independent of the others. They all work just fine on their own, without need for the others. The way they work together is what makes my system powerful.

In my system, entity number one is *cash*, entity number two is *investment and reinvestment*, and entity number three is *real property*.

The relationship among the entities is flexible. Cash and investment/reinvestment apply to any wealth-building business. If you seek wealth through some source other than real estate, substitute the security or source of income you've chosen.

Before you start buying and selling paper, you need to understand how each entity relates to your situation, and how each entity relates to the others.

The following diagrams show how the entities relate to each other and how they interact. You'll notice that the arrows go both ways from each entity to the others.

The arrows represent a flow—how you can shift your emphasis

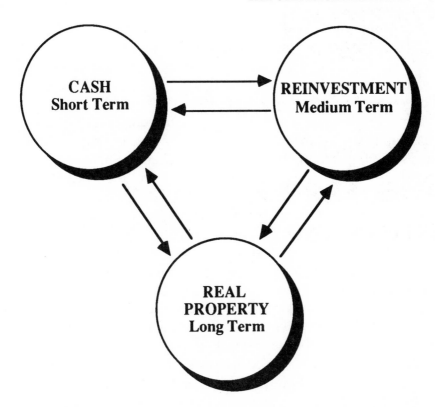

from any entity to the others depending on your financial needs.

Paper is not just the success of one entity, but of all three working together to create your financial success. You're not bound into any rigid relationship of equal emphasis on any entity, but can freely balance the entities against one another according to your needs.

Your ability to manipulate each entity separately and all three together to your own advantage is the key to the Stefanchik Method.

We'll examine the entities separately, then look at how they work together.

Entity One—Cash

Cash from buying and selling paper can solve your short-term financial problems. Cash is also the ultimate goal of this or any other successful business. When I had my negative cash flow problems with nothing-down real estate years ago, paper generated the cash I needed. Cash is the most liquid form of return you can get from any investment. It's what we all want from our investments. Cash is accepted by everyone. No one will turn you down when you buy with cash.

In paper investing, as described in the last chapter, the most basic technique is to buy, or contract to buy, a mortgage or trust deed and then sell it for more than you paid. The difference between the price for which you contracted to buy the note and the price for which you sold it is your profit.

Flipping notes is the most basic way to use paper to create a cash flow, but it certainly isn't the only way.

Cash when generated and used in this manner is short-term. It only takes three or four weeks to produce cash from flipping a note—hence the short term.

Flipping paper is a great way to generate cash. This short-term process can be repeated over and over to generate as much cash as you can find paper to buy and sell.

The flip technique is the cornerstone of the Stefanchik Method. I will, of course, talk about it in detail in a later chapter.

Entity Two—Investment and Reinvestment

Investment and reinvestment are really the same thing, but people often think of them as separate: first you invest, then you reinvest the profit from your investment.

Actually, "reinvestment" is simply another investment. I'm using both terms because so many people (and too many businesses) seem happy to take all the profit from an investment and spend it. If you want to build wealth, all or part of the profit from each investment (or reinvestment, if you prefer) must be added to your investment capital.

In first-grade arithmetic terms, if you have two and invest it until you have four (a profit of two), but then spend all four, you're two behind where you began. If you spend two of your four, you're back where you started. If, however, you add your profit of two to your original two, you can now invest (reinvest) four.

If you need part of your profit for living or operating expenses (as most of us do), you might spend one and add one to your investment capital. Now you can invest three.

Investment is the ability to take the money you're making and put it into something that will make you more money. Reinvestment is doing it over and over again.

When you purchase paper for your own portfolio, you're making an investment that will pay you cash each month. You can sit back and collect the checks. You don't have to do anything else. This is where we all want to be, and can be, by using entity number two.

When I was taking physics in school, I learned a simple principle: Everything in life wants to move to the lowest energy level possible, which is at rest.

Applying this to investing, the best we can achieve is to do as little as possible to gain maximum results. In physics, this is achieved by cutting back on wasted energy. The less energy wasted, the more efficient the process, whatever it may be—including investing.

The efficient investor doesn't spend time and energy chasing low-yield investments. Neither does he or she invest where he or she has very little expertise and could lose money.

When you begin your career in paper, you'll most likely start by flipping paper for cash. As soon as you've generated enough cash, you should look for a place to invest it. Why not invest in what you've been dealing with every day?

Most people invest as a two-step process. They find something in which to invest, then purchase it for their investment portfolios.

In paper, you've eliminated the first step. You already have something in which to invest. You can do it yourself, because you've already become an expert in paper. You don't need to go to a stockbroker or trust some other "expert." You need only concern yourself with finding paper with an acceptable yield. You have more time, energy, and money to create greater financial growth.

Entity Number Three—Real Property

Real property is the long-term solution to your financial problems. It's a long-term investment because it takes a longer time to make money from real estate than from flipping or investing in paper. Real estate's value is always the security for your paper. Here are the three entities at work together.

If you insist on thinking of one entity as the most important, this would be it. Without the security provided by real estate as collateral, paper investments would be as risky as any other financial investment, or perhaps far more so. The long-term key to your success in paper is the security of the real property. You need to understand the true value of this collateral, and how you can be certain of it.

The true value of real estate changes. Does this make your security suddenly insecure?

It can—if you're careless about determining the value of the property, and if you're careless about the loan-to-value ratio of the mortgage or trust deed you purchase.

How do you know the value of real property?

One of the interesting things about real estate is that it does rise and fall in value. That's where investors who count on short-term increases in real estate values can lose, big. But, while there may be a rise and fall in values, over a long period of time there is always an overall rise.

The overall rise is one half of your best insurance against loss. The other half is the discount for which you buy the paper. I'll talk about the importance of this discount in later chapters.

No matter whether the value of your real estate security rises or falls, if you knew its true value at the time you bought the mortgage, you're protected against all but the most disastrous collapses of the market. You're protected against collapses like those seen in Houston or Denver in the early '80s. You're protected against all but the worst collapses ever seen, including the Great Depression.

You can see that it isn't enough to just have a loan secured by real estate. You have to know what that real estate is really worth.

It doesn't matter whether you buy paper secured by a single-family home, a multi-family dwelling, a commercial building, or a piece of raw land, just so long as it's real estate and you know its present value.

Always remember: Real estate is only worth what someone is willing to pay for it. It doesn't matter what you feel it's worth or what someone tells you they think it's worth; it's only worth what someone is willing to purchase it for.

This is a very basic lesson that I learned a long time ago, when I first got involved in paper.

A lot of people will tell you that a piece of real estate is worth a certain amount of money. You hear everybody talking about that. "Oh, my house is worth $300,000. Oh, my house is worth $57,000." Everybody talks about the value of their real estate.

You'll hear people say anything if they imagine it can add to the value of the real estate. I've had people call me and say, "Clint Eastwood lives on my block." Why would having Clint Eastwood as a neighbor raise the property value of your home?

They'll say people want to live near Clint Eastwood. That's rarely the case. You're not going to pay an extra $50,000 just to live near a movie star. If anything, many people might prefer *not* to live near a celebrity, assuming that there may be parties, a lot of noise, or just a lot of traffic from tourists who want to see where the famous person lives—which would probably bug Mr. Eastwood or any other celebrity just as much as it bugs the neighbors.

Real estate is going have a certain value that is attributable to the real estate itself and to its location. You'll hear real estate professionals say that the three most important things about a piece of property are location, location, location. The presence of Clint Eastwood or any other celebrity on a block would certainly suggest an upscale neighborhood, but wouldn't add to the value that existed when they bought their homes. They, after all, are looking for location and value, too.

Some other things a paper buyer should look for or beware of are:

- Current local values
- Has there been a dramatic rise or fall in values in the last three months?
- The economic condition of the area
- Trends of movement around the area
- What will the property rent for?
- How easy would it be to sell the property if you had to foreclose?

These questions apply whether you're buying paper secured by a property or are buying a property for a residence or for investment.

Real estate value has little to do with whether you're in an up-and-coming area or whether someone lives on the block or other intangible factors that may never be realized. Real estate value depends on what someone's willing to pay for a property *today*.

CHAPTER 4

The Three Entities in Action

To understand how the three-entity approach to paper differs from other investments, let's look at a typical investor.

He's successful and fairly well off; he owns a few car dealerships. He buys and sells cars for a living, knows that business inside and out, and has done really well. The dealerships hold big sales every month and advertise heavily on TV. Business has been good. The investor already has a great house with a pool, two or three luxury cars, a vacation home, and takes three vacations a year. His family has everything it wants.

One day our successful car dealer wakes up and sees the need to do something more with the extra money the business is making. Money is supposed to make more money, after all. It's clearly time to start investing the excess cash. He loves selling cars, but doesn't want to do it forever. He starts looking for a good place to put the money, a place that will provide the best return. The cash could be put into stocks, bonds, mutual funds, the bank, or into some form of limited partnership. Every investment option is available and open.

The only limit is knowledge. Our car dealer knows how to sell cars, not now to invest, and has been too busy making a living to learn the principles of investing.

The stock market looks good. Everyone talks about their stocks, so how tough can the stock market be? He invests in some stocks his brother-in-law said were good—and before long is losing money.

No car dealer can become successful without knowing when to

dump a loser, so it's out of here for the stock market! A mutual fund is next, but the growth rate is so slow you could be dead before it makes any sizable amount of money.

In total frustration, the car dealer puts the money into a bank, even though bank interest is rarely more than a percent or two better than inflation, and may even be *less* than inflation. He needs help. The problem is, help costs money.

Our frustrated car dealer goes to a stockbroker and tells his tale of woe. His lament is just what the broker wants to hear. The broker gets paid for playing with other people's money, whether he makes money for them or not. First the broker charges a fee to set up the investment account; then he charges a percentage each time he buys or sells a stock. If the stock loses money, the broker still gets paid.

This process is called "two-step" investment. The car dealer is involving someone else in his investment. He made the money in the car business, step one; then had to pay someone else for advice to invest, step two. Not only did step two cost money, but the decisions about the future growth of his money are left in someone else's hands.

Aren't you likely to look after your own money more prudently than someone else? Compound the problem of using a stockbroker to look after your money with the time that person must devote to all the other people who invested money with him. The "expert" is too busy looking after his many accounts to focus any amount of time on any one account.

You begin to see why people can lose large amounts of money on "safe" investments, made with the "best advice possible," and why really safe investments usually produce an unacceptably low yield.

The problem is the two-step process, in which one step involves paying someone else to make decisions about your money.

What Makes You Money Is What You Should Invest In

The beauty of paper is that it is a one-step process. You make the decisions and have the expertise to do so wisely. You're already making cash through paper. Doesn't it make sense that what makes you money is what you should be investing in?

That statement is so powerful and important I'm going to repeat it: What makes you money is what you should be investing in.

The cash (entity number one) you make from paper should be reinvested into paper (entity number two). You're the only one controlling your investments. Because you're in control and handling your own investments, you're making more money. You aren't sharing the profits with a broker or anyone else. Your investments are secured by real estate (entity number three), which is a lot safer than stocks, bonds, or other high-yield investments.

Investment/reinvestment is the medium-term solution to your financial problems; successful repetition of reinvestment is the key to attaining your long-term goals.

It's absolutely imperative that you don't discount the importance of investment and reinvestment. People who don't reinvest are continually behind in meeting their financial needs.

I've seen this many times. People work all their lives for a company, like I almost did. They depend on the company's retirement plan and social security. If the company goes bankrupt, or social security doesn't keep up with inflation, they can't do anything about it. They have no money to do more than barely survive their retirement years. They can't afford to enjoy life.

If they had investments working for them, their situation would be entirely different.

Where to Invest First

As I discussed above, there are many potential investments, but I've found most people have no idea how and where to invest. Even when these people invest, they encounter major problems trying to reinvest any money. They don't have the expertise or the time, nor do they usually invest more than small amounts of money.

One of the first things I say to people who ask me for investment advice is, "Well, if I had a small amount of money, perhaps an extra $2,000 or so, the quickest, easiest way to get that money working for me safely, at a higher rate, is to pay off my credit cards."

They're often surprised and say, "Huh?"

I explain that if you pay off your charge-card debt, on which you may be paying, say, 15 to 21.5 percent interest, you save. You're actually investing money at that rate.

People don't look at it that way, though. At seminars, I've asked large groups of people how they think one can best invest $2,000.

Most people say to me, "If I had two million I could get going. Or even if I had $200,000, I could get a business started—$20,000 would at least be a good beginning. But $2,000? I wouldn't know where to put that."

They don't see the problem. If you don't know where to put $2,000, you're definitely not going to know where to put $20,000 or $200,000, much less $2 million.

The best example of this is people who win the lottery. Many either blow the money or invest it in something they have no idea about. They wind up losing it.

You could put your investment money into something tax-related. That's an investment that depends on tax benefits for profit. The problem with tax-related investments is that you have no control over your money. And, if you put it into something that's tied to some sort of limited partnership based on current tax law, a small change in the law could wipe you out. A lot of people were hit hard when the 1986 tax-law revisions took effect. Many of those investors found themselves in trouble because the tax-law changes revised their profits out of existence. Some were wiped out. People who bailed out of limited partnerships wound up losing money, too. Many people who created such partnerships went bankrupt.

The core of the problem is understanding that you need to put your money into something that is safe and returns a high yield. To solve the problem, you need to know which investments fit that description.

There aren't many; paper, treated wisely, is one of them.

Get Your Money Working Safely, With High Yield

As you learn and begin to practice the Stefanchik Method, you'll find it becomes easier and easier to get your money working for you safely, with high yield. You're going to buy paper at a discount—there's no reason to buy if you can't. This is a real estate secured investment on which you can determine the value of the property that secures the paper.

Banks have understood and accepted the value and security of real estate for as long as there have been banks. While they stuck to that, they did fine.

Banks and S&Ls had problems during the '80s, when relaxed federal regulations let them lend on risky commercial properties, junk bonds, or large-scale developments like huge condominium complexes and vacation resorts. These types of projects had previously been restricted to specialized lenders who could tell you in the blink of an eye whether or not a proposed project was a good risk or not.

Lenders who were used to lending money against single-family, owner-occupied homes purchased with a large down payment or federal FHA or VA insurance began investing in areas where they had no expertise. They often acted as if the default rate on these risky investments would be no higher than on owner-occupied residences. The S&L bailout mess shows how wrong those lenders were.

When developments didn't develop and junk-bond mergers lost money, the borrowers just shrugged and walked away, leaving the lenders holding the bag—a bag almost as empty as some banks found themselves holding during the Great Depression.

This irresponsibility caused problems not only for lenders but for anyone looking for a safe, high-yield investment.

The Stefanchik Method allows you to get exactly that kind of high yielding, secure investment—paper. You are not limited by low interest rates or the sudden caution of lenders. Not only are you saving an investment step (because you are not in the same position as our car dealer), but you get safety and high yield too!

Beginning

When I first started working in paper, I bought paper and sold it. I'd find a deal, sell a deal, find a deal, sell a deal, and so on. You are going to learn how to do it, too: find a deal, sell a deal, find a deal, sell a deal.

You'll make cash, lots of cash: entity number one.

But I always wanted to get my money working for me. I just didn't have money to put to work. So, when I finally did have money, I looked for a place to reinvest it.

That's where entity number two comes in.

You don't have to learn all about the stock or bond market. You use your cash to buy deals you might otherwise have sold to another investor. You take your pick of the best you find.

I'll never forget the first paper deal I bought. It was a small deal, but it was *mine*! It was a second mortgage that a real estate agent had taken in lieu of a commission in order to make a deal work. It paid only $60 a month, but I could afford it. It was paid off a few years later when the house sold, and I got my money plus a profit that gave me a nice yield.

What's More Important: Cash or Investment and Reinvestment?

When I travel across the country giving seminars, I often ask my audiences, "What's the most important thing? Cash or the ability to invest and reinvest?"

I ask it early in the seminar, before I give them the information you've gained by reading this far. You can see that it's really a trick question, intended both to find out *how* my audience thinks and to *make* them think.

Ninety-nine times out of a hundred, I get people telling me, "The most important thing is getting my hands on cash. Cash is the most important thing!"

I'm sure many of you feel the same way. Cash is a lot more important *right now,* because cash pays bills, pays the mortgage, and makes possible the life-style you prefer. It gives you the power to make things happen.

This isn't exactly wrong, because without cash you can't invest and reinvest.

But what happens if you have cash and *don't* or *can't* reinvest? You're right back at square one, where you started—no cash and a need to make more.

You see, investing and reinvesting is just as important as making cash. Yes, you have to make cash *first,* but first doesn't mean more or less important. That's why I ask my trick question.

We all have a tendency to think in terms of the biggest, best, most important, and so on. It's part of the way we learn to live life in the twentieth century, but that kind of thinking can ambush us when we least expect it if we don't think things through. I hope you can see why none of the three entities of the Stefanchik Method is more important than any other. You need all three.

When You Have Cash

So, you have to make cash first. Once you have cash, you'll want to buy your own paper. If you don't, your cash will mean no more than the salary trap you're trying to escape. You'll have it, spend it, and it will be gone.

When you buy paper, you're not only buying the lump-sum profit when the loan is paid off, you're also buying a stream of income.

All you have to do is collect payments every month. It's a unique situation. You're buying debt at a discount, and the debt is paying you. It creates a wonderful situation.

Imagine buying a mortgage that pays you $132.27 per month. Then you buy another mortgage that gives you a payment of $427.98. You buy another mortgage and it gives you $382.58. As you buy mortgages, you'll find this monthly income starts to add up.

It's easy to set financial goals when you understand that you're making money and reinvesting it in something that's going to make you more money. You can plan to reinvest your money every month. You can keep doing it over and over again.

Reinvestment is a very focused plan, not some vague hope that one day you're going to do this, or one day you're going to do that.

It allows you to generate cash now and reinvest it at higher rates. That's how people become wealthy. The difference between someone who's merely well off and someone who's wealthy is the ability of wealthy people to get their money working for a higher yield.

I saw the best illustration of this a few years ago, in the Forbes 400 list of the wealthiest people in America.

An article proclaimed that no one on the list was an entertainer. I was amazed. I mean, you read about how much money Michael Jackson makes, how much money Madonna makes, how much money all these entertainers make, but *not one* entertainer was on the list that year. *Why*, I wondered. The reason, *Forbes* wrote, is that these high-income entertainers had absolutely no idea how to invest. They know how to make money but not how to invest it. If, over time, they'd been making that kind of money and had made it work for them at higher and higher rates, they'd have been on the Forbes 400 list without a problem.

It doesn't matter who you are or how much you're making. Whether you're making an extra few bucks a month or you're some superstar who commands a ton of money every time you produce a film or go on tour, you face the same problem. You need to invest your money, no matter how much or how little you have. If you don't, your cash will be spent—gone.

As you read this book, keep saying to yourself that you need to invest and reinvest. Visualize yourself buying paper and reinvesting the income from it. Visualize the deals you'll make.

When I first began buying and flipping paper, I noticed an interesting thing.

I'd buy a mortgage, sell it to an investor, and feel real good about my profit. The investor would often call me a month or two later and said, "Hey, John, thanks a lot for selling me that mortgage. It paid off early. Do you have more like that?"

At first I wondered why they were so happy; then it made sense. When you, I, or an investor buys a mortgage, we determine its value based on the payoff to maturity. If there are twenty-nine years left on a thirty-year mortgage, we have to assume, when we quote a price, that it will be paid off in twenty-nine years. We have to assume, based on past experience with the time value of money, that a dollar twenty-nine years from now will be worth less than a dollar today.

That means that if we're paid off early, our yield goes up. Remember that we figured a profitable yield based on payoff to maturity. When the note is paid off early, we get our money back in today's more valuable dollars. We have our capital back to invest again.

When you realize that the average American family moves once every five to seven years, you can see that early payoff is a real benefit. You can't count on it when you buy a mortgage, but when you buy a number of mortgages you know the odds are that most of them will pay off early, producing a higher yield.

Early payoff is tremendous asset. It's part of what makes paper an absolutely phenomenal investment.

When I realized this, I looked at what I was doing and said to myself (and then to Ricki), "Gee, we can't buy and keep *all* the deals we find, but if we could have just bought that *one* deal we would have made a heck of a lot more money than we did by selling it."

Ricki agreed. We decided that no matter how many mortgages we bought and sold, we were also going to keep as many mortgages as we could. We wanted to make the high yield of early payoff work for us. As a beginner you'll face the problem of deciding whether you want to sell a mortgage and take the cash or whether you should keep it for the monthly cash flow and hope that this mortgage will pay off early for a high yield.

Either way, you'll make money. Short term, medium term, and long term are all earning you money at the same time. Paper will continue to make money for you as long as you keep dealing in it.

How We Succeeded

Ricki and I saw what we needed to do. Sure, the cash coming in from finding and flipping notes was great, but that was just the tip of the paper-profit iceberg.

We knew we had to buy and hold notes to really make money, so we set up S.E.S. Funding Corporation to do just that. Now we have a company that both buys and sells and buys and holds mortgages and trust deeds nationwide and in Canada. We get profit both ways.

We didn't set up S.E.S. Funding the instant we did our first paper deal, of course. We'd made enough deals to take care of our real estate cash-flow problems and give us the funds we needed to invest.

I recommend that you plan something similar. It's a five-step process:

1. First, find notes and flip them.
2. Take care of any pressing debts or cash flow problems.
3. When you've made enough money finding and flipping notes, buy notes for your own investment.
4. When you own enough notes, set up a company to manage them. Check your state's incorporation laws and determine whether you need a license to buy and sell more than a limited number of mortgages each year. Get the advice of an attorney and your accountant on incorporation and on

state and federal tax law considerations.

5. Keep on doing it!

A Problem We Didn't Expect

We can laugh at this problem now. It's always easier to laugh about problems after you've solved them than when you're in the middle of the crisis. At the time this problem arose, it gave us a really strange feeling—but it illustrates the kind of profit you can make from paper.

We had this infinitely growing pool of money being invested at higher and higher rates, so we decided we needed a larger office. We looked around and found the space we wanted.

The broker representing the building asked what company would rent the space. We told him and provided him with a financial statement of the corporate entity we were pledging. That's routine in setting up any office lease.

A financial statement shows the company's assets and debts, and the amount of money it takes in and pays out. Subtracting debt from assets give you the company's net worth. Adding up the cash the company takes in each month and subtracting what it pays out in expenses gives a rough estimate of profit and cash flow. You've probably done this when you got a loan for a car or house or anything like that.

My accountant produced a simple one-page financial statement. He showed that we had X number of mortgages worth X dollars that produced X amount of money each month. He showed how much we took in each month. And he showed that we had *zero debt*. No debt whatsoever; no money at all paid out for debt service! We thought that was pretty impressive.

We had no debt or money owed because our company owned debt as an *asset*. We owned paper, and the paper was debt owed *to* us. So we had no liabilities, only cash flow.

The financial statement went to the landlord. He looked at it and rejected us!

We asked our agent to check. Surely, we said, this can't be right.

The landlord told our agent he thought we should have a meeting.

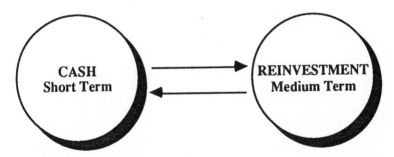

The landlord sat us down, got us comfortable, and said, "Look, I'm not trying to offend you or anything, but how is it possible that you have money coming in every month without money going out for debt service? It looks like money laundering to me."

You've probably read about money laundering. It's something the Mafia and druglords do to conceal the source of their illegal income. They've made all this cash that they don't report as taxable income. They need to make it work for them, just like you and I need to make our money work.

When they buy something, they buy with cash. They have no overhead whatsoever. They own everything outright. And they have no debt.

The result is that when you have no debt it looks *very* suspicious to a landlord. He can lose the property to federal confiscation if he knowingly rents to an illegal organization or to organized crime or drug traffickers. He may even lose the property if federal agents believe he *should* have known what the renter was doing. If you're a commercial landlord, you need to be cautious and check out your tenants!

You can see why our prospective landlord was worried. It hadn't occurred to us until he pointed out the problem. Of course, we were able to explain what we were doing and how we did it. He listened and it made sense to him. He knew that, as shown in the diagram above, if you earn cash in the short term, you have to reinvest it in the medium term or you won't grow.

He understood one of the true, fundamental principles of financial success: If you can quickly and inexpensively get your money working for you, you no longer need to work for your money.

He gave us our lease.

I haven't told this story to say that the Stefanchik Method will make you more money than a Mafia capo or a druglord would make, but it does show that you can make a lot of money without carrying a lot of debt.

While this creates a very favorable situation for us, it also can cause misunderstandings among people who aren't familiar with the Stefanchik Method.

How Can You Assure Yourself of the Value of Real Estate?

Real estate isn't worth much as security if you don't know its true value. You can't take someone's word for it. You can't trust the most recent sales price, even if it sold only six months or a year ago. Real estate is only worth what someone will actually pay for it today.

The only reliable estimate of value is a current appraisal of the property.

An appraisal looks at the current market value of comparable properties. "Comps," or "comparables," as they are called, are similar properties that have sold in the same or a similar area recently. Using the comps as a basis, an appraiser looks at the property, evaluates its condition and any special problems or benefits, and estimates an *appraised value.*

Suppose the property is a single-family home. Picture a street somewhere in suburban America. Let's say it's a cute little three-bedroom, two-bath house on a quarter-acre lot. We're looking at purchasing the mortgage. The property sold two years ago. We know what it sold for then, and the current balances of the loans against it. We need to know what it's worth now. Is it worth more than when it sold? Has it lost value? In either case, how much?

We'd go to an appraiser. We're considering buying the mortgage, not the property, so the appraiser can't go inside and check it out as would be routine if the house itself were being sold. Instead, a *drive-by (or windshield) appraisal* is made.

A drive-by appraisal takes about three to five business days and provides a full analysis of the property and its current market value. The appraiser looks at the house, makes notes on its appearance and apparent condition, takes a couple of pictures, checks out the neighborhood, and then looks up comps for the area.

The appraiser first looks at comps on that same street, preferably on the same block. If the only available comps are several blocks away, the appraiser should drive by them to make sure that the area is similar and the houses are in similar condition. Suppose that across the street and three houses down is a three-bedroom, two-bath house on a quarter-acre lot that was sold recently. Maybe there's one a block or two away. The closer and more similar the properties, the more accurate and reliable the appraisal. The appraiser will give more weight to the comps according to how similar, how close, and how recent the sale was.

From this information, a competent appraiser can provide a very accurate estimate of value. Use this current appraised value, not the old sale price or what anyone else tells you the property is worth.

When you understand the current market value of the real estate, you have a sound basis for evaluating the relationship between the loan and the actual, realistic value of the property. It doesn't matter whether the loan is a first, second, or third mortgage; the relationship of that loan and the total of all loans to the value of the property is what's important.

You want to avoid a situation where the mortgage(s) could exceed the value of the property. Obviously, that could cause a situation in which you couldn't get your money back if you had to foreclose. You don't want the total loans to even come close to the value. I'll talk about acceptable loan-to-value ratios (LTV) in a later chapter.

You want to have plenty of equity in the property. When somebody puts a lot of money into a piece of real estate, they are less apt to walk away from the property. They've put more in, so they're more apt to stay and make that property work.

Because real estate is a collateral so universally understood, you can (as I do) live in New York and work with paper on real estate in Seattle or anywhere else.

There's a whole continent between New York and Seattle, but we can call up an appraiser and get an estimate of value just as reliable as if you called an appraiser to give you a value of the house down the block. You can get that value very quickly and easily.

It doesn't matter if it's a single-family house, an apartment building, or raw land. Real estate has real value. If I buy a mortgage on a piece of real estate in Arizona, I know it will stay in Arizona. I don't have to wonder each day if it's still there. Real estate doesn't drive away in the middle of the night, as a car could possibly do.

A car is not good collateral for our purposes, because it depreciates in value and it can drive away. Real estate does not move, and it appreciates in value.

Some Things That Don't Add Value

Let me tell you a story.

A person sent me a deal on a mortgage secured by an apartment building. They said it was a multi-unit complex, but all the apartments were vacant. Then they said the property was owned by John McEnroe, the great tennis player, as if that was supposed to make it worth a lot.

I had to explain that we looked at the apartment building and the mortgage first. Only if the building and mortgage met our standards would we consider who owned it and whether they had resources and were credit-worthy.

We didn't do any investigation into this deal. To this day, I don't know whether John McEnroe really owned an apartment building where all the apartments were vacant. That's not the issue. The issue is to consider what the person was saying to me.

They were saying, "Hey, look, John McEnroe owns this property, and you know that John McEnroe makes a lot of money, so you know that he can afford to make the payments on the mortgage!"

Our reply was, "Yes, sure, but no one lives there now. There's no income. It doesn't matter what the owner's going to do with this property. It doesn't matter how great an area it is. It doesn't matter if John McEnroe plans to fill the building with every tennis player he knows. We have to look at it right now. If anything goes wrong with that piece of real estate, if the owner doesn't make payments for any reason, we're stuck with this totally vacant apartment building. Sorry, we can't be interested in the mortgage."

Another example is a mortgage we bought in Fairbanks, Alaska. It was on a nice piece of land. The owners were half done building a house on it, and were working to complete the job. When the mortgage holders asked us to evaluate the property, we said we could only evaluate the land.

They said, "But the house is half-built! It will be finished soon!"

We said, "Can you live in a house that's half-built? Would you want to move into a house that's half-built?" They agreed that they couldn't. We said we'd buy the mortgage if the price was right, but they had to understand that we could only quote on the mortgage secured by the land. Until it was finished, the half of a house added no value.

They understood. We gave them our quote and they accepted.

Beware of Inflated Prices

We all want our real estate to be worth a lot more than we paid for it and quite often it is, but don't let yourself get caught by someone's inflated prices.

Suppose you want to buy a mortgage on a house that has three offers to purchase for $500,000 each. Through your own research and appraisal you have determined that the most you could get for this house if you had to sell it is $400,000.

What is the house really worth? The three $500,000 offers or $400,000?

Until one of the $500,000 offers is accepted and the deal closes, the property is worth $400,000. Until then, the offers are only offers. Your appraisal tells you that the potential buyers are offering more than the property is worth. You'll see this in hot markets, for example the San Francisco Bay Area in 1989 and early 1990, where it was not uncommon to see a property go on the market and instantly have four or five offers, all for more than the asking price. It was a really *crazy* time to buy.

As a wise paper buyer, you'll only buy a mortgage based on the value of the property, not on inflated offers. If you buy a mortgage based on the appraised value and one of the inflated offers is accepted, that means that your mortgage pays off early and you've got quick yield. If it doesn't sell, you bought the mortgage based on real value and will make a real profit.

Suppose the property sold for $500,000, and the seller took back a mortgage to make the deal work. Now you're offered that new mortgage. Do you base your quote on the sale price or on the appraisal? Base your quote on the sale price, unless you suspect it was inflated. In this case, since there were three $500,000 offers, you can trust the sale price.

Remember that property is long-term. It just sits there, doing nothing more then serving as collateral. You may hold this mortgage for thirty years, so buy accordingly.

If You Have to Foreclose

Most mortgages are paid regularly, and paid off before maturity. Those are what you want, expect, and plan for. But what happens when the payments stop?

Foreclosure is your ultimate weapon and protection. In some cases, the simple threat of foreclosure will bring the payments up to date. In others, you have to foreclose.

In foreclosure, there are two possible outcomes:

1. Your mortgage is paid off from the proceeds of the foreclosure auction.
2. You acquire title to the property at or before the auction.

In the first case, your only risk is that the property won't sell for enough to pay off the remaining balance of the mortgage. If that seems likely or possible, your best defense is to take the property yourself and either keep it for income or sell it under better conditions than a foreclosure auction.

In the second case, you have a keep-or-sell decision to make. Your needs and the value, salability, and rentability of the property will make most such decisions easy.

There's plenty of money to be made by taking the property back, but it involves more work and requires different skills from buying, selling, and holding paper.

I'll spend more time on foreclosure in Chapters Fifteen and Sixteen, explaining the foreclosure process. You'll see that foreclosure can bring you even greater profits.

CHAPTER 5

Planning and Goal-Setting: Your Road Map to Success

Without planning and goal-setting, the Stefanchik Method will not work. Without a plan and realistic, achievable goals, the three entities don't matter. You won't achieve any of them.

The plan is your road map to wealth. Goals are where the road map takes you.

Everyone wants wealth, but few attain it.

Why?

Most people lack a plan. Simple as that.

Without a plan, goals are, by definition, unrealistic.

If you want to get anywhere, it is inconceivable that you can get there without a plan. Sometimes people get to the right place or attain wealth by blundering accident or incidental good fortune. Do you want to trust your future to accident and blind chance?

And yet many people seem to think wealth "just happens" to people. They can't see the need for a plan.

If the only thing you learn from this book is that you need a plan to accomplish anything worthwhile, then the book will have been worth every penny you paid for it.

Paper Goals

My three-entity approach to paper, or any plan to attain your financial goals, doesn't mean a thing if you don't set realistic, attainable goals. And, even more important, all the realistic, attainable goals in the world won't do you any good if you don't follow through and reach them. But first you have to set the goals.

Financial success is the same. The only way it happens instantly is through a massive inheritance or winning the lottery. Since I assume you have no prospects for those or any other means of becoming an instant zillionaire, let's plan—realistically.

How I Learned to Plan

I find that each time I set goals in whatever I'm trying to do, they serve to keep me on target and increase my chances of success.

In the early 80's I was trying to do a number of things at one time: I had a full-time job as a scientist; I was trying to get a master's degree in biochemistry; and I was running close to a hundred miles a week training for marathons.

You can see that I had a real load to carry. Trying to balance all these activities at one time was very, very difficult. It forced me to learn planning and goal-setting.

Early one Monday morning, when I was on my way to work, I started to think about all the things I had to do that week. I had a number of tests coming up at graduate school, and I don't need to tell you that tests at the graduate level are never easy. I had a number of projects that had to completed that week. If I didn't find time to run my planned miles, I'd never be ready for the next marathon.

I was driving and thinking, and driving and thinking, and driving and thinking. I thought I had more things to do than there were hours in the day.

I started to panic. I got really nervous, because I didn't know how in the world I was going to accomplish everything without something very important falling apart.

I arrived at work a little early, took out a piece of paper, and wrote across the top of it, evenly spaced: A.M., LUNCH, and P.M. Along the vertical, I wrote "Monday," "Tuesday," "Wednesday," etc., all the way through Sunday.

I blocked in the hours I had to spend at my job and times I had to be in class, and the time I had to spend driving to work. I assigned things that I could do in my free time. I could run at lunch and study in the evening. Or I could study in the afternoon and run in the evening. Or do a combination of a number of different things to accomplish my projects, keep running, and study for the exams. I assigned all the things that I had to do that week. I filled in the blocks for school. I had classes on Tuesday and Thursday, so I put those in first. I assigned study time for the exams, and put those in. I decided when I would run, and how far, each day. I sat back and looked at how much space still remained. I was shocked!

I couldn't believe I'd panicked twenty minutes earlier. With a few minutes' work and a little planning, I now had a very sensible, workable plan for that week.

Not only did I survive that week, I was able to do well on my exams, maintain my running schedule, and keep all my projects on track at work.

On the day I sat down with that sheet of paper to outline my week, I learned a very valuable lesson: not just how to effectively plan and set goals, but the power of goal-setting and planning to not only bring calmness and order to my life but also to increase my productivity and enjoyment of life.

There Is No Way You Can Achieve Success Without Goal-Setting

I was forced into learning the value of goal-setting. It's a lot easier to incorporate goal-setting and time-planning into our lives than to face a crisis and panic.

I no longer panic about not getting things done, unless it's my own fault—and even then it's a controlled panic, because I know I have the organizational tools to deal with the crisis in the best possible manner. I do my best to effectively plan everything I do.

My only source of possible panic is something that comes up at the last minute that I didn't know about and couldn't predict. Those panic moments are few and far between. There are some of them in everyone's life, but such moments are easier to deal with because everything else is under control.

On the day I sat down with that piece of paper, I learned that if I systematically plan what I want to do, continually revise what I'm doing as things change, and stay on top of things, I will be much more successful at anything I try to do.

You Can't Succeed Without a Plan

Why can't we achieve success without being a good goal-setter and planner?

The reason is simple. There is no way to achieve success without a plan. A plan must be followed or you won't reach the goals you set. You need a road map to success.

What's the difference between planning and goal-setting?

Planning is thinking through what you want to achieve and how you can achieve it.

Goal-setting is developing a timetable for when you're going to achieve each part of the plan. Now, how are we going to set one up?

The plan is easy. I think most people can sit down and set up some sort of plan for how they're going to achieve a desired goal. Now is the time for *you* to sit back and think through what you want to achieve. We're going to talk about different types of goals and how you can make them part of different types of plans.

If your goal is to make a million dollars, there's nothing wrong with that, but you're not going to do it in two months. Making your first million is a long-term goal.

You'll achieve goals only if you understand the timetable involved in doing whatever task you want to get done. If you expect to achieve a six-month goal in six weeks, you're setting yourself up for failure.

Planning is easy when you ask yourself the question, "What do I want to do?"

Once you have asked yourself this fundamental question, all you need to do is assign a timetable to it. Assigning the timetable is easier than you think. You simply estimate how long it will take to achieve the desired result and schedule that time in your planning. The easiest way to do this is to break it down into its component steps.

Taking the Steps to a Goal: An Example

On one of my many airline flights, I got to talking with the man sitting next to me. We were both very tall and obviously athletic, so it was logical to talk about sports.

He liked golf, and he asked if I played. I said I hadn't.

He said, "You know, it used to be I wasn't interested in golf, either, but once I tried it the game really fascinated me." He described how he'd become quite successful in about a year.

I asked, "How did you do that? I've always heard golf was a hard game to play really well, that it takes a long time to learn."

He said, "Well, a friend of mine said the game was simple if you broke it down into the important steps. The most important thing is learning to get the ball near the hole on your drive. If you do that, you've got a good chance of getting the ball in the hole in two putts, and that's what they allow for par. That means that if you can drive close to the hole, you're ninety percent there."

That's easier said than done, from what I'd heard. My new friend agreed, adding that putting was easier said than done, too, but it was also easier to learn.

"I wanted to learn fast," he said, "so I hired a coach." He described how he and his coach went to the driving range four times a week. For an hour or two, the coach watched him drive and worked on teaching him good habits and correcting bad ones. He was fortunate to have the money to hire a good coach and the hours to spend on a range. (Although I have to admit that he spent less time on the driving range than I spend on the road training for marathons.) The coach said being tall was a real advantage in getting power into hitting the ball, as long as he learned to focus his power on driving the ball in the right way.

Day after day, for eight or nine months, all he did was hit the ball. After that, the coach decided he was ready to go to a golf course. The two of them went to a course, and again he practiced, now working on his putting. After a year he was ready to face his buddies, who'd been playing the game for years.

His buddies knew he'd just started playing golf, but didn't know that he'd developed and followed a plan to learn in a few months what they'd learned from a lifetime of trial and error.

To their shock and amazement, he beat every one of them.

That's the power of a very focused plan followed through with dedication. He achieved success because he had a definite, strict, patient plan and adhered to it rigorously. His plan was to become a very good golfer in a very short time. In order to reach his goal he had to sacrifice money (for the coach and driving range) and a lot of time, but he achieved success.

Planning Your Own Success

How can you relate this story to your own path to success?

Look at the steps the golfer took.

First, he identified what he wanted to do.

Second, he learned what he needed to do to achieve the goal.

Third, he decided that he wanted to do it and that he could do it.

Fourth, he developed a plan to reach the goal.

Fifth, he committed the time, energy, and money needed to carry out his plan.

Sixth, he carried out his plan.

Seventh, he followed through on his success, continuing to do the things that brought him even more success, so he continued to improve.

You might say, well, how many people are going to have the patience to spend long hours for many months just to learn how to hit a golf ball? That's not a good example at all!

But that's just my point!

Look around you. How many successful people do you see? How many people do you see who have achieved the success you want to attain?

Not very many, right?

Perhaps about as many as might focus as much time and energy as my friend focused on learning golf? Or on learning something else important to them?

Most people want to run out to the golf course and have a good time. They have their fun, but don't achieve my friend's level of success. Most people bring that attitude to most of life, which is why they don't achieve success.

My friend simply set a goal, created a realistic (for him) plan, and carried it out.

You can do the same. All you need to do is think realistically about what you want to do and how you can do it, and then act.

Let's come back to success in paper.

Buying and selling mortgages can become very time-consuming.

Like my friend's dedication to golf, you have to work at it.

So, how can you achieve success in paper?

You need to create a plan. For your plan to work properly, you need to break the plan into short-term, medium-term, and long-term goals.

Short term is the achievement of something in a few weeks to two months.

Short term is very, very important. Short term is much more important than medium or long term. If you do not achieve short-term goals, you'll never get anything in the longer term. Short term is fundamental, the foundation for everything else you do.

To obtain short-term goals, break down what you want to achieve into steps you can take in up to two months. Identify the steps, plan for them, and take them.

Medium-term goals are the things you can do in three to twelve months. This is where short-term successes combine to produce larger successes. You continue to do everything you did for the short term, but now you can expand and repeat your efforts.

Long term is one to two years. That's about as far as you ever want to plan with any degree of specificity. The reason is that anything more than two years, to me, is a dream. You may be different, but I find my life changes considerably within two years, so I have a hard time planning beyond that, except in a very general way. It's okay to block out a general plan for longer, but remember that it's general and you'll probably change it.

If you'd like to extend your long-term plan to three years, there's nothing wrong with that. Just remember that anything beyond two or three years really does become a dream.

There's nothing wrong with dreams. If you didn't have a dream you wouldn't have a goal. Dreams give a reason to set goals and make plans, but dreams in themselves are not what a realistic plan is all about.

Write Down Your Goals!!!!

Yes, that's right, writing down your goals is important enough to justify four exclamation points. Because so many people can't be convinced to write down goals, maybe I should throw in four more for good measure: !!!! (And you should be glad most people won't write down goals—it means you have less competition!)

Why is it important to write down your goals?

If you don't write down and date your goals, you'll never achieve success.

The simple fact that you are writing something down and dating it, says to yourself that you are now committing yourself to achieving the goal.

If you sit back and say, "I'd like to do this," and, "I'd like to do that," there is no reason on earth why you would ever achieve those things. You're dreaming, not committing yourself to doing anything.

Until you've taken your dream out of your head and put it on paper, your dream will remain just a dream. You won't do the things needed to achieve it.

When you finally sit down, write down your plan to achieve your dreams, and date it, you've made a commitment to yourself. When you write down and date your plan, you can look back and see how you're doing at any time. Your written, dated plan means you know what you have to do and when you have to reach each goal. You know you've either achieved or not achieved your goals. If you've achieved one, you know what you need to achieve next. If you failed to achieve one, you know you need to look at why you didn't reach the goal, whatever it was, and decide whether you need to realign your priorities or go on to another goal.

This can't happen unless you write down your goals and date them.

Please do not ever, *ever,* try to achieve goal-setting and planning without committing everything to writing (!!!!).

Planning Achievement in Paper

Let's identify our short, medium, and long-term goals.

The way to begin is to say to yourself, after you've finished this book and know what you have to do, "What can I achieve within the next couple of months?"

A number of things are reasonable and possible.

First, finish this book. Write that down now, estimating how long it will take you. When you've achieved that goal, you may want to review the book. You don't want to begin until you're sure what you're going to do.

Second, you might go down to the county recorder's office and look up names. Another aspect of this step would be to place ads in local newspapers and begin any other form of advertising you may want to get rolling.

Third, send out letters to the names you generate.

Fourth, plan to be ready to respond to letters or phone calls generated by your letters or ads.

Fifth, prepare yourself to respond positively and confidently when the calls and letters come in.

As you can see from this list of steps, I want you to get something done within a short period of time. All of these things can easily be achieved within a month or two.

The simple fact that you've taken these actions, even if you have not yet received your first response or purchased your first discounted mortgage, will give you confidence that you can do it. As you take each action, check it off the list and date the checkmark. You'll feel great each time you date a checkmark, and you'll feel your energy building to continue on the path to success.

For medium-term goals, you may want to look at closing two or three deals within the next six months or so.

These goals are closely related to your short-term achievement.

If you did not go down to the county recorder's office or run an ad, there will be no mortgages for you to buy or sell. Remember, the short term and the medium term are very closely related to each other.

So what do we do for the long term?

Well, this is what I do. When I first started in paper, I looked at a long-term goal of one to two years. Within that time, I wanted to quit my job. I wanted to do paper full time. The only way I could do that was to achieve a number of successes in the medium term. I needed to close a number of deals, not only to make the money, but to assure myself that this system worked.

After all, when I first started, I thought it would work, but I hadn't done it yet, so I didn't *know* it would work for me. If I was going to quit my job I wanted to make sure that I had something that really worked. I didn't want to just jump into something without knowing I could do it successfully. I *strongly* suggest you do the same. Like me, you'll want to be sure paper works for you before quitting your job.

The plan that I've outlined worked. Within two years of starting in paper I was able to quit my job.

It worked for me, so I know it can work for you.

I can't emphasize too strongly that if you do not achieve short-term successes, you'll never achieve medium-term goals, much less long-term goals like quitting your job.

This is a very realistic plan, but if you put forth no effort in the beginning, there is no way that you'll ever reach your long-term goal. It will remain a distant dream.

Don't Try to Do Too Much—But Do It!

It's not the most difficult thing in the world to sit down and make a plan, write down your goals, and date them.

The problem almost everybody seems to have is actually doing it. Writing down goals makes doing it easier, but writing down, while essential, doesn't give you the energy to put your plan into action.

You need to take action.

Taking action will bring you that vital short-term success.

What Happens When You Try to Do Too Much

Without short-term successes you'll probably quit and decide it wasn't worth the effort. You not only won't achieve your overall plan, but you'll also begin to get depressed because of your doubt. That's not a favorable indication of success to come.

I want to caution you against setting too many short-term goals. If you set too many short-term goals, you'll find, every time, that you'll never achieve what you expect of yourself. When that happens, even if you're achieving so much your friends can't believe it, you'll get discouraged, disappointed, and distracted, and stop believing in yourself and your system.

When you start to get discouraged, disappointed, and distracted, your mind begins wandering, trying to figure out what went wrong or what else you should do instead. That's deadly to success.

This problem happens to most of my students. When I meet them, they say, "I'm going to get started *again*, soon." Then they ask me how to do that. I ask them what happened. And they say they started off just fine. They were very excited. But then they set up one too many things they wanted to do in too short a period of time, and all of a sudden they were achieving nothing.

I think that in many cases some part of them was really afraid of success and change. That fear ambushed them on their path to success by helping them convince themselves that they had to do more than was possible in their lives, under the circumstances in which they found themselves. When they failed to meet the commitment they made to themselves, they felt like failures.

Please, never forget that as much as you need to reach your short-term goals, cut yourself some slack. If you don't give yourself a little slack, if you set too many things to do in too short a period of time, you'll never achieve success.

Your goal-setting and goal-achieving has to be something you can do. Set what seems to be a reasonable goal. If it turns out not to be reasonable for you, scale back your expectations.

It's imperative that you think through, realistically, how much time you can devote to achievement of your short-term goals in the next three to eight weeks.

Write these down right now. After you've done so, think how achievement of these short term goals will build into medium and long term goals, and write that down, too.

Short Term

_____

_____

_____

_____

_____

_____

_____

_____

Medium Term

_____

_____

_____

_____

Long Term

_____

_____

If you do not write these down, right now, and date them, the enthusiasm you're feeling at this moment will be lost. You may never get it back.

What If Things Change?

You may not really know, at first, what a realistic goal for you actually is. If you plan and set goals and discover that, for any reason (time is the most common), you can't do all you planned, sit down with your goals and change them to reflect the reality you've discovered.

For example, suppose you discovered that you simply couldn't find enough time to spend at the county recorder's office. You might have expected to find a hundred names in your first outing and only located twenty mortgages in the time you could spend searching the records.

Well, okay. That's how many names you can find in your courthouse in the block of the time you have available.

Adjust your short-term goals and plans accordingly. If a goal that I or someone else might achieve in three months is going to take you a year, then plan to take a year. Don't feel you've failed because it took you longer; just keep doing it until you learn how long it really takes you to reach the goal of finding one hundred names.

When you change a goal, *write it down!*

When we set goals, like planning to finish this book in a week, or to put a deal together this month, we increase our chances for success.

Short-term goals, when achieved, give you momentum to keep setting new short-term goals to keep on achieving success in small steps.

You'll probably find that you change your medium-term goals too, as you learn what's a realistic short term goal for you. Many people, I think, will find that they've planned to do too much and will have to scale back a little. Others will find that they've been too cautious, and surprise themselves by how much more they can achieve than they expected and planned.

It doesn't matter which group you're part of, or even if you achieved exactly what you planned. The first short-term goals are an exploration, learning what you can expect of yourself.

Now, though, you really want to pick up speed to success. How do you do that? Look at your medium-term goals and set achievable standards for yourself. Your short-term goal achievements will lead to medium-term successes.

For example, if your medium-term goal is to produce $50,000 in the next fifteen months, that can only be accomplished by finishing this book and going out and doing a deal (short-term), and then repeating the process of closing more deals to add up to your medium-term goal of $50,000. If you hit the goal early, great! If you're in the fourteenth month and have only done two deals worth $10,000, then it's time to reevaluate your short-term goals and begin again, if you haven't already done so.

Don't let yourself think you've failed! You've achieved $10,000 worth of success. That's $10,000 more than most people! You just didn't do it in the medium term you anticipated. You've learned what you can expect of yourself and, I hope, you've learned how to be a better paper buyer.

Is it realistic to set your medium-term goal for the next fifteen months at $20,000? More? Another $10,000? Only you can answer that.

You may reevaluate your short-term goals and see that you have not spent enough time to achieve the success you desired. Okay, *can* you spend more time? What would give you more time? Is there a way to make better use of the time you have? Perhaps you need more advanced information about paper. Evaluate everything you've done, looking for ways to do it better.

Don't fall into the trap of looking for things you did wrong! That only reinforces the negative and makes you feel bad about yourself.

Do what you've decided will give you greater short-term success and try again. Now you have a much higher probability of reaching your goals.

"True" financial success (being able to quit your job; having more than all the money you need, etc.) is reached by achieving your long-term goals.

If you set a long-term goal to be a billionaire in five years, your chances of success are as good as winning the lottery, or less. Set your sights on something realistic.

A realistic long-term goal might be to quit your job and have $260,000 to invest in paper. That's achievable in five years. But you might be able to do it in two years (you'd be pretty exceptional), or you might need ten.

Perhaps the most important part of the planning and goal-setting process is the feedback it gives you about what *you* as an individual can realistically do, and what changes you can make to do more.

CHAPTER 6

Understanding Paper: A Deal

The previous chapters have given you an understanding of paper as an investment. Before you can do paper deals, you need to clearly understand how and why a deal is put together and what makes it work or not work. This includes knowing how real estate is financed, how and why privately held mortgages and trust deeds come into existence, and why those who hold them are willing to sell at a discount.

I like to think of learning to succeed in paper as a little like learning to run a marathon. I'm a long-distance runner, so I like to use running analogies. To someone who has never run at all, or who has only run shorter distances, completing a marathon may seem an unattainable goal. If you've never bought a privately held mortgage, you may likewise look at my success and see it as unattainable. But just as I had to run my first step before I could think of running a mile, much less a marathon, you have to do your first deal before you can think of achieving the level of success you want.

This chapter is about those first steps toward running the first mile.

Someone who wants to run a marathon may already run, but they need a firm running base to build from so they can train for the marathon. Without that firm base of training, they'll either never finish the race or they may injure themselves.

In paper, you don't want to hurt yourself financially and you do want to succeed. Your firm base of training is understanding how paper works, so you don't hurt yourself while doing the deals that prepare you to go the distance.

I'll go through a paper transaction in detail to show you how to get short-term cash.

Let me introduce the players who are part of our hypothetical deal.

First, meet Mary. Mary has a piece of real estate she wants to sell.

Next is Bill. He wants to buy Mary's real estate.

In a little while we'll meet David, who is a paper buyer like you, and John, who, like me, buys mortgages and trust deeds from people like David.

Mary's real estate is a single-family home, which she's selling for $130,000.

Bill has agreed to purchase it at that price. He has $50,000 cash to use as a down payment. He needs to finance an additional $80,000 in order to buy the house.

Mary owns the house outright, free and clear. There are no liens or back taxes against the property. This means that when the sale is completed, Mary will have $130,000 cash out of the deal, less her closing costs.

I'm assuming, to make this transaction simple, that Mary owns the house free and clear. You don't have to have a transaction free of other debt to profit from paper. In most cases you won't be dealing with free-and-clear property, but to make the numbers simple, let's make it free and clear.

Bill needs to borrow $80,000 to make this deal work. Where does he go for the money?

The Transaction with Standard Financing

More often than not, Bill will go to a bank for his loan to purchase Mary's house. And why not? That's what banks are there for; that's what everyone does.

Bill sits down with the banker, describes the property, and explains how much down payment he has. The banker does a little figuring and tells Bill his payment on a fixed-rate loan of $80,000 will be $775.00 a month for the next thirty years, assuming the property appraises okay and he qualifies for the loan.

Note: This payment may be high or low, depending on the interest rates actually available when a loan was made. When you buy paper, you'll find that the interest rate on the paper will relate to rates as they existed *at the time the loan was made,* not whatever the current rate happens to be.

This banker is offering Bill a *fully amortized loan. Amortization* on a loan means that *principal* and *interest* are paid simultaneously, but at different rates. The amount of principal (the money borrowed) paid back per payment increases over time, and the amount of interest paid (rent paid to the bank on their money) decreases over time. As the years pass, the principal gets paid off faster and less interest is charged. At the end of the thirty years, there is no principal left to pay. The following graph of a fully amortized loan of $80,000 with payments of $775.00 per month over thirty years illustrates what happens to the amounts of principal and interest over time. The payment stays constant at $775.00 per month over the life of the loan.

The exact number of payments with the corresponding amounts of principal and interest are given on an amortization schedule (see the example in Appendix 1). We can look at each payment or set of payments to learn where the borrower is in paying off the loan.

Before the bank agrees to lend Bill the money, it checks him out and approves or disapproves his loan. This normally takes anywhere from four to eight weeks.

The bank goes through Bill's financial life with a fine-toothed comb. It wants to be very sure Bill has the means to actually repay the money. The bank will ask for a net-worth statement, two years of tax returns, a credit report, verification of employment, etc. The process takes a long time. The bank does not want to lend money to just anyone, especially someone who has bad credit or little net worth.

The bank wants to make sure Bill has enough money, somewhere, for the down payment. If Bill borrowed the down payment, he'd be financing the entire purchase price. While the bank is in a safe foreclosure position by holding the first mortgage, it doesn't want to foreclose. Foreclosure takes time and costs money, even if the bank gets back its full principal and back payments. It looks at a borrowed

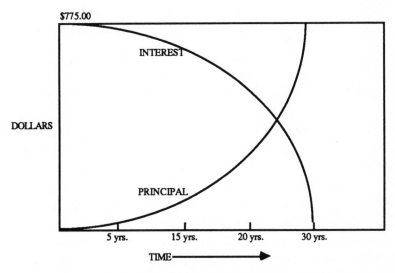

down payment as an additional debt it hadn't counted on, and one much too likely to send its security—the property—into foreclosure.

That's why banks are very careful, take a lot of time, and, as you know if you've ever bought a piece of property, are always asking for one more piece of documentation about something or other as the loan gets close to funding.

The bank also checks out the property itself, just as you will when considering purchasing paper. They do an appraisal on the property to learn whether the true value of the property supports the loan Bill is requesting.

They also do a title report on the property. The title report tells them what other liens, if any, are against the property, what positions those liens hold (whether first, second or third mortgages, for example), and whether property taxes have been paid. If there are taxes or outstanding liens when Bill buys the property, then at settlement those taxes and liens must be satisfied (paid off) so that the bank has first position, taxes have been paid, and insurance is current. The title report also reveals whether Mary holds a clear title, whether there are any covenants, conditions, and restrictions on the deed, and whether there are any easements on the property, among other information vital to determining the value of the property that will secure the bank's loan.

The bank will be very happy with Bill's $50,000 down payment provided the appraiser confirms the accuracy of the selling price.

But it also wants to be sure Bill has an income/debt ratio that will allow him to make the payments.

Finally, the bank calls Bill and tells him his loan has been approved. The banker goes over the details with Bill one more time. The banker explains to Bill he will be paying $775 each and every month for the next thirty years, or 360 payments, in order to pay off the loan of $80,000, unless he sells the property sooner, at which time Bill pays off the remaining principal balance from the proceeds of the sale.

A date is then set for closing. At the closing, in mortgage states, Mary, Bill, their attorneys, and a representative of the bank sit around a large table to review the documents and sign the papers that transfer ownership of title to the property from Mary to Bill.

Mary transfers the right of ownership of the property to Bill for cash. Bill gives Mary $50,000 of his own money and the bank gives Mary the remaining $80,000.

When closing is completed, Mary has $130,000 cash to use as she pleases. Bill owns the house and has signed a mortgage and promissory note. These state the terms of his loan from the bank.

If Bill decides that he wants to leave the property, sell the property, transfer the property, have someone assume the mortgage (if it's an assumable loan), or whatever, he's no longer liable for the rest of that money. It's either paid off or someone else legally assumes responsibility for the loan.

You can't take $775 and multiply it by 360 payments to learn the amount of money actually owed. The amount of money actually owed is the principal amount: $80,000. It's payable in installments of $775 each, a fraction of which goes to interest and the remaining fraction goes to principal. In the early years of the loan, most of Bill's payment is interest. The principal is being paid down slowly, so each month Bill will pay a little less interest and a little more principal.

If Bill decides to sell the property, he gets the difference between what the property is worth at that time and the remaining balance (principal) of the mortgage.

Bill has signed a promissory note. This is a legal promise to pay back the money. In this document all the terms are stated, such as interest rate, monthly payment, amount borrowed, as well as the parties' names and addresses, and of course the address and legal description of the property. Bill signs this document at closing and the bank puts it in a safe place. The promissory note is like a check worth $80,000 plus interest, payable at $775 a month for thirty years.

The note is combined with another legal document called the mortgage or trust deed, which is recorded—placed on public record—at the county recorder's office. It spells out, in detail, what Bill has agreed to. It also includes the legal description of the real estate Bill has purchased—the collateral the bank uses to secure the loan—listing the lot and block number of the property. It details what will happen if Bill doesn't make his payments.

The mortgage document is a contract between Bill and the bank. It's fairly standard all across the United States and Canada. In a number of states, mostly in the West, this contract is called a trust deed. California and Arizona are major trust deed states.

A trust deed serves the same purpose as a mortgage. It, too, has a promissory note associated with it, but instead of two parties (Bill and the bank) there are three parties, Bill, the bank, and a neutral third party, the trustee. The trustee is an independent person or company who holds the legal documents *in trust* for Bill and the bank. If it is necessary to foreclose, however, the procedure is usually faster in trust deed states than in mortgage states, which can be an advantage for anyone who holds paper.

For a paper investor, it really doesn't matter whether the note is secured by a two-party mortgage or a three-party trust deed. You still have someone who is selling a property and someone who is buying the property.

When closing is completed, Mary has her $130,000 cash, Bill has the property, and the bank has the mortgage or trust deed and promissory note. (For a further explanation of terms, see the glossary at the end of this book.) This is a basic cash transaction.

Bill's $50,000 cash down payment and the $80,000 cash from the bank loan Bill obtains gives Mary cash for her full equity, in this case the full value of the house. If she had owed money on a mortgage, say she had a $40,000 balance remaining on her loan, she would have gotten cash for her equity (the difference between the sale price and the remaining balance of her loan), and the rest of the cash would have paid off the mortgage.

Mary sells the property for cash. When she gets her cash, she goes on to buy her next house or does whatever she wants·with the cash. Mary, in this example, is choosing to do nothing more than sell Bill the property under a standard transaction.

A large percentage of all real estate transactions, whether for single-family homes, apartment buildings, commercial property, or raw land, are done in this way, with bank financing. The bank lends the money and the person who's selling the property is cashed out.

Now let's look at the alternative, which makes the Stefanchik Method possible.

The Creation of Paper

Let's change this scenario slightly. It's the same property and the same people are involved.

Bill still wants to buy Mary's property. All the amounts are the same, but instead of going to the bank for a loan of $80,000, Bill goes to Mary and asks her to hold the $80,000 first mortgage.

When Mary says, "Yes, I'll hold the mortgage," she is creating paper—a personally held mortgage. Mary would then be lending Bill $80,000, though she would not give it to him in cash.

The technical term for this is a *purchase-money mortgage*—this is a mortgage that is given to assist the purchase of real estate. It is a fairly universal term for paper. Even in trust-deed states, we refer to this kind of transaction as a purchase money transaction, involving a purchase money mortgage.

Mary gave Bill an $80,000 mortgage to assist in the purchase of the real estate.

Let's look at this deal from both sides and see why Bill and Mary might want to arrange financing between themselves and not involve a bank.

Why would Bill rather go to Mary than the bank? There are many reasons. One could be that it takes a lot less time to arrange a mortgage with Mary than it does to get a bank loan.

Mary doesn't have to go to a loan committee to get approval to lend Bill money. Mary won't charge Bill points or fees for the loan. She won't require an appraisal, because she and Bill have already agreed on the value of the house. (That can save a couple of weeks.) Mary won't check Bill out the way a bank might. Sure, she should do a credit report to make sure he is a good risk, but it won't be anything like the bank might do. Bill and Mary can sit down and work out all the terms and conditions between themselves. They can decide the interest rate, the terms of the mortgage, and how much Bill will pay Mary each month. The bank is not nearly as flexible as Mary can be.

It's clear it would be a great deal for Bill to go to Mary instead of the bank. But is it a good deal for Mary to hold the mortgage?

If Bill had gone to the bank and cashed Mary out, she would have had an additional $80,000 cash. What's she going to do with this money? Unless she has something specific in mind, like paying cash for another home, she'll probably put it in the bank and earn 5 or 6 percent on the money. If she holds the mortgage herself, she'll earn more than 11 percent on her money, using the figures in our example. She'll collect $775 each month for the next 360 months.

There aren't many investments around that will guarantee you a return in excess of 11 percent. So, one reason Mary might hold the paper herself is for the cash flow over time. If she's looking for retirement income, this is a wonderful deal for her.

Even if she plans to buy another house, she might want to carry the paper for income. Her $50,000 in direct cash from Bill's down payment would be more than enough for a down payment on another house, especially if she's looking for something smaller. She might find it a tax advantage to deduct mortgage payments on her new house while collecting interest from her loan to Bill.

Another reason this might appeal to Mary is that she will be getting a lot more than $80,000 back over the next thirty years. In fact it will be over three times the original $80,000, for a total of $279,000. This makes holding the paper very attractive.

The third reason Mary might hold this paper is the tax advantages involved. She may go to her tax advisor and ask his opinion. He will weigh the benefits of taking the $80,000 now and paying capital gains and the other associated taxes against collecting the money over time. Mary's tax position may change over the years, but it may be wiser to collect the money over time instead of cashing out. Now, Mary has three very good reasons to hold the note herself.

Mary has agreed to hold the mortgage. She is now acting like the bank. Since this transaction is just between Mary and Bill, they could have negotiated any kind of deal they wanted. The loan could have been amortized for twenty years, or ten, five, or any other period. They could have computed payments as if the loan were amortized over thirty years but required that the full remaining balance be paid after five years—a balloon payment. They could write the loan in any legal way they agreed to. No one else is part of this deal. It's just the two of them. At the closing there is no banker, just Mary and Bill, and possibly their attorneys.

Bill gives Mary his $50,000 and signs the promissory note and mortgage or trust deed for the balance of $80,000. Bill owns the real estate. Mary owns the $80,000 promissory note, mortgage, and $50,000 cash. The actual mortgage and note used by Mary is exactly the same as the one the bank uses, except that Mary's name is on it. There is no bank involved.

Mary is now free to move to the other side of town or the other side of the United States. As long as she stays in the fifty states, it will only cost Bill a first-class stamp to send her the $775 check each month. If Mary moves out of the country, she'll probably set up a U.S. bank account to handle her funds, so Bill would mail his check to the bank or the trustee of the account. Either way, Mary gets her money and Bill has no hassle making his payments.

Let's review what has happened in our paper transaction:

1. Bill wanted to buy a piece of real estate that Mary had offered to sell.
2. Bill asked Mary to carry the paper.
3. Mary decided she wanted to hold that paper. As we've seen, there are many reasons why she may want to do so.
4. Bill and Mary negotiate on the terms and conditions of how much cash down and how much of a mortgage Mary is going to hold. This is fully negotiable. They decide that Bill will put down $50,000 in cash and Mary will hold the balance as a purchase-money mortgage (paper) against the real estate for $80,000, payable at $775 per month over the next thirty years. At closing, when everything comes together, Mary will transfer her right of ownership to Bill for cash and paper. Bill will own the real estate. Mary will own the mortgage (paper) and cash.

5. Everybody walks away from this happy. Both Bill and
   Mary are ready to get on with their lives.

Oh, How Life Can Change in a Year

Let's skip forward and assume that twelve months have gone by
since Mary sold the property to Bill. He's made twelve payments,
always right on time. Everything is going fine.

Mary has just heard about a great new investment she would like
to get involved with, but she will need more cash than she has available. She may need cash for any reason, even so she could go Las
Vegas and gamble, but let's assume that her son-in-law is starting a
business and needs cash. She trusts his judgment and sees it as a
great investment, with a possible return far greater than she's getting
from Bill's payments.

As she tries to figure a way to get some cash in a hurry, she realizes, or a financial advisor tells her, that the paper she holds could
be a way to get some fast money. Mary wants to sell the paper and
cash out.

Bill still owes Mary twenty-nine years of $775 monthly payments
(since one year of payments have been made). That cash flow should
be worth quite a bit to the right person.

Mary has been going through the newspaper classified ads every
week. She sees an ad like this one that simply states:

> ## "I Pay Cash for Mortgages
> ## Call Mark at 994-3683"

Mary calls David and says, "I have a mortgage I'd like to sell. Do
you want to purchase it?"

David asks for the details of the mortgage.

Mary explains that a year ago she sold a house to Bill and took
back a mortgage for $80,000, with monthly payments of $775 for
thirty years, but she now would like to sell it.

David writes all this down and asks a few additional questions so
he can understand all the facts.

After giving David all the information, Mary tells him that at the closing a year ago she was given an amortization schedule listing each of the 360 payments she was to receive. Since it was a fully amortized mortgage, it showed each month's payment with the corresponding remaining principal balance after each payment of the principal and interest. According to her amortization schedule, after twelve payments have been made, the remaining principal balance is now $79,658.84.

Mary says, "David, if you give me a check for $79,658.84 I'll sell you my mortgage."

At this point, David has a little explaining to do.

David doesn't plan to buy this mortgage for $79,658.84. David won't pay that amount because he'll be receiving his money over the next twenty-nine years. The time value of money affects the value of paper. David has to explain to Mary why her mortgage is not worth face value, and why the dollars she receives twenty-nine years from now will not be worth as much as the dollars she receives today.

The Time Value of Money

The time value of money states that by paying cash today to receive cash tomorrow, you have to get a discount because you have to wait to collect your money.

The longer you wait to get your money back, the less you can pay today.

The shorter the time before you get your money, the more you are willing to pay today, though you still must get a discount.

Whenever you pay cash today to receive cash at some future date, you have to get a discount because time erodes the value of the money.

Let me give you a simplified example of the time value of money.

When someone has a baby, a frequent gift to the new child is a U.S. Savings Bond. It's a great gift, because it matures in twenty years, when the infant will be an adult, either in college or perhaps starting a family and setting up a household.

Suppose you buy the child a $100 savings bond. Do you pay $100 for it? No. The bond is worth $100 at maturity, so you pay much less. Would you pay $100 for that twenty-year bond now? Would you pay $100 today to receive $100 in twenty years? Of course you wouldn't! You'd pay maybe $50 or $60 dollars today.

This is exactly how the time value of money works in a very simple example, familiar to everyone. It's paying less for something today because you will get your money back at a future date.

When you buy a bond, the certificate states that it will pay a certain rate of compound interest. The compound interest will result in the $100 payoff at maturity. If you cash in the bond before maturity, you get less than the face amount of $100 because it will not yet have earned enough interest.

Most people understand compounding, or can understand it with a simple example like the savings bond. If you bought the $100 bond for $60, the amount you paid would be the principal. The $40 difference between $60 and $100 is the interest earned over the life of the bond. That would figure out to a 66.67% yield over twenty years, or 3.335 percent per year—a much lower yield than you'll get in paper.

Discounting is the reverse of compounding, but many people have a hard time understanding this. Using our savings bond example, when we bought a $100 bond for $60, the $100 face value was discounted 40 percent ($40) because we were buying the future value of $100. We have to wait twenty years to get the face value.

Compounding is the process of computing a rate of interest that will create the future value. Discounting is the process of computing how much we can afford to pay for an existing future value, whether in a savings bond or in a personally held mortgage.

David still isn't quite sure Mary understands, so he asks her how much it cost her to go to a movie ten years ago. Mary isn't exactly sure, but says it was probably around two dollars. David asks how much she paid the last time she saw a movie. Mary says it was about seven dollars.

In ten years, the cost of a movie has gone up five dollars! The only real difference is that it's ten years later. Have movies gotten so much better that they can justify a five-dollar increase? Or is the dollar just buying less today?

With this or similar examples, David can show Mary that the money her mortgage will earn ten, twenty or thirty years from now will be worth much less than it is today.

This is how she will see that David's offer is a fair price. David is not discounting Mary's paper because he just wants to. He's discounting it because he *has* to, for sound economic and financial reasons. The discount is completely negotiable. Whatever price David and Mary agree to is the price that will be paid.

Not Everyone Will Sell

One key point is that many private mortgage or trust-deed holders will find that it is *not* to their advantage to sell. They don't need the money that much. You'll talk to many such people. The most lucid explanation in the world won't convince them to sell if it isn't to their advantage. There are more than enough people who need to sell their paper to make you quite wealthy. Don't waste your time after you've determined that it's not in a person's interest to sell.

David's Offer to Mary

Now let's look at why David wants to buy Mary's mortgage, and how he plans to use the Stefanchik Method to make money.

David fully understands a number of key concepts that I'll discuss in detail in later chapters. These include, in addition to the time value of money, the value of real estate, and the importance of the loan-to-value ratio (LTV).

He knows he can only offer a certain percentage of the face value of any mortgage or trust deed. By applying these concepts, David knows how much he can offer—or whether he should make an offer at all.

These concepts are the heart and soul of the Stefanchik Method. When you have finished this book, you'll understand them as well as David does.

David knows that if he can buy the note for the right price he'll make money whether he sells the paper or holds it. In this example, he plans to sell the mortgage to John. We'll get to John's part in the transaction in a moment.

Now he has to make an offer to Mary.

The amount David can offer her is fully negotiable. The price is whatever he and Mary agree upon. There is no fixed amount, no legal amount, no amount he is required to offer.

If he were to buy a used car, he might go to one of the blue books that give average values for used cars and decide from that what he would offer to buy the car. He has a basis for his offer, but the car will sell for whatever he and the other party negotiate and agree upon. The owner can give the car away if he wants to. If it's rare or a classic car, the owner may ask and get many times the original price. The price is fully negotiable.

I've written an entire workbook, with cassette tapes, on exactly this point. I call it *Negotiating: The Key to Success,* because this is crucial to the Stefanchik Method. If you can't negotiate, you'll find it hard to buy paper. I've made the workbook available to my students as a separate set of materials. Negotiation is a skill anyone can learn. I'll talk more about it later.

Before David begins his actual negotiation, he gets as much information about the mortgage, the property, and Bill's payment record as Mary can give him. If Mary doesn't have all the information, he will ask her to get it and call him back.

David uses a mortgage worksheet (see example in the Appendix) to ensure that he remembers to ask all the questions and get all the answers. When he has the information he needs, he's ready to negotiate. He doesn't negotiate from lack of knowledge, which would be terribly risky.

The mortgage worksheet is one of David's most important tools, because it enables him to get all the information he needs on one sheet of paper. It provides him with a chart of the things that will determine whether or not the deal is worth doing. Even more important, John will ask him the same questions when David calls to ask whether John is interested in buying the mortgage. After David has done a few deals, he'll be able to look at a mortgage worksheet and tell at a glance whether the mortgage is worth buying.

Because he's making an offer based on what Mary tells him, and he doesn't know whether the information is accurate or whether Mary is hiding something from him, his offer is *conditional* upon the validity of the information and the appraisal, and his approval of everything.

David tells Mary he can offer $50,000 for her $80,000 mortgage.

Mary, understandably, is shocked. Even with David's explanation of the time value of money, she'd expected a lot more. Now David has to explain why that's the most he can offer.

Mary may decide she doesn't need to sell, or she may realistically look at the benefits of cash now versus cash twenty-nine years from now.

In most cases, Mary and David will negotiate back and forth on how much David will pay. David might offer $45,000, so he has room to negotiate upward. For this example, we'll keep it simple and assume David offered $50,000 and Mary accepted.

When Mary first called David, she expected to get the full face value of her mortgage, but she didn't understand the time value of money. Now she does and realizes that if she wants to cash out, she'll have to take a discount to sell her mortgage. She needs the money, so she decides to go ahead with the deal at $50,000.

David asks Mary to provide the proper preliminary paperwork so they can proceed with the deal. At the closing Mary will get $50,000 in cash, everything conditional on whatever David has stated when he made his offer.

Now, David can go to John and say, "I've found a good mortgage you can buy. These are the details. How much will you pay for it?"

Who Is John?

John now becomes part of our scenario. He's a paper buyer, like myself. He buys personally held mortgage notes and trust deeds (paper) all over the United States and Canada. He does this every day. It's what he does for a living.

Whenever possible—and it usually is—David calls John *before* he gives Mary a quote. He tells Mary, in their first conversation, that he will have to analyze and check out the figures she's given him before he can make his offer. He calls John, prepared to give him the numbers and other information on his mortgage worksheet.

David tells John he has a note with twenty-nine years left with monthly payments of $775. That sounds good to John, but before he gives a quote he'll ask David the same questions David asked Mary. David has that information on the mortgage worksheet.

John will consider Bill's creditworthiness, since Bill is making the payments. He'll ask what area of the country the property is located in, how the property values have been there, what the future looks like, and a series of other questions that will help him determine if this is a deal he wants to purchase. When all of John's questions have been answered, John provides David with a quote. John says he'll pay $60,000 for this mortgage, conditional on everything checking out and the appraisal coming in okay.

This gives David the information he needs to proceed with Mary. He confirms his offer, if he made it before talking to John, or makes the offer and negotiates a price if he talked to John first. Mary, as we discussed above, agrees to accept $50,000.

For the purposes of this example, we'll assume everything checks out and the deal closes. In actual deals, you'll find that things check out far more often than not, and sometimes when things are not exactly as you were told, they still aren't far enough out of line to wreck the deal. When you do discover a hidden deal-wrecker, you should probably go buy a bottle of champagne (or whatever you prefer) to celebrate the fact that you escaped a bad deal. That's why checking all the details is so important.

When the deal closes, Mary assigns her mortgage to John. She's paid $50,000 and walks away. She has nothing further to do with the note or Bill or her old house. John owns the mortgage, the right to twenty-nine years of $775 per month, and all other rights written into the mortgage. The title company goes to the county recorder's office and requests it to record an *assignment of mortgage*, which shows that Mary has assigned her mortgage to John, and John is now the owner of that mortgage.

David collects, in cash, the $10,000-dollar difference between what John, the investor, is willing to pay, and Mary, the note seller, is willing to accept.

This is the short-term solution to David's financial situation. Entity number one, cash, is at work. David will collect his $10,000 cash at closing. All he has to do is bring the deal to a close.

This Is Real

This deal is not fantasy.

Deals like it take place all over the country each and every day, some with more than $10,000 going to the David in the deal, some with less.

There are people just like Bill, Mary, David, and John in every city in the country. The aggressive buyer and seller of paper is out there looking for the deals all the time. It wouldn't take very long to become wealthy with paper. The Stefanchik Method provides this kind of potential.

At this point at seminars I usually am bombarded by questions about Mary.

It may seem that David is taking advantage of Mary, and that Mary would never agree to a deal like this. Wrong on both counts.

In the next chapter, I'll talk about that and some other aspects of this deal that I didn't take time to explain in detail here.

What Made this Deal Work?

The deal between David and Mary, with John providing the funds, worked for several reasons.

1. The time value of money.
2. Mary's need for money now, not in the future.
3. David's ability to explain the time value of money, which enables Mary to understand why she can't get face value for her mortgage, and to negotiate a price.
4. David's connection to John, and his ability to evaluate Mary's mortgage as one John will purchase.
5. John's ability to fund the purchase of Mary's mortgage for more than David was offering Mary.

What Special Knowledge Does the Note Seller Need?

None.

David (you) needs a great deal of knowledge, and needs to know it well enough to explain it clearly to the note seller, but the seller, in the beginning, only needs to know that the note can be sold.

It's not that Mary should be ignorant, but she doesn't *need* specialized knowledge of finance or money or anything else. She just needs cash.

She probably won't sell until she knows how the time value of money works and sees that David's offer is fair, and that the price she accepts is to her advantage.

She *does* need to know why she needs the money and why the deal would be to her advantage. Otherwise, she's just selling blindly—but that's her concern, not David's.

Why Doesn't Mary Go Directly to John?

This question comes up quite frequently. The simple answer is that she doesn't know who he is. She has no idea who John is, nor, more important, where to find him. Most people don't know who buys mortgages. David is doing Mary a service by linking her to John's funds. He's doing John a service by locating Mary's mortgage. The money he puts in his pocket, whether the $10,000 in our example or perhaps $1,500 on a smaller deal, is his fee for his time, effort, and knowledge.

If Mary knew about John, would she go to him directly? Maybe. The point is that she doesn't, and John doesn't know about her. David is the person who puts them together.

Does Mary think that David is buying the mortgage? Maybe. It depends on the way the deal is structured. The reason I say, "maybe" is because she may feel a rapport with David that she doesn't get from John. Maybe David can understand her need for cash better than John can. Or maybe she just goes to John directly and never contacts David.

If Mary asks, David must disclose that John is funding the transaction.

Could David buy that mortgage for his own account? Yes, if he has the personal funds to do so. Will David buy the mortgage in this case? No. He'll flip it to John. Cash is cash. Whether Mary is getting the cash from John or whether Mary is getting the cash from David, cash is still cash. She gets $50,000 in cash no matter who provides the funds or shows up at the closing.

David could buy the paper and resell it in a simultaneous closing. He could also write the contract so that he could assign it to John. To do this, instead of writing just his name in the contract as the purchaser, he would write "David Miller *and/or Assigns or Assignee.*" He can then assign the contract to John for whatever price John will pay. Mary gets her $50,000 no matter how this is structured.

The outcome of this deal is that Mary will get $50,000 in cash. David will make $10,000 just for the connection, and John will buy twenty-nine years of $775 a month secured by a house that Bill lives in.

Is David Taking Advantage of Mary?

Absolutely not!

This is an important consideration because many states have laws against taking unfair advantage of a distressed seller. These laws are mostly intended to prevent abuse of people facing foreclosure, and there's often a wide gray area in their interpretation. These laws apply to buying and selling real estate, not paper.

I know of no similar law applying to buying and selling paper. However, if you encounter a situation in which the "Mary" of your deal is selling the mortgage to avoid foreclosure on his or her current residence or to prevent bankruptcy, I'd advise caution and suggest that you obtain good legal advice. And, though you can't be a charitable organization while making money in paper or anything else, if you find such a person, I'd suggest that you give them as much benefit as you can. Take a minimum profit and be glad you've been able to help someone.

Our internal research indicates that few people sell mortgages because they are in financial difficulty. Almost always, they have a good, clear reason why they need cash now, not payments later.

David is not taking advantage of Mary. She was freely offering her mortgage for sale. David made an offer that she could have refused. She was not under pressure to accept. They negotiated fairly to arrive at the purchase price.

David is not concerned with why Mary needs the money, unless he picks up an indication that she's in financial distress.

So, why is Mary going to discount that mortgage? Because she needs cash. She has her own reasons for needing the cash.

Why is she going to work with David? Because she needs cash now. David is providing that cash (through John).

Mary may be able to get a better price somewhere else. She may not be able to get a better price somewhere else. In this case, David is the only game in town if she wishes to convert the long-term payments of her mortgage to short-term cash today.

Does she really feel the discount? It depends. If Mary takes the money to Las Vegas and gambles it away, did she lose the value of those dollars? Yes. But suppose she takes that money and invests it in a growing company her son-in-law has started up. The company prospers and within two years she triples her money. Did she effectively see the discount on that mortgage? No, because she used the money wisely. In two years she earned more than 50 percent of the money she'd have gotten in thirty years from the mortgage.

Who are we, David, or anyone else to judge what she should or should not do with the money? It's totally up to her. We do know one thing: she's going to sell her mortgage, not because of ignorance, but because she needs the cash now. David is able to provide that service. A bank will not provide it. No lending institution can provide it. They will not lend against a personally held mortgage.

Banks buy mortgages from other institutions on a large scale, if they buy at all. Banks buy millions and millions of dollars' worth of mortgages, but it doesn't make sense for them to buy one mortgage. It's an inefficient use of a bank's time and resources; if it can't work with millions of dollars worth of mortgages or trust deeds, it isn't worth its time.

We carve out our niche in the mortgage market using the Stefanchik Method. Our niche is not based on Mary's ignorance but on the fact that there are millions of people like Mary across the country who need ready money—for perhaps as many reasons as there are people—and who want to cash out on their mortgage.

CHAPTER 8

Protecting David's Position

David can sometimes find himself in a very awkward and precarious position. He's standing between Mary, who wants to sell her mortgage, and John, who wants to buy it. He's the man in the middle. He could make $10,000, but what if John doesn't come through? If you've wondered and worried about that possibility, you've worried right.

When you were a child, was "monkey in the middle" a common game on your playground? The idea is that two kids grab something belonging to a third child (the monkey), and when he attempts to get it back the other two kids toss it back and forth, high over his head, so he can't get it.

If you were ever the monkey, you remember how frustrating it was to be trapped in the middle, unable to do anything about it.

David doesn't mind being in the middle, because he's about to make $10,000, the difference between what John is willing to pay and Mary is willing to accept. But he's at risk of becoming a financial monkey in the middle if he doesn't keep control of the deal and close it properly.

David is the orchestrator of the deal. His responsibility—to Mary and John, as well as to himself—is to make sure it works.

Fortunately, it's easy to do things right. There's a lot involved in David's orchestrating of the deal, which I'll discuss in later chapters, but ultimately it isn't difficult.

But what happens if something goes wrong? Sure, there's a clear profit there for David, but what happens if David offers too high a price and there's no John who will allow him to recoup it?

If David offered $50,000 to Mary, but the best price any John will pay is $55,000, David would only make $5,000. That still isn't bad. But what happens if David offers $50,000 and the best price any John will pay is $45,000? Will David lose $5,000? Or maybe John sees something David missed and won't buy the mortgage at all! Will David be left holding the bag for $50,000 he doesn't have?

The answer is NO!

David, if he's done it right, is fully protected from such disasters. David has told Mary that purchasing the mortgage and the price he offers is subject to everything checking out. When David makes an offer to buy any mortgage, his offer is always subject to verification of all the pertinent information necessary to do the deal *and to David's approval of the information.* If David doesn't like what he sees, he doesn't have to explain why he is canceling the deal. The fact that he doesn't approve of something is sufficient. For example, the property may be rundown, or in a really bad area, or he learns that he has not been told everything about the property and mortgage by the mortgage seller.

If David realizes he offered too much for the mortgage (or can't find a John to buy it), he can simply drive by the property and call Mary back to report, "I've looked at the property and don't like what I see. I don't want to do the deal."

David has a legitimate, legal, ethical, back door built into each offer he makes, because all offers are subject to everything checking out properly and approval by the buyer. David must only ensure that he makes this clear to Mary, and that any offer he signs contains the appropriate language.

On one recent transaction, we made an offer to purchase a deal through a student of mine in the Boston area. We offered $38,000 to purchase a mortgage secured by an owner-occupied single-family home in Vermont.

For the first week after the offer was made my student sent in all the preliminary documents, and everything checked out. We always ask for a recent picture or two of the property, but the pictures furnished to the student were from a year before, when the property was last sold. The home looked great.

We ordered an appraisal, as we always do, to get a current estimate of value. The appraisal came back with a few current pictures of the property. (Usually an appraiser sends two pictures, but this time we got quite a few photographs.) To our astonishment, the new owner had painted each side of the home a different color. There was a mural on the garage that looked more like graffiti. That was why the appraiser kept shooting pictures. He couldn't believe what he saw.

We immediately called our student and asked if he had personally seen this property. He replied, "No, I live in Boston and haven't been to Vermont in years."

We explained what the appraisal revealed and said that our offer of $38,000 was revoked. The property had lost significant value because of the owners' peculiar artistic tastes.

The student understood, because we explained that if we had to take the property back, we'd have to spend a great deal of money to turn this property around into something anyone but the present owner could love.

Any time you make an offer, everything must check out. If it doesn't, the deal won't go through. You, as David, will not be left as the monkey in the middle, holding an empty bag.

How Does It All Come Together?

That takes care of one side of protecting David's interests. He won't be caught with a binding contract to buy a mortgage that is worth less than it originally appeared.

Now, how does he make sure John will fund the deal?

You can see the potential problem. John says, "Sure, as soon as you buy the mortgage from Mary, I'll write you a check for $60,000. Go ahead and write her a check. You can cover it with my check."

Whoops!

Suppose David writes Mary a check, and John says, "Sorry, I changed my mind." That's not going to work! The Stefanchik Method is not about taking that kind of risk!

Paper investors have taken that kind of risk. You may hear someone assure that "everybody does it," and you shouldn't worry. Wrong! Usually, everything works out just fine—but if it doesn't, David has just knowingly written a bad check for a very large amount of money. This breaks a number of laws. He could go to jail for it.

David can prevent this from ever happening.

He does not proceed to closing with Mary until he has a signed contract with John. He either purchases the mortgage with his own funds, or borrows the funds, short term, on the security of his contract with John.

The scenario described above is called a *double closing* or *simultaneous closing.*

In a double closing, David meets Mary at the title office. He writes Mary a check for $50,000 and she signs over the mortgage and note to David. Mary is now finished with this deal and leaves with her money. She is out of the picture. David owns the note and it's his to do what he wants. The only problem is that, technically, he doesn't have $50,000 to cover his check.

John arrives at the title office and writes a check to David for $60,000. David assigns the mortgage and note to John. Now David can cover his check. David only owned the note for a few minutes or less, but made $10,000 for his efforts.

The two closings took place within minutes of each other at the same location almost simultaneously. David did actually own the mortgage for a few minutes, without having the money to back up his check.

In practice, double closings are regulated by the laws of each state and by some federal agencies when their money is involved. The title company is aware that a double closing will take place, and will not only assure compliance with the law, but will not complete either closing until it holds funds for both. Because the title company knows that David's money is coming from John, they won't close his purchase of Mary's note until they have John's funds and verify that his check is valid.

Perhaps David is worried that Mary will find out where his funds were coming from. It's true that with this kind of double closing the odds are astronomical against her ever learning about his source of funds. She's got her cash. She doesn't own the mortgage. She has no reason to check. In her eyes, everything is fine.

Let's look at alternatives to a double closing.

One method is to put John in contact with Mary and let her sell the mortgage to him directly. David still gets a fee for his work, because John understands the value of what David is doing and will sign a written agreement for the deal. John is happy to let David negotiate whatever price he can with Mary.

David puts John and Mary together after he has reached agreement with Mary on price and has obtained a signed commitment from John to purchase the mortgage. At that point, David tells Mary who will buy the mortgage and brings the two together.

In his first conversation with Mary, David should say something like, "This sounds good. I'll review the figures and get back to you with a quote." In the second conversation, when he gives the quote, he should disclose that John is the actual buyer and he (David) is acting as the agent. That avoids any misunderstandings later.

But what if Mary finds someone like John and sells it directly to him, bypassing David, the middleman? If Mary knew where to find John, she'd skip David. She'd have no need for his services.

Normally, however, Mary doesn't know where to find John. The only way she found David was by seeing his ad in the newspaper or getting his letter. She is dealing with David because he advertised that he was available for this kind of deal, made the contact, and did the negotiation.

It doesn't matter how he made contact. He could have run an ad in the newspaper or sent a letter to Mary, or used some other kind of advertising to let her know he wanted to buy her mortgage. Mary is dealing with David and no one else.

Another common method is the *assignment of contract*. In this method, David gets a price and a signed commitment to purchase from John *before* he quotes to Mary. Then David signs a *mortgage purchase agreement* (MPA) with Mary. In the MPA, David puts his name in the form I mentioned earlier, "David Miller and/or Assigns or Assignee." David then assigns the mortgage to John for the difference between John's quoted and committed price and the price David and Mary agreed to in the MPA.

This is the method we, at S.E.S. Funding, recommend you use when working with us.

How Does David Know John Will Pay Him?

What's to prevent John from buying Mary's mortgage and forgetting about David?

Self-interest, first. John makes money buying a lot of mortgages, not just one or two. He knows that if David has found one good mortgage, he'll find more. John wants an ongoing, profitable relationship. He's glad to see David making that $10,000, because he knows that a good profit will keep David looking for more mortgages.

Second, Mary and David will sign a written contract (MPA) committing each of them to the deal. This protects both John and David.

Third, David must keep control of the deal. That means that he runs the deal on his end, even if John and Mary are now dealing directly with each other. John may not be in the city where David and Mary live. David sets up the *settlement* or *escrow*—the term used in trust-deed states—with the title company and is John's contact to obtain whatever reports and papers are needed. David makes sure everything goes right. He doesn't depend on John or anyone else to close the deal and send him a check. He controls the settlement or escrow to assure that when the deal closes he'll get his share of the deal.

It's very important for David to control escrow or settlement because, unfortunately, there are people out there who don't understand their own self-interest, who may try to take advantage of him.

I recently received a letter from a student who had encountered just such a person. This student chose *not* to work with S.E.S. Funding.

The letter arrived not two days after I mailed a newsletter in which I advised students to keep control of their deals and never rely on someone else to take care of everything and pay them their share when it closed.

When you're beginning, you may find it very easy to assume that the other person is experienced and knows what to do, and therefore it seems to make sense to let them handle everything.

Wrong!

The other person may know more than you and may be perfectly honorable, but if you let them do everything you'll never learn how to do it yourself. You'll be left wide open to anyone who wants to rip you off.

My student had just been the victim of exactly what I was talking about. She said, "Please let people know what happened to me, so it doesn't happen to them."

She didn't maintain control of the deal and didn't have the agreement in writing. She gave control to the buyer, who said, "Don't worry, I'll take care of everything." She expected to get paid by that person, but that person was not buying the mortgage with his own money, like John. Instead, he was another person like my student who was finding deals and flipping the deal to someone else for funding. This created a daisy-chain deal in which too many people were trying to make a profit from one deal. When the deal closed, he didn't pay her. She wound up losing almost $2,000.

So, what I want to say to you, from her and from me, is *be careful!* Check out everyone you do business with. Keep control of your deals. If someone tries to take away your control, get out of the deal!

I don't understand why people rip off other paper buyers. It's just bad business practice. The guy who ripped off my student will never do business with her again. Think how much more than $2,000 he could have made with a long-term profitable relationship! Not only will he never do business with her, she told me, and everyone else she knows now knows about it. As I said earlier, paper buyers are a relatively small, close-knit community.

CHAPTER 9

How to Use the Best-Kept Secret

By now it should be obvious that David would not do any business without his advertising (or marketing) efforts. Business of any kind doesn't happen by itself. The businessperson generates business by his or her choice of product, location, advertising, and so on.

Finding and buying paper is no different. It's a business, and you should treat your paper buying career like one.

David's product is his ability to buy mortgages. He has to find ways to market that product to people who want to sell mortgages. He also has to market his ability to find good mortgages to investors like John.

It's not hard.

Marketing Is the Key

David needs to get his name out there, letting people know that he has cash for their mortgages. He is a cash-flow-to-cash conversion machine. David is telling everyone who sees his advertising that he has cash today for their future cash flow.

How does he do this?

As I've said earlier, one way is to place an ad in the local newspaper. The ad would be brief and to the point:

> ## We PAY CASH For Your Mortgage.
> ## Call Mark 967-1313

Or he might use something I've had a lot of success with:

**WE BUY MORTGAGES
FULL AND PARTIAL**

I'll discuss what a partial is in a later chapter.

The classified ad didn't cost David much money, but it was worth $10,000 because it put him in touch with Mary. This is a very inexpensive way to let people know you are available to buy their paper.

The weakness of newspaper advertising is that it only reaches people who are actively looking to sell their paper, people who know where to look.

You won't get the response you could expect from more direct marketing, but you'll get enough to be more than worthwhile. You'll get calls from people who think you want to buy the mortgage they're paying on. That sounds crazy (and it is), but these callers never think how ridiculous it would be for you to buy the privilege of paying off their mortgage without getting the benefit of living in the house.

You'll also get calls from people like yourself, who want to find, buy and flip mortgages, and a few calls from investors like John who are prepared to buy mortgages from you. Those few calls can be just as useful as calls from people with mortgages to sell.

Using the Best-Kept Secret

There's nothing wrong and a lot that's right with using a classified ad, but there's a place where all mortgages are listed. If you go there, you'll find far more mortgages than you'll locate through classified ads.

Even better, it's free. The only catch is that you have to spend the time to look up and write down the mortgages you want, which can take a lot of time—but it's highly rewarding time, time well and profitably spent.

I've spoken earlier about going to the county courthouse to look up mortgages. That's where all recorded mortgages are listed. Throughout the United States and Canada we have a public process for recording legal transactions such as these. Every mortgage taken out by a bank or individual is recorded on public record for anyone to read. The names of everyone receiving mortgage payments is a matter of public record.

I call it the best-kept secret on public record because so few people even know it exists, much less how they can use those records to find paper and make money.

All you have to do is go into any county recorder's office anywhere in the United States and look up the names and addresses of these people and copy them down. Then you send each of those note holders a letter asking whether they'd be interested in selling their mortgage for cash.

At the Recorder's Office

When you go down to your local county recorder's office, don't expect to go in and ask the clerk for the list of names and addresses of private individuals receiving payments on mortgages.

The clerk will definitely reply, "We have no such list."

This is true. Mortgages are not listed that way.

Most county recorder's offices call their list a *mortgagors' index*. (The mortgagor is the person making the payments—Bill, in our example.) If your county uses a different name, a description of what you're looking for will usually get you to the right list. The list, usually compiled every year, alphabetizes all the people who are making payments on mortgages.

When you open up the mortgagor index for whatever year you are interested in, you will see a list of all people making payments to all the entities that hold mortgages. The entities receiving payments on a mortgage are call mortgagees. The entities could be banks, mortgage companies, large corporations, pension funds, credit unions, and individuals. These entities are also listed. (It wouldn't make much sense to list the person making payments without also listing the person or entity receiving the payments.)

You're looking for individuals, because you want privately held paper. You're not interested in buying and selling paper on the scale engaged in by banks and other institutions.

To find these mortgages, simply look down the list of mortgagees till you find a person's name instead of an institutional entity. That's the one you want.

Copy it down. Now look to the left of the person's name to see the corresponding reference number. The reference number often refers to a book and page number. The next step is to go to that book of records and turn to the page. You should find a copy of the mortgage document. There you will see the mortgagee's (note holder's) name and address.

Now you have the name and address of someone who is receiving payments from a mortgage. Continue down the list, repeating the process as long as you have time to look. If you've set a goal of finding a certain number of names, keep looking until you reach this number. Your goal is to locate as many private note holders as you can.

Why get a large number of names? The more names you have, the more people you will contact. The more people you contact, the higher the probability that you'll find paper you can buy.

Once you have this information, all you do is send the mortgage holders a letter or a flyer telling them you will pay cash for their mortgage.

Not everyone will respond. You're doing a direct-mail advertising campaign to a targeted audience. It's strictly a numbers game. Direct-mail professionals consider a 1 percent or 2 percent response quite good. With a carefully targeted audience, the percentage may go a little higher.

If the idea of sending out a hundred letters to get one or two phone calls seems like too much work, ask yourself if it would be worth that much of your time to make $10,000.

Making Your Marketing Work

You have to be creative in your marketing.

You can mail a letter, but if the note holder doesn't open it, or opens it and doesn't read it, you've wasted your effort.

There are some standard techniques for getting your letter opened. Some people put a colorful stamp on the envelope. (The recent Elvis stamp was a favorite when it came out.) Others use an odd-sized or bright-colored envelope. You can put a message on the envelope. Three examples:

IMPORTANT INFORMATION ENCLOSED!

TIME-SENSITIVE MATERIAL! OPEN AT ONCE!

DON'T PASS UP THIS OPPORTUNITY!

Or you can use any other message intended to either grab the reader's attention or to say something about what's inside.

The letter should be simple and to the point, like the example that David might have written to Mary.

It pays to have some stationery and envelopes printed with your letterhead (the letterhead should be simple) so you look like someone who is serious about doing business. Use your letterhead and envelopes.

Do not use someone else's letterhead or a letterhead that is confusing to the mortgage holder. For example, suppose you have a software company called Complex Programming Solutions. If you used that letterhead to save money when sending letters to mortgage holders, you'd confuse them. They might not know whether you were selling software to help them buy or sell mortgages or whether you were offering to buy their mortgage. When you confuse mortgage holders, they will not act.

DAVID MILLER FUNDING CORPORATION
123 Bay Street
Los Angeles, CA 12345
(213) 555-5555

Mary Smith
5678 Main Street
Long Beach, CA 16182

Dear Mrs. Smith,

It has come to my attention that you hold a trust deed on 1234 Green St., Centerville.

How would you like a lump sum of cash *now* instead of having to wait for all your payments to be made? This money can be used for many things, like that addition you want to make to your home, other investments you may have wanted to make, or even a well-deserved vacation.

The amount of cash you can receive is determined by the size, length, and terms of your trust deed.

If you are interested in obtaining more information, with no obligation, please fill out the enclosed trust deed data card and return it to me. I am in the business of purchasing trust deeds such as yours for cash. I would be pleased to discuss your trust deed and offer you a fair quote.

Thank you for your time.

Sincerely,

David Miller

P.S. If you are not interested in this opportunity at this time, please file this letter for future reference.

Follow up the letter with a phone call about a week to ten days after mailing the letter. If the county records didn't include the note holder's phone number, look in the phone book or call information.

The follow-up phone call is a powerful tool. It enables you to explain more than a letter can—that is, if the person is interested in listening. The call may make the difference between a mortgage or trust-deed holder being willing to sell or deciding to hold on to the paper. A mortgage holder who might not respond to a letter may respond to a phone call.

You can use the phone call as a screening tool to identify those who probably wouldn't sell under any circumstances, those who show varying degrees of interest, and those aren't ready to sell now but who might in the future.

Follow-up, as you can see, is crucial.

Sometimes a note holder will need time to think about the benefits of selling, or a need will develop that didn't exist when you made your first contact.

Follow-up doesn't mean just a call a week or so after you mailed the letter. After three months, send a follow-up letter, and follow that up with another phone call. If you find you're getting short of time, call only those you identified as possibilities the first time.

Try another follow-up in three months for those who were probables, perhaps in six months for those who were only possibilities.

Educating the Paper Holder

You are engaged not only in a marketing campaign but in an educational process. Your marketing is designed to educate the note holder about the possibilities and benefits of selling his or her mortgage.

You see, most people holding paper have no idea they can sell it. They think they have to hang on to that paper until the final payment is made.

Since they don't know they can sell it, they don't know what it's worth. There's no magic formula that will tell them the true value of their paper. There isn't a blue book like the one used for the resale of cars.

Your strategy is to help them realize they can sell the paper, and then explain what the paper is really worth. You can see why I've stressed your need to understand and be able to explain the time value of money. Just as David had to help Mary understand the value of her mortgage, you will have to explain this to the people you contact.

The note holder must understand that the value of their paper is fully negotiable. The price will be negotiated between you and them. There is no minimum or maximum price set by law or custom.

Obviously, you walk away from the deal if you can't get a discounted price that meets your standards and those of the person buying the mortgage from you.

Assuming that the mortgage holder has a good reason to sell, the best thing for both of you is to agree on a fair price and proceed to close. Just as Bill and Mary agreed on a price for the house originally, Mary and David agreed on a price for the mortgage. Concurrently, David and John also must agree on a price for the mortgage. Each meeting, in our example and in real life, takes a little time and some negotiating, but a good price was finally reached on all sides. This is the same way you'll work with your clients.

How Much Paper Will You Find at the Courthouse?

The first time you go to the courthouse to look up people personally holding paper, you'll probably be amazed at how many there are.

I can't tell you exactly how many billions of dollars there are in personally held mortgages (there's no way to accurately determine the total), but it's incredible. A good estimate is that *anywhere from 15 to 30 percent of all mortgages, in most areas, are held by individuals.* This will vary in different parts of the country and at different times. Economic conditions play a major role in determining how many personally held mortgages are created in a given year in a given county. It is always a significant number, and new ones are constantly being added. You can keep going back to the same courthouse over and over. The business just keeps growing.

David's Choices

When David makes the deal with Mary, he has to make a choice. He can call John and sell him the paper, as we've been describing. David's other choice, if he has the funds to do so, is to keep it for himself.

He must decide whether he wants the $10,000 he can get by selling it to John, or whether he wants to buy twenty-nine years of $775 a month for $50,000, with the probability that it will be paid off sooner, thus increasing his yield.

How would you answer if you were David?

You see, the interesting thing about David's decision is that no one but David can answer it. If David came to me and asked what he should do, I wouldn't have an answer. I could only give him general advice and guidelines, as I'm giving you. Only his personal financial situation will determine what he should do.

I'd suggest David consider these guidelines, and any others his personal needs might dictate.

1. If David is in need of cash, he probably should sell the paper to John.
2. If he doesn't have the capital required to purchase and service the paper, he'll have to sell it to John.
3. If he has the ability to buy and hold the paper and doesn't have an immediate need for cash, he may want to hang on to it.

David's circumstances determine what he does.

After David has met his immediate (short-term) cash needs, if he had any, I recommend that he start to very selectively buy the paper he finds for his own portfolio. By the time he's done enough deals to solve short-term cash needs, he'll probably have done enough deals to be a very good judge of which deals are the very best ones. Those are then ones to buy for his own portfolio.

When he begins to buy paper for himself, he's reinvesting his money (medium term). He has reached a point, like the car dealer in the earlier example, where he needs to make his money work for him. Investing in paper for his own portfolio makes his money work for him at aggressively high yields.

If he just keeps buying and selling paper, he'll make nice money, but he won't reach his medium-term goals. If he fails to reach medium-term goals, he can forget about long-term goals.

The Joy of Being the Man in the Middle

The middleman position is a great place to be. David has great options, all of which are winners. It's up to him which one he takes on in his deal with Mary, or in any other deal. He's in a super financial position. He'll earn good money whatever choice he makes.

In this way you, too, are going to make money in paper. Find the leads and then go after them. There's money to be made with the Stefanchik Method in the county recorders' offices of this country. It's still the best-kept secret on public record.

Going Big-Time into Paper Buying

We've seen how David operates. David's medium and long-term goals are to buy and hold paper, to become like John. So, let's look at John. What are his motives, how does he make money, and how does his part of the paper business work?

John buys paper because he wants a return on his cash investment, a yield on his money, just like David's medium and long-term goals. John has two major concerns about his investment.

1. Safety for his money. He doesn't want to lose what he has worked for.
2. He wants the highest possible yield or return on his money.

Paper satisfies both needs. It's a safe investment. Paper is very high-yielding.

When you compare paper to any traditional investment, paper comes out on top. Let's do a comparison of paper as an investment against five traditional investments. We'll compare paper to:

1. Putting your money in the bank.
2. Buying stock.
3. Buying municipal bonds.
4. Buying junk bonds.
5. Putting money into a limited partnership for investment or tax purposes.

Remember, paper is a real estate secured investment. There is always real property backing it up. The security and/or yield of other investments can't compete.

How Does Paper Compare?

Savings.

Most people deal with excess cash by putting it in the bank, either in savings or CDs. This investment satisfies most people, but does it meet John's requirements? Banks are fine for safety, about the safest place there is, but the yield is low, rarely more than 1 or 2 percent above inflation, sometimes less than inflation. John can forget banks if he wants a significant return on his investment.

Stocks.

How about in stocks? We've touched on this in an earlier chapter. Stocks don't meet either of John's requirements. They're neither safe nor high-yielding.

As far as I'm concerned, investing in the stock market is just like gambling. You never know what's going to happen. You have no control over your money. Even if you get someone who has a "hot tip" for you, it usually turns out to be wrong. There are just too many outside variables that influence the stock market, among them world affairs, inflation, the price of gas, the threat of war, the value of the dollar, and many, many more.

The real problem is that we have no control over these economic variables. The situation gets absurd when a group of leading economists get together to make predictions about the economy and the stock market. They rarely agree. The economists have such a varied view of the financial outlook that we don't know who to believe. No matter what they tell us, the stock market will still rise and fall.

There are a group of "blue chip" stocks that have a great track record and are a safe investment. The only trouble is that the yield is usually low. You won't lose any money and the yield is usually better than bank interest, but you sure won't make money very quickly, either.

I tend to lump mutual funds with stocks because most mutual

funds invest heavily in the stock market. You're depending on some financial guru to invest your money for you. You have no control, other than pulling out of the fund, if you don't like what's happening.

If I can't control my money in an investment, I'm not really very interested in investing it. I never want to lose my money, but if I'm in control and I lose money, at least I should know why I did. With a mutual fund, all you get is a report every few months telling you what happened to your investment. You still won't know why you made or lost money.

Municipal Bonds.

These bonds are really interesting because they're secured by a highway, bridge, or some type of municipal project. Then bonds are issued against it as collateral. Overall, these bonds are safe and secure.

But what about the yield? The best you're likely to do is 8 percent or maybe 9 percent over the life of the bond. These bonds are usually twenty or thirty years in length. Doesn't make for a very good yield over such a long time, does it?

Junk Bonds.

But is there a bond that does pay a high yield on your money? There certainly is—junk bonds.

Don't you just love that term? A name like "junk bonds" really makes you want to run out and buy some, doesn't it?

I think the name is extremely accurate. They *are* junk! Oh, I know they have a very high yield, but they're about as safe as a stick of dynamite with the fuse lit. You don't know when it's going to blow up. You just know it's going to.

The problem with junk bonds is that they're secured by highly leveraged companies. As long as the company makes money, great! The bonds pay off. If the company experiences any dip in cash flow, any at all, you're going to lose money.

Junk bonds were popular in the '80s, with the rise in LBOs (leveraged buyouts). LBOs occur when one company buys out another by taking on a huge amount of debt secured by issuing junk bonds.

As an example of how profitable the entire junk bond industry is to us today, look at Drexel Burnham Lambert, the largest seller of junk bonds on Wall Street. This company's junk bond department, headed by Michael Milken, rode very high during the roaring eighties. In 1989, Drexel declared bankruptcy and is now out of business. Milken was indicted for fraud, convicted, and sent to prison.

The reason for junk bonds being worthless is the lack of security. You've got a highly leveraged company that has taken on a huge load of debt. They've issued bonds secured by that company and they've raised the yield on the bonds. The bond yield is high, but the collateral is unsafe.

Junk bonds may promise you a high yield, but what happens when someone can't pay? The yield is zero. It really doesn't matter what yield they're promising. All that matters is the yield they can deliver.

The collateral behind the bonds is a company with very high debt. The probability of the company actually surviving and making money isn't good. If you can't get paid, then the yield is inconsequential.

Limited Partnerships.

Limited partnerships are kind of interesting. Usually they involve a limited number of people getting together and investing their money collectively. They may invest in oil wells, real estate, even the stock market—anything that looks like it will produce a good yield.

This may not be a bad way to go, but again someone (not you) makes the decisions about where your money goes.

Before the Tax Reform Act of 1986, all kinds of limited partnerships were created. Many were formed to take advantage of loopholes in the tax laws. Limited partnerships invested heavily in real estate and were able to shelter most of the income produced. When the tax laws changed in 1986, many loopholes were closed and real estate tax sheltering was eliminated. Many real estate limited partnerships collapsed and a lot of people lost large sums of money.

I prefer to stay away from limited partnerships for two reasons. One, you have to rely on someone else to invest your money, and two, you're usually tied to a specific investment plan that is based on the current tax laws or something else that could change but that is out of your control.

In paper, you're fully in control. If you don't like a deal, you can walk away from it. If it's a good deal, you can control it and your money.

Is John's Paper a Liquid Investment?

Is there liquidity in the paper John (and we) are purchasing? Yes, but it's not quite like having cash in the bank and writing a check on it.

Liquidity means how fast an asset can be converted to cash. For example, your checking account is liquid. A CD with a penalty for early withdrawal is less liquid. A piece of raw land that might take several years to sell is not liquid at all.

John must find a buyer for the paper. That normally won't take long. The transfer could take a week or so, once you've located the buyer and agreed on a price. To me, this is not a problem, because I keep an active record of paper buyers who might purchase paper from me. If I need cash, I call a few buyers and resell any paper I no longer want to hold and collect payments on.

By the time you're buying paper for your own portfolio, you'll have made many contacts with paper buyers.

Where Does John Find People Like David?

Everywhere I go, students ask where I find buyers, and where they can find paper buyers. The answer is remarkably simple.

Most people think the best way is to go out and advertise for buyers, an advanced variation on the way David advertises for paper sellers. The problem with this approach is that you have no way of knowing whether the people who respond have either money or knowledge of paper.

John is looking for someone who not only has money to buy mortgages but also understands paper as an investment. This sharply reduces the number of people he wants to hear from.

His ad will most likely draw people who have money but are used to dealing with traditional investments. If John tries to introduce them to paper, they're probably going to want to do things the way they're used to, and run everything by their attorney, financial planner, or some other person who probably knows as little about paper as they do.

John may teach a certain number of such people about the benefits of paper and show them the right way to do it. After all, these people didn't acquire their wealth by being stupid or unable to recognize a good new investment when they see it. He may develop some very good, valuable sources in this manner, but it will take time to find and educate them.

What John's really looking for is someone who has money, or access to money, and also understands paper. How and where can he find someone like that?

This gets interesting when you stop to think it through. Ask yourself, Where can I find someone who's already been through a paper transaction? That's the only qualification you really need. If a person has done a paper transaction, you know at once that they have money or access to it, and that they know at least enough about paper to have done a deal.

Since it's more important to find somebody who's been through this process and understands paper than to simply find people with money, where do you suppose you'd look to find such individuals?

If you thought you might find them at the county recorder's office, you're right. You've avoided making a simple process complicated.

The only place you can find a person who has already bought paper is at the county recorder's office. Remember what happened when Mary, David, and John closed their deal for Mary's mortgage? The change in ownership was recorded as an *assignment of mortgage*.

Thus there is a public record, available to anyone, showing the people and institutions who have purchased mortgages! (The assignees.)

When you go to the county recorder's office to search for privately held mortgages or trust deeds, also look for assignments to individuals. Write down the name and address of each assignee. Keep track of how many times a name appears. By the time you've found enough mortgages to begin finding some you can buy, you'll probably have found a significant number of assignments. Look over your list. Do the same names appear a number of times? Those individuals are the ones with expertise in paper and the money to buy it. If you don't find these repeat buyers of paper in your first surveys at the recorder's office, keep looking. There won't be nearly as many of these buyers as there are holders of mortgages, but the more you look, the more you'll find.

This information is invaluable to both David and John. David needs it to find John, even if he has already contacted my company or some other source of funding. David should have more than one source of funds. He may find a great deal on a mortgage and go to John at a time when John isn't in a position to buy, or he may find that what he thinks is a great deal doesn't fit John's standards. In either case, he needs additional sources of funding.

John needs this source of paper buyers to locate people he can sell paper to, as well as to find mortgages in the first place. He multiplies his efforts by using people like David to find paper, but he also keeps looking for himself in the courthouses near his home and office.

When John has his list of people who have already taken an assignment of mortgage, he can send a letter to them or call them and say, "I have a mortgage. Would you be interested in purchasing it?" Or, "I'm always looking for paper. Are you interested in buying what I find?"

You'll find dozens or even hundreds of these people when you search through the county recorders' office. The larger your community, the more likely it is that you'll find a lot of people. Wherever there's paper, you'll find people who buy and sell it. You'll find plenty of investors in your area.

The nice thing about finding investors in your area is that sometimes local investors will bend their rules a little farther than an out-of-town investor. The property is close to them and they know local trends and values. They can check it out personally.

If the property is located in Oregon and I live in New York, I'll have more problems dealing with foreclosure and owning and managing the property. The distance involved makes me more cautious. When you have more experience and deal carefully, distance becomes less of a problem.

Most other paper buyers, including you when you begin buying for yourself, work the same way. You can see the benefit of locating local paper buyers.

Wherever there's a courthouse, you'll find assignments. Wherever you find assignments, you'll find investors. That assures John, and you, that whenever you need liquid cash instead of the cash flow of a mortgage, you can find a buyer and sell your paper.

Who Is John?

"John" (the paper investor) can be anyone: your doctor, your mailman, auto mechanic, your child's teacher—or you. He's anyone who has money to invest and wants a secure, high-yield return on his investments. He may have a lot of money to invest or he may not have much at all. You should never have to worry about finding John.

John probably got into the paper business for the same reasons as you. He most likely heard about it from someone else and tried it. Once he discovered how much money there was to be made, he got into it big time. You see, there aren't any college courses you can take to learn about paper. Few people grow up knowing they want to buy and sell paper for a living. Quite often, John had tried other investments and got sick and tired of losing his hard-earned money. He wanted something safe and lucrative. Once he found paper, he stayed with it.

Going Nationwide

Let's go back to my personal story. You'll see that much of it parallels what I've been describing.

After a year or so of buying and selling to just collect cash, I started to get back on my feet financially. I used the money I was earning in paper to pay off short-term debt like charge cards and to support the negative cash flow from my real estate purchases. (If only I'd learned about paper before I ever thought about buying investment real estate!)

As more deals came in, I started to pump the money I was making back into the business to find more paper.

The more letters I sent out and the more ads I ran, the more people knew I bought paper, hence the more paper I bought and sold.

One of my first short-term goals was to quit my job. If I'd been a little more experienced and realistic, I might have seen it as a medium-term goal, a result of achieving the short-term goal of making cash from paper.

After only six paper deals, I reached that goal. I was making money from paper and could see that it would give me a consistent, healthy cash flow, enough to live on comfortably, cover my negative cash flow, and provide money to invest. That made it possible for me to quit my job to pursue paper full-time. Now I had time during the day to go to the county recorder's office to research names and write letters.

When I quit my job, it was a banner day. It was wonderful, and I'll never forget, as long as I live, walking away from a full-time job, from a secure income, into a world where I could make as much income as I wanted to work for. I walked into a world where I was my own boss and where I was in complete control of my own destiny.

But a few problems developed. The first became apparent when I was in the Westchester County Recorder's Office searching for paper. I was not in Brooklyn, Queens, the Bronx, or other places where I'd looked for paper, and where I knew there was a lot to be found. I'd quit my job to have freedom to do paper full-time, but there was only one of me and more than one county recorder's office.

I was only getting as many names as I could write down per day, but there were many more to be found than I had time to look for.

The second problem was that while I was in the recorder's office searching for new names, I couldn't answer calls from people who received my letters and wanted quotes on how much I could pay for their paper. I could have said in my letter to call only in the evenings (which would eliminate callers who worked a night shift), or that I'd be "in my office" to receive calls on certain days of the week. If I waited by the phone on Tuesdays and Fridays, for example, I wasn't looking for more names on those days. And if I spent all my time in the recorder's office, when was I going to get the letters prepared and mailed?

I felt more limited when I had all my time to devote to paper than when I only had lunch hours, nights, and weekends. I faced the problem of wanting to get my name out there as fast as I could and I wanted to cover as much ground as I could, but I couldn't do it all. I wanted to create a situation in which I didn't have to totally and directly involve myself in every aspect of paper. I realized that my time would be better spent doing other things.

The solution was for me to clone myself and put the clones in the county recorders' offices. I decided to hire college students to search the recorders' offices. (You might try this, too, once you've made a few paper deals.) I paid them by the hour and let them work flexible schedules, coming and going from the county recorders' office as their time permitted.

I created a form they could fill out with each mortgagee's name, address, city, state, and zip code. They mailed the completed forms to me at the end of each week. I sent them a check for the hours it took them to produce those names.

Now I was flooded with potential customers that I could mail my letter to. I was so inundated with names of mortgage holders that I had to hire my parents to assist me in sending out more and more letters. My mother typed the mortgage holder's names onto labels and my father folded, stuffed, and sealed the envelopes.

Suddenly I was putting a nice operation into place, but it was only the beginning.

As I covered more and more territory around the vast New York metropolitan area, I realized that if I could cover the New York market so well, I could expand to other states. The thought entered my mind, Why not go nationwide? Why not buy paper, not just in the greater New York area, but all across the fifty states?

Great idea, but how could I possibly cover all the county recorders' offices in fifty states? How could I place ads and collect phone calls from around the country?

I realized very quickly that it would be extremely costly for me to hire enough employees, run ads, get 800 numbers, etc. to cover the nation. At this point I had a breakthrough idea.

Hitting the Seminar Circuit

Why not give seminars to groups of people interested in making money? I'd become so successful so fast, and so few people even knew it could be done, that there ought to be a real market for teaching people all over the country how to find paper. Then, when the paper fit my parameters for purchase, I could buy it and my students would make a finder's fee, like David.

So, with my paper-finding-and-buying operation in New York in full stride, off I went to other cities around the country giving a talk each night on how to find paper for profit. I worked on the talk constantly to pack in as much detailed information as I could into two hours, so the people would go out the next day and find paper.

I taught my students how they could call me and I'd give them a price I would pay for the paper. Like David, they'd offer less to the note holder, earning the difference.

What a great idea! Right?

Not quite. There was only one problem.

No one called me!

I was spending time, money, and effort to give the best talk I could with as much information as I felt they could absorb, but no one was calling me.

After careful investigation, I learned why I wasn't getting calls from the people who attended my seminars. It was actually quite simple: *Fear!* The people who attended my talks were not confident enough of their knowledge of paper after a two-hour seminar. Consequently, they wouldn't go to the courthouse, find names, or call the note holders from fear of not knowing what to say and do.

Knowledge is power, and knowledge also breeds confidence. Lack of knowledge, or fear of inadequate knowledge, breeds insecurity and inaction. You know that the more you know about something, the better you feel about doing it.

I faced a real problem. How could I get people the information they needed to build the level of confidence necessary to go out and find paper?

At that moment I thought of a home-study package of workbooks and cassette tapes—workbooks to outline all the exact steps to finding, funding, negotiating, and selling paper, and cassette tapes to enhance the workbook information with ideas, stories, do's and don'ts, etc.

I started to sell books and tapes at a modest price in seminars around the country.

Then my phone started ringing!

My phone started ringing because people were going home and devouring the information. They couldn't take my talk home with them and study it (unless they took far better notes than most people ever learn to), but they could read the workbooks and listen to the cassette tapes as many times as they needed. I got calls from people who said they'd read the workbooks two and three times. They'd listen to the tapes three, four, five times on the way to and from work and while they were sitting at home at night.

I called my home-study course the Stefanchik Method.

Some students have told me they listened to the cassettes so many times that not only did they know my voice, but they felt I was actually there with them helping them study this information. People wanted to reinforce their knowledge of the information because it was new to them. When they'd read and listened enough, they had the confidence to go out and find paper.

The reason my phone began to ring and then started to ring more and more and more was because people started to take this seriously. People started to take the information they learned from the Stefanchik Method and do the things that would make them successful.

Today, I have students making money in paper by finding the paper, negotiating a price, getting some preliminary paperwork going, and letting me buy it. Since my students come from all over the entire country, Canada, and even Australia, I've purchased paper in almost every large metropolitan area as well as some very small areas such as Yerington, Nevada; Gauer, Missouri; Lithonia, Georgia; Cortland, New York; Willits, California; and many others.

I realized that marketing was key. The more I could get my name out there, the more I could get my home-study courses into people's hands. The better I could present my information, the more mortgages I could buy.

I faced another problem. Each time I got to another level of marketing, I found I needed to do more. I'd never expected my business to grow like this when I quit my job to invest full-time.

I got to the point where I was selling a lot of books and tapes at seminars around the country and my students were sending out letters and finding mortgages. The only problem was that I could speak only so many times a week and to only so many people at each seminar.

Yet thousands of people were just dying for information on how to make money in their spare time or full-time. They showed up at my seminars looking for an entrepreneurial way to make money. They listened to me speak and bought the Stefanchik Method. Then I went back home and they'd go out and find paper in their area.

That was neat, and very satisfying, but besides accumulating a lot of frequent-flyer miles I soon realized that there was a limit to the number of seminars I could give and the amount of places I could travel.

Going On the Tube

I was approached by a group of people who wanted to put together a TV infomercial to help get my system out to more people. We'd sell the materials to people around the country, putting the Stefanchik Method into the hands of people I couldn't reach with seminars.

This really stepped up my level of marketing. At midnight, while I might be sleeping, reading, or out at a restaurant, my TV show would be selling my materials, reaching people in all areas of the U.S. and Canada, not just in one city where I could give my seminar.

Getting your name out there through TV is a really powerful way of marketing yourself. Millions of people see you. Many people bought my course and went out and started to "do" paper.

Those of you who've seen me on television (and those who haven't) may call 1-800-621-0283 for a special offer to purchase my books and tapes. I want any of you who is interested in paper to have all the information I can give you to go out there, find paper, and consistently make money.

If you've seen me on TV, you know that I'm so confident of the success of the Stefanchik Method that at the end of the show I offer each person who purchases my materials the chance to earn a rebate.

The idea came to me one day when I was out for a run through a beautiful wooded area. It was the kind of place that helps my mind get into a quiet, restful state where the cares and worries of the day go away and ideas come out. Sometimes I wonder why I didn't think of them before.

I'd been trying to think of a way to get more people to try paper and bring me deals, and I'd also been wondering what I could do to convince more people of the value of my materials and my confidence in the power of paper.

All those thoughts came together and produced the idea of a rebate—not the kind the auto makers offer, which sometimes look like the amount you might have gotten anyway if you bargained hard with the dealer, but a realistic working-agreement rebate.

A rebate made so much sense I wondered why I hadn't offered it sooner. I'd been making the point, over and over, that the amount of money a student could make from his or her first deal would be far more than the cost of my materials.

"Okay," said the lightbulb that flashed on in my head, "if a student brings me a deal, *why not rebate the entire price of the course?*"

What a breakthrough!

Not only would the student make money on the deal itself, not only would I make money on the deal, but I'd make enough money that I could easily afford to repay the student for the cost of the materials he or she bought. After all, if I knew that each person who took the materials home would actually bring me a deal, I wouldn't bother charging for them in the first place! I'd know that the first deal would more than pay for them. So why not reward students who bring me acceptable deals with a full rebate?

I finished that run with a burst of energy and a feeling like I'd just won the Boston Marathon.

It worked. I've paid out a lot of rebates. Essentially, the rebate takes away the problem some people have with spending money on the course. I rebate, to a student who brings me a deal I purchase, the money they spent on purchasing the course, and sometimes a little more. This is a reward for using the course and bringing me a deal.

After that, the student can bring deals to me or to whomever else he or she wants. I just say, by offering the rebate, "Use the materials, find paper, and give me a shot at doing a deal with you." The rebate makes sense for both of us. The student makes money, gets back his or her money for the course, and gains confidence from doing a deal with me. I, of course, get to do the deal and everybody's happy. It's a real win-win situation.

The agreement works to rebate the money the student spent on the course when the student simply uses the materials successfully.

You can see that my success has been based on marketing. By getting my name out there and getting people to work with me, I've been extremely successful.

You don't need to grow as big as I have, or to do so as rapidly, but the same principle applies to creating your paper business. You can use my marketing techniques, or you can develop your own, but a marketing plan must be a part of your short, medium and long-term goals.

Buying Paper Anywhere

Do you think you might want to buy paper over a wide area, like I do?

I wouldn't recommend trying it until you've done a number of successful deals in your own area and learned how to be a good judge of paper's true value, how to negotiate, and how to control your deals. But once you reach that point, you may, as I did, want to increase your opportunities.

There are no limits for a paper buyer. I, and you, can buy paper in all parts of the country, as easily in New York or Los Angeles or Chicago or Tallahassee. All we really care about is that the mortgage payments come in the mail every month.

My paper-buying company is based in New York, but I get mortgage payments from every state in the country. I choose to live in New York and run my business from there, but I could live anywhere and run my business just as well.

When you really get into paper buying and you look at paper buying around the country, you can live anywhere you want. You have access to the world through a fax machine, a phone line, an overnight delivery service like Federal Express or UPS, and a post office box where you collect checks.

I could even run my business in New York, live in Hawaii, and have everything working for me just as well as if I lived at the business address. I could live in Kansas, Texas, or Montana and run the business across the country. It really doesn't matter, because I have a post office box to collect the checks.

When you're successful, you can live wherever you want. Wherever you live *now*, you can start and run a successful, profitable paper business.

As I've mentioned, real estate experts often say that the three most important things are location, location, and location. In paper, one could say that the three *least* important things are location, location, and location.

If you'd rather live somewhere else, paper can be the way to make it possible. That's a longer-term goal, of course, but when you achieve success you can decide where you want to live and move there, whether or not you move your business address.

The nice thing about buying paper nationwide is that you can pick and choose the paper you buy. I don't buy every mortgage or trust deed that's offered. I only buy the ones that make sense for me.

You won't want to buy every mortgage or trust deed offered to you, either. You only buy the ones that can make you a good profit.

CHAPTER 11

When the Mortgage Holder Says No— The Paper Salvation: The Partial

What can you do when the note holder won't accept your offer? Is there anything to do but walk away and try to buy the next mortgage?

Yes, there is. It's called a *partial*.

A partial is the purchase of *part of the cash flow* of a mortgage. It can be for any period of time during the mortgage; the next three (or any number of) years, the balloon payment, or for a future time period of any length. In practice, it's rare to purchase, for example, the fifth through tenth years of a mortgage now in its second year, but you could do it if you found a reason. Purchase of balloon payments is not uncommon.

When I first learned that I could buy a partial, it really blew me away. I already knew paper was extremely flexible, but this made it seem almost too easy. I started viewing every paper deal differently. All of a sudden, I didn't have to buy the entire cash flow if I didn't want to or if the mortgage holder wouldn't sell.

The real fun was introducing potential paper sellers to this fact. At first they didn't believe they could sell only part of their mortgage. I found it wasn't really too hard to convince them, especially when I showed them how little principal they will be giving up. Whether you buy the entire mortgage or just a partial, you're going to make money. Isn't that what it's all about?

Let's return to David and Mary and see how their deal would work as a partial.

Suppose that when David offered to buy Mary's $80,000 mortgage for $50,000, she says, "No way! You're out of your mind!"

David does all he can to help her understand why she needs to discount her mortgage, but she won't budge. David negotiates with Mary the best he can to let her know exactly why he can't offer more than $50,000. He gives her all information he has to convince her to accept his offer.

She still says no.

Now what does David do?

At this point, a lot of my students have found it difficult to make progress, which really isn't surprising. Sometimes the problem is a simple lack of negotiating skills. Not everyone is a natural negotiator, though anyone can learn. More important, many people have never been taught or developed negotiating skills.

My students needed to learn how to negotiate, so I produced (as I mentioned in an earlier chapter) a set of materials, cassettes and a workbook, called *Negotiating: The Key to Success*. I wanted to answer the question, "How do I get more people like Mary to accept my offer?"

In the workbook and tapes I go through negotiation, step by step, and teach you a number of techniques that will make everyone a better negotiator. I give you an understanding of how you can get someone to say yes. It takes technique and it takes practice. Anyone can learn.

But no matter how skilled a negotiator you become, there are some negotiations where you can keep pushing, pushing, and pushing, using all the information, negotiating skills, and logic at your command—and the person will still say no.

There's always a reason why people say no. Sometimes it's a perfectly good reason, and you and the person can agree that it wouldn't be in their best interest to sell. Usually you can determine that early on and save time for both of you. More often, when a person comes to you asking about selling their mortgage, there's a reason they need money, as well as a reason they don't want to sell the mortgage for what you can offer.

A lot of times people will fumble around and let you think it's just about the money. "I can't sell for that. Can't you offer more?" You've already offered as much as you can, so now what do you do?

One of the keys to negotiation is to find out what the person really needs. They're selling the mortgage because they need money. That's simple, you both think. You might assume you should ask what price they'd accept, but that's not the right question. It gives them the opportunity to state a price you can't pay, ending the negotiation.

It's easy for David to assume that when Mary wants to sell her $80,000 mortgage, she needs the entire amount, especially if she won't sell. He might, operating on that assumption, gradually negotiate up, knowing he can get $60,000 from John. He might figure that if he can at least take $2,000 out of the deal, that's certainly better than walking away after putting all his effort into getting this far. Gradually he raises his price to $58,000 . . . and Mary still says no.

This is where David's perfectly logical assumption could cost him the deal. Every time you make an assumption in negotiations, you'll probably lose.

In *Negotiation: The Key to Success*, I teach you to get as much information as possible about the other party in any negotiation, whether for paper or anything else. The more you know, the better you can negotiate. One of the ways you get that information is to ask the right questions.

Suppose, as I suggested above, David asks Mary, "Okay, for what price would you sell your mortgage?"

What's she going to answer? She'll answer *that exact question!* Yes, this may seem obvious, but think about it. Remember your mother, or perhaps some teacher, warning you to be careful what you wanted, because you might get it? That's good advice (if you want to be a success in paper, you probably will be), and it certainly applies to questions you ask in negotiation. The other person will answer the question you ask. He or she won't read your mind and give you the answer you want unless you ask the right question!

Mary may answer the "what price" question by grudgingly saying she might part with her mortgage for $75,000, but she'd have to think about it overnight.

That's not what David wants to hear. At this point David has limited choices. He can raise his price to whatever Mary will accept, or he can hang up the phone without a deal. That's why David, in his negotiation, never asks that question. It's asking for an answer he doesn't want to hear. Worse, it asks Mary to state a position she'll have to defend when he tells her he can only offer $50,000.

David avoids the "what price" question by saying, after he explains the time value of money and other factors that make it necessary to buy paper at a discount, "Mary, I can offer you $50,000 for your mortgage." He's made a positive statement, not asked a question that will produce the wrong answer.

But now, after Mary has refused to accept his offer, what's the right question?

The right question for David to ask is, "How much money do you really *need*, Mary?"

You can see how this changes the assumptions we (and David) have been making so far. We've assumed Mary needed the entire amount, or all she could get for her mortgage. That's helped keep things simple in explaining how a deal works. Now we're looking at a solution for the times when the deal doesn't work so neatly.

It's important not to assume the "Mary" in your deal needs all the money, or needs a lot more money, or that the more money you offer the more likely you'll get your deal accepted.

You may think that Mary will go to somebody else for a better offer. If she knows someone to go to, she may. But Mary usually doesn't know of anybody else who will buy her mortgage. She has no place to go for a better offer. You may be the only offer on the table, but you may not have the right offer. That's where the all-or-nothing assumption can hurt you. You need negotiating flexibility.

Suppose Mary answers, "Well, all I really need is $10,000, and it's just not worth giving you a $30,000 discount to get that." Anyone can agree with that logic.

Now you can see why I say it's important to ask the right questions, and why you need to listen carefully to what the person is telling you. One of the important things about negotiating is to be a good listener. If you listen carefully to what the person's saying, you may hear them say that they don't need all the money, or may not need the money all in one lump sum, as you propose to give it to them, or they may not need to sell you the mortgage outright. There are all sorts of things they may be saying to you, perhaps without even realizing what they're telling you, but you *do* need to listen carefully.

The two biggest "secrets" of negotiation are asking the right questions and listening carefully and closely.

When David asks Mary how much money she *needs*, he is no

longer assuming Mary needs *all* the cash she is asking for. She's selling her mortgage because she needs cash for something. It doesn't matter to David what she needs the cash for, except in the sense that if he knows she has a really pressing need he can use that information to convince her of the benefits of accepting his offer.

What happens if she really doesn't need all the cash this mortgage will bring her? What if in reality she only needs part of it?

Perhaps Mary wants to send her daughter to Yale next year. Maybe she wants to surprise her husband with the boat he's always wanted. Maybe she needs a new car, has medical bills, has a chance to take a trip around the world, wants to help her child with a down payment on a house, or wants to go to Las Vegas and play poker.

Most likely, when David asks her how much she needs, Mary won't understand the question. She can't see any alternative to selling the entire mortgage.

The Partial to the Rescue

Does David have an answer? Yes—the partial.

When you buy a *partial assignment of mortgage,* you buy the rights to the cash flow of a mortgage for a certain time, for a certain price.

David's answer to Mary's need is to offer to buy the next three years of her cash flow from her mortgage for $10,000. This means that for three years (if he keeps the mortgage) David gets the payments. Mary gets no payments during that time, but after three years is entitled to the remaining twenty-six years of payments and the remaining principal. Since little principal is paid down in the first years of a mortgage, she loses very little of her principal.

This creates a very easy way for Mary to obtain cash now while retaining most of her principal.

Splitting Up an Asset

David understands the opportunity he's offering Mary. He was willing to buy the entire mortgage for $50,000 to get a cash flow of $775 per month for twenty-nine years. He reminds Mary of this. He goes on to tell her, "I can get you the $10,000 cash you need. It will cost you almost no principal, just some interest. Sell me the next three years of payments and I'll give you $10,000 today."

Mary doesn't understand what's going on, so once again David explains the whole process to her: "First I was offering to buy your mortgage for $50,000. The mortgage still has twenty-nine years to go on it and the monthly payments are $775. Now I'm offering you to buy the next three years of payments from you for $10,000 cash today. At the end of the three years the mortgage reverts back to you and you continue to receive the remaining twenty-six years of monthly payments of $775. How does that sound to you?"

Mary is still a little bit confused and asks, "How does that work? Can you *do* that? Is it legal?"

David explains, "Sure it's legal. All I'm doing is buying part of your mortgage, not the whole thing. For the next three years you won't receive payments on your mortgage because I get them. The payments come to me because I bought them from you for $10,000 today. At the end of the three years, the payments revert back to you. If you look at your amortization schedule, you'll notice that after the next three years your remaining balance is still in excess of $78,000. You've discounted your mortgage even less than if you sold me the whole thing for $75,000."

Mary may be a bit dumbfounded by this idea and still not sure she understands what's happening.

David, being a good negotiator, reminds her that she really does know what's going on but is not giving herself credit for understanding it.

She says, "I'm not really quite sure what you mean."

David says, "Well Mary, let me ask you something. Do you have a home right now?"

She says, "Yes."

He says, "Do you pay a bank on a mortgage for that home?"

She says, "Yes, we have a thirty-year mortgage."

He says, "Mary, did you ever look at an amortization schedule on that?"

She says, "What do you mean?"

He says, "An amortization schedule describes the amounts of principal and interest in each payment. The payments stay the same, but the amount of principal and interest changes over time. Where is all of the interest on mortgages like this?"

She says, "It's all up front. Most of my payments are interest."

He says, "Didn't you ever look up your mortgage amortization schedule and see that even after three or five years' worth of payments you've still hardly reduced the principal amount that you still owe?"

She says, "Yes. I hate paying all that interest. I'd rather be paying down the principal, but at least the interest is tax deductible."

He says, "Mary, now do you see how that works against you because you pay a lot of interest to support that principal that you borrowed?"

She says, "Oh yes, I can definitely see that."

He says, "Mary, it's simple to see what's happening with your mortgage from Bill. You're receiving payments on a thirty-year mortgage."

Mary says, "That's right."

David says, "Well, where do you pay all the interest you're seeing?"

She nods and says, "Up front."

David says, "That's right. So if you sell me three years of payments, what are you discounting?"

Now she begins to understand. She says, "The interest."

David says, "That's right. You're forgoing the interest you would have received in order to get the $10,000 in cash up front. Your principal has barely changed. Your principal is now $79,656.22. After three years more it would still be $78,361.47."

Mary says, "Oh, now I understand. Now I can see what you're talking about. I'm just forgoing some interest."

"Right," David says. "That's correct."

Mary sees what's happening, but may still feel something's wrong, depending on how well she understands interest and amortization schedules.

If her understanding is not good, she may think that adding David's $10,000 to her remaining $78,361.47 of principal means she's getting $88,361.47 for her mortgage instead of $80,000. That certainly seems to work in her favor, but it doesn't seem right—and of course it isn't, because it ignores interest.

If she doesn't understand interest, David must explain. If she does, he can show that the deal works both in her favor and in his favor. *He can show her that he's creating a real win-win situation for both of them.*

At this point Mary will probably have more questions, but unless she's one of those people who won't let go of a penny, David probably has a deal. It will depend, again, on how much Mary needs the money, and what she needs it for.

David is not trying to talk Mary into doing something against her best interests; he's trying to find a way to satisfy both his interests and hers.

If Mary had said she needed $20,000, David would offer to buy more payments.

It must be a win-win for both parties. If not, it won't work.

The Partial Assignment of Mortgage

Much of a partial purchase works just like a full purchase. Like a full purchase, it is a recorded document. Like a full purchase, it is handled by a title company with a similar set of legal papers.

Unlike a full purchase, the papers state how long David will receive the payments and when the mortgage and payments will revert to Mary. It's quite simple—just like a full purchase except for the terms of the agreement.

The documents also state what happens if Bill sells the house or decides to pay off the mortgage early. That's likely to be one of the key questions Mary asks. "But David, suppose Bill defaults and I have to foreclose? Or suppose Bill pays off the mortgage during the three years you're buying. Would that mean you'll get my whole eighty thousand?"

"No," David would explain, "it doesn't mean anything like that. All you give up is the three years of payments of principal and interest I've purchased. If Bill pays off during the three years I'm receiving payments, the purchase agreement spells out how I'm to be compensated for not getting the balance of my payments. It also spells out what happens if Bill defaults."

Mary, of course, wants to know how that works. Even if she doesn't ask, David must tell her as matter of good standard business practice. This disclosure is often legally required as well. Most states have disclosure laws that either apply specifically or could be made to apply if David fails to explain and Mary decides she doesn't like the results and brings legal action.

Let's look at how David explains how a partial purchase of paper works.

"First, let's look at the possibility of foreclosure. I don't think either of us has much worry there. I wouldn't be buying part of the mortgage if I thought Bill was a bad risk. You wouldn't have given him the mortgage if you had any doubts.

"The size of Bill's down payment is the best guarantee we have against needing to foreclose. If Bill has financial problems, he can either get an equity loan large enough to carry him over, or he can sell the house for enough to pay us both off and have money left over to carry him until he recovers from his problems. If Bill is either dumb or panics, like some people in financial difficulty seem to do, then we foreclose and I get my money and you get back the house you originally owned. We're both covered, no matter what happens."

"Okay," says Mary, "I'd never really thought about foreclosing on Bill, and I really wouldn't want to, but I guess you're right. If I had to, my investment would be protected. Now tell me what happens if he pays off early. I really do think he's smart enough to sell if he has financial problems, so that would mean he paid off early."

"Right," says David. "An early payoff is far more likely than foreclosure. If I bought the entire remaining twenty-nine years, it would be simple: Bill pays off the remaining principal balance and I get it all. I don't get the interest I would have earned on the money after the date of payoff.

"It's little more complicated when he pays off before my three years are up, but it works pretty much the same way. Bill still pays off the remaining principal balance. He doesn't care who owns all or part of the loan. He isn't affected by our agreement. He owes the same amount either way, and it's divided up and distributed at settlement or close of escrow. We're the ones who have to have an agreement about what happens."

"Okay," says Mary. "How do we do it?"

David says, "We create a new amortization schedule for just the three years I own the rights to the payments. It's figured at the same interest you charged Bill, so that doesn't change, and Bill's payment doesn't change. It will show how much I get and how much you get if he pays off at any month during the three years, just as your existing amortization states how much he'll pay you if he pays off at any month during the next twenty-nine years."

What David is offering to do is called a *partial assignment of mortgage*, which means David is going to take only part of the cash flow, not all of it. If David was going to buy the entire mortgage it would be called a *full assignment of mortgage*.

The partial assignment of mortgage is really a great tool. It allows Mary to have her cake and eat it, too.

Mary will get the cash she wants today and David will get the cash flow from thirty-six payments on Mary's mortgage. Mary will still get almost the same amount of remaining principal, even after David has his three years of payments.

David's three years of payments enable him to almost triple his investment in three years. How many safe investments can you think can do that?

David's Choices

At this point in the deal David is in a great position, but he needs to make a decision. He must choose whether he wants to take advantage of entity number one (cash) or entity number two (reinvestment).

David can sell his portion of Mary's mortgage (the next three years) just like he could if he bought the entire thing. He can still call John and offer him the partial assignment of mortgage.

Let's say John offers David $18,000 for the next three years of $775 per month. What does David do? He has to decide between making $8,000 right now on the deal (the $18,000 offered by John minus the $10,000 Mary needs) or keeping the partial as an investment, using his own $10,000 to purchase the partial.

The yield on David's $10,000, with the numbers we are using, is extremely high. It's in excess of 80 percent (that's right, 80 percent per year), and that's phenomenal.

What would you do if you were David? For some of you it could be a tough decision, for others it may be easy. The answer is determined by your individual goals and needs. If you need cash, that's what you take. If you don't need the cash now, you might want to hang on to it for the yield over three years.

Of course, there's a simple way to decide what to do. Take a look in your check book. What's your balance? If it's more than $10,000, you should probably buy the note. If it's less than $10,000, then you ought to consider selling it. Either way you win.

What if Mary, for some reason, balks at selling three years of payments? This deal can also be done with two years' worth of payments. For two years' worth of payments at $775, you could also give Mary $10,000 cash. It would still put you in a position where you could get a good return on your investment; not 80 percent, but certainly better than most investments, somewhere around 68 percent. That's a strong rate of return.

It's really just a matter of negotiating.

A (Risky) Way to Buy for Yourself

I'd like to mention one other way that you could think about doing this deal. Some of my students have asked me about this technique, but I have mixed feelings about it. This technique can work if you're fully aware of what you're doing and do it right, and are willing to take a certain extra level of risk.

These students come to me and say, "Hey John, if I can make 80 percent and I'm buying the next three years of payments and only need $10,000, could I go to my charge cards and borrow the money (get cash advances) to buy the deal and enjoy the cash flow? Even if I have a really bad credit card with 21.5 percent interest, I'd be making almost 60 percent more than I'm paying for the money. The better the rate on my card, the better my rate of return. Right?"

My answer is, "Yes, you certainly can do that. You can borrow $10,000 with your MasterCard, Visa, or other card, assuming you have a card or cards with a limit that high and enough available credit. With that $10,000, you can buy this mortgage. Since you're making 80 percent on your money and you'll probably pay the charge card companies 18 percent, average, would you be making 80 percent minus 18 percent?"

The answer is no. You'd be making an infinite rate of return because you're using borrowed funds. You're using somebody else's money to make yourself money. You've invested no funds of your own, and the mortgage payments you purchase will pay the credit card interest.

Theoretically, an infinite rate of return is a wonderful thing. I say "theoretical" because this assumes the payments come on time for all three years and everything is fine. You take in $775 and you pay out whatever part of that amount it costs to pay off your charge cards. You just have to be sure you budget enough to clear the credit cards in three years. No problem, right?

Sorry, wrong.

If the payments come in on time, you're fine. You look like a financial genius. Problems occur when the mortgage payments stop. What happens then? Do you still owe money to the charge-card company? You sure do. Can you call the charge card company and say, "Listen, I bought a mortgage with that cash advance, but they're not paying me. I can't pay you until I foreclose and sell the property. Do you mind?"

You bet they mind! They'll cheerfully sock you with late payment fees, report your late payments to TRW and the other credit reporting agencies, and eventually turn your account over to a collection agency. Do you want that on your credit report?

No, you don't want that!

So you have to realize that credit cards can be a nice way of getting an extremely high rate of return, but they are *not* risk-free. An infinite rate is certainly better than 80 percent, but the theory is only as good as the payment record of the person paying on the mortgage. You're depending on someone else to keep your credit record clean. If you can't make the credit card payments if the mortgage payments stop, this is not a good idea. I wouldn't suggest you get yourself in that position.

Is there a way out, should you find yourself unable to carry payments? There are several possibilities.

You can sell the mortgage quickly. You'd need to have a buyer of delinquent paper lined up, and hope that he or she would want the mortgage at that time, and would pay enough to clear your credit cards. If you have a relationship you can depend on with such a person, the risk may be worthwhile.

You can plan for the possibility that mortgage payments will stop and you'll have to carry the credit card debt. You might put the first twelve months of payments, after paying the credit card minimum, in a separate bank account. Then, unless the mortgage payments stop in the first few months, you'd have resources to carry the credit cards.

There's a further possible problem. Suppose you had two cards, each with a $5,000 limit. You withdraw the entire credit line in a cash advance, and your monthly minimum payments are $125 each; a total of $250. Subtract that from $775, and it looks pretty good: $525 per month profit.

Yes, but will your credit cards be paid off in three years at that rate? Sorry, no. You have to budget money to clear the cards before you can take your profit. The longer you pay on the cards, the more interest you pay to Visa, MasterCard, etc. Remember that credit card interest is like mortgage interest in that the interest is highest when the balance is highest. Your payment may be two-thirds interest. (The actual percentage varies from card to card, depending on min-imum-payment policies.)

So, you have to pay off the balance as quickly as you can, or the credit card interest will eat away at your actual dollar profit, never mind that whatever you make has a theoretical infinite rate of re-turn. It will probably take you twelve to fourteen months to clear the credit cards if you apply your entire mortgage payment to the credit card debt until the entire balance and interest are paid off.

You can still get a very nice cash return—assuming you encounter no problems. To cover the risk of problems, you're better off making minimum payments until you have enough in the bank to cover a foreclosure and resale period. Remember that time to foreclose var-ies from state to state, and time to resell the property if you have to take it back varies according to the property and the local market. Be conservative in the cash cushion you allow.

You still have the problem of what to do if payments stop before you've collected enough payments to cover foreclosure and resale. For that, the only answer is to already have some cash in the bank.

I can't see any way you can entirely eliminate the risk of using credit cards to buy a mortgage. You can minimize the risk, as I've described, but you can get hurt financially doing this. If you're will-ing to take those risks, I want you to go in with your eyes open and a firm plan to extricate yourself from any problems than might arise.

Splitting Up an Asset

The partial assignment of mortgage is a wonderful tool because you're splitting up an asset.

Many assets are difficult to split up. It's hard, for example, to buy half a car, a third of a refrigerator, or one fifth of a boat. If you own one hundred shares of stock, you can sell half of them or any number you want, but usually you can't sell half a share. In all these cases, two or more people can share in the ownership of the asset, but that's not what we're talking about.

Let's think about buying a house. You're out with a realtor, looking for a piece of investment real estate. The realtor pulls up in front of a three-story house and say, "You know, this is a really good deal. I think you could do well by buying this property."

You look at the property and say to the realtor, "I think I could make you a pretty interesting offer."

The realtor says, "Go ahead. I'll listen to anything." (They often say that, but most of them don't mean it.)

You say, "It's going to be a little creative."

The realtor says, "I've heard creative offers before." (Many of them haven't.)

You say, "Okay. I'd like to buy just the third floor."

The realtor suddenly gets a shocked look on his face and says, "I don't know how we do can that."

There are ways it can be done, for example condos and tenants-in-common (TIC) agreements, but if the house or building isn't already legally divided, most realtors don't know what to do next.

But if you look at splitting up a cash flow, as we're doing in the partial assignment of mortgage, it becomes much easier. You can buy discrete amounts of cash flow: The next five years, the next two years, or the next thirty-nine payments before a balloon occurs—whatever looks like it will work for that particular purchase.

There are all sorts of things you can do because you're splitting up the asset and discounting the cash flow for a certain time period, for a certain amount of cash today.

A wise and prudent paper buyer like David should always have the partial assignment of mortgage available as a fallback. In a lot of cases you'll find that the person selling the mortgage doesn't really need to sell all the payments to get the cash they need. They may ask for the full amount simply because they didn't know they could sell part of it.

A simple question like David's—"How much cash do you really need?"—can produce a lot of money you might not have otherwise made.

Remember this and use it in your advertising, as I did in the ad I showed you earlier:

We Buy Mortgages
Full and Partial
Call John 962-4137

This ad gives me great results because most people call and ask, "What's a partial?" (See "Breakthrough Deal Number Four.")

Another ad that I've found pulls well is:

Don't Discount Your Mortgage
Call JOHN 962-4137

The intent of this ad is to offer purchase of a partial assignment of mortgage. Because you really aren't discounting the mortgage (principal), this is a true statement. You're barely discounting the principal of the mortgage and are not being misleading in your advertising. You're discounting the interest, not the principal. This ad produces a lot of inquisitive phone calls.

Paying Off a Partial Early

David and Mary discussed the need for an amortization schedule and a contract that would spell out what happened if Bill either sold the property early or defaulted.

How does that work? You, as the "David" in the deal, will have to explain it to "Mary."

If David had bought the entire twenty-nine years of payments from Mary and Bill wanted to pay off the mortgage, he would pay David the remaining principal balance according to the amortization schedule.

This is a clear and simple transaction. But if David had only purchased the next three years of payments and Mary still owned the remaining twenty-six years behind David, who gets paid what and when?

This seemingly simple question has created a major stumbling block for a lot of people who'd like to work with partials. If you can't answer the question who gets paid what when, then you're not going to take advantage of the great opportunities in partials.

In the last chapter in this book I'll talk about doing deals in Canada. When I first did Canadian deals, I learned that they didn't do partials, not because there was any law or policy against it, but simply because they didn't have the proper legal documentation to support the answer to exactly this question: who gets paid what, when?

The person who's selling the mortgage and you, the person buying the mortgage, *must* know who gets paid what, when.

If either of you doesn't know, you've created a situation that can cause a major legal battle. That's why no province of Canada (to my knowledge) did partial assignments of mortgages until my company introduced the documents and concepts.

Bill is not affected by the existence of a partial. He still pays the same payoff amount from the original amortization schedule he was given at the closing from Mary. The only thing that changes is where the money goes.

David, when he wrote up the deal with Mary, knew there was a chance Bill might pay off the mortgage early.

Remember what I told you in Chapter Two about the benefits of getting paid off early? Whether you own the entire mortgage or some of the mortgage, early payoff drives up the yield on your investment.

The reason, of course, is the time value of money. The faster money comes back to you, the more it's worth.

The document that David uses to secure this deal is an *assignment of fractional interest.*

This term is used because Mary is assigning a fraction or a portion of her interest in the mortgage.

She's assigning a fraction of her interest in the cash flow of the remaining period of her thirty-year mortgage. She could assign any fraction, of course, but in our example she's assigning three years, or one tenth of her total interest.

The assignment of fractional interest spells out the terms and conditions involved in this particular fractional-interest assignment.

David will also calculate, for that document, the present value of the future cash flow. The document will spell out what cash flow David's buying, whether it's the three years of our example, five years, ten years of a twenty-year mortgage, or whatever. David has to figure out what the value of that mortgage is worth today.

To do that, he does a calculation called the present value of the future cash flow. That term sounds complicated, but basically it means what the cash flow is worth today. If the cash flow is paid off early, how much would David receive? If it's paid off at any time while David owns the cash flow, how much does he get?

The document also spells out who gets paid what in the event of an early partial-principal payment. If all the principal is paid off, there's no problem. But suppose Bill comes into some money and pays off $20,000 of his remaining principal balance.

Who gets the money?

Mary, who owns the first?

David, who owns the payments for the period?

Bill would send the payment to David, because the assignment of fractional interest says any monies collected up to the present value of the future cash flow is paid directly to him, to reduce or pay off the principal amount owed (the present value of the future cash flow), which is what David bought when he bought the partial.

This may sound complicated, because a lot of possible actions have to be covered. It's really pretty simple, which you'll see after we go through the steps. David has to cover everything in order to protect himself.

When Bill bought Mary's property, he and Mary set up an amortization schedule on the original $80,000.

Because David is buying three years of payments, a new amortization schedule for the partial is created from the existing one. This new schedule is based on only three years of payments. The schedule uses the interest rate Mary is charging Bill (David's purchase doesn't change that rate) and it will be based on what the present value would be to David, at that stated interest rate, on the promissory note for the $775 payments.

If the mortgage is paid off early, Mary has an agreement with David that the remaining balance will be paid off at a certain pre-determined amount at any given date. This amount is stated in the new amortization schedule that David has created with Mary.

If Bill pays off the mortgage early, David would get a set amount and Mary would get the difference. Obviously, if David's three years were already up and Bill paid off the mortgage, Mary would get the full amount.

When you write up a partial assignment of mortgage, you need to include this amortization schedule for the mortgage being paid off early. It's not hard to do and really is just a matter of a few simple calculations.

If Bill was to pay off the mortgage to Mary after exactly three years (thirty-six payments) have been paid, Bill would pay her $78,361.47. If Bill was to sell the property for $160,000 cash to a new buyer, Harold, Bill would get a profit of $81,638.53 ($160,000.00 minus $78,361.47). Bill's sale price doesn't mean a thing to Mary or David and has no effect on what they receive.

When Bill sells the property, he pays off the mortgage. That's still the $78,361.47 remaining balance of the principal, according to the mortgage he gave Mary. That payment satisfies the mortgage. He's out of the deal entirely.

The difference, when a partial is involved, is that Mary must now give some of that money to David, since David purchased three years of cash flow.

How much does she owe David? The new amortization schedule determines this, preventing disagreements.

Let's assume Bill sold the property three years after he purchased it. Remember that one full year of payments were made to Mary before she called David to sell the mortgage.

David has received two years of the cash flow he purchased and is still owed one year's worth.

The amortization schedule Mary and David set up has a three-year starting balance of $23,598.16, which is the present value of the future cash flow. We make this calculation to determine what the mortgage is worth today, or at any time during its life.

David has purchased thirty-six payments of $775 a month. What is that worth to him today, the day Bill pays off the mortgage? This is a time-related return. On the day David buys the three years of cash flow, he calculates that value to be $23,598.16, the amount of money that he would have to get if the note was paid off the day he bought it.

The amortization schedule lists what he would get on each payment date over the three years he's purchased. The remaining balance decreases to zero at the end of three years.

If David has received two years of $775 and will not get the last year because the mortgage is paid off early, the amortization schedule shows that David is owed $8,758.76.

Therefore, when Bill pays Mary $78,361.47, Mary pays David $8,758.76. Mary nets $69,602.71, and David's yield increases because he gets his money sooner. Everyone wins.

When I say that Bill pays Mary $78,361.47, of which Mary pays

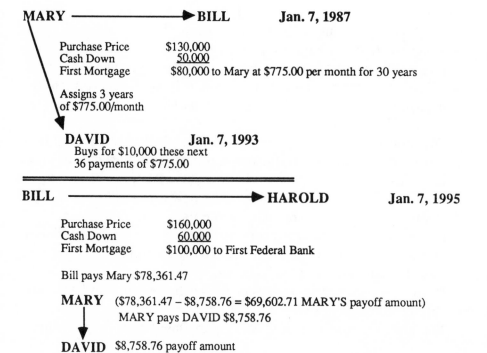

MARY ──────────▶ BILL   Jan. 7, 1987

    Purchase Price $130,000
    Cash Down   50,000
    First Mortgage $80,000 to Mary at $775.00 per month for 30 years

    Assigns 3 years
    of $775.00/month

    DAVID   Jan. 7, 1993
    Buys for $10,000 these next
    36 payments of $775.00

BILL ──────────────▶ HAROLD   Jan. 7, 1995

    Purchase Price $160,000
    Cash Down   60,000
    First Mortgage $100,000 to First Federal Bank

Bill pays Mary $78,361.47

MARY   ($78,361.47 − $8,758.76 = $69,602.71 MARY'S payoff amount)
       MARY pays DAVID $8,758.76

DAVID $8,758.76 payoff amount

David $8,758.76, I'm doing that for illustration, to make it sound simple. What really happens is that David is paid first at settlement or close of escrow. Technically, since David bought the next three years of payments, he has to be paid first and Mary is paid after that.

The priority of payment is of practical significance only if there isn't enough money from Bill's sale to pay off the mortgage, which doesn't happen in normal transactions. The priority of payment could become significant in a foreclosure, however, where the sale price may not cover all the loans against a property. In that case, David would be paid first and Mary would get what was left.

The diagram shows the course of this transaction.

For exact amounts from each amortization schedule, please refer to Appendices 1 and 2.

Appendix 1: Bill and Mary amortization schedule.

Appendix 2: Mary and David (three-year) amortization schedule.

Creative Use of a Partial: The Arizona Deal

I put this deal together fairly early in my paper career. It will give you more insight into what you can do with partials.

I had just quit my job and was ready to really gear up in the paper business. I moved into a small office on Twenty-sixth Street and Broadway in New York City. I was proud of this office, though it was really just a little crackerbox of a place, because it was my first, and it was all mine. I thought it was big time.

I hadn't been in the office long before I got a call from a developer in Arizona. He'd heard I bought paper and wondered it I'd be interested in buying his trust deed.

How had someone in Arizona learned about me and my little office in Manhattan? My parents live in Arizona. They told a realtor friend, who knew the developer and told him about me. This was networking in action even before I really knew what networking was, or how to do it.

Developers are an excellent source of paper. They often build properties and hold the paper themselves in order to get a quick sale. They always have a need for cash. They're always running from one deal to the next, because if they don't develop, build, and sell, they aren't making money. Quite often they have four or five projects going at once. They can afford a limited number of projects that merely break even. They can even afford an occasional slight loss—but not too many losses, and not too much. They're often better off breaking even on a deal and moving on to the next project rather than sitting and waiting for the right price while their work crews sit idle.

The developer asked whether, since I was in New York, I bought paper in Arizona.

By this time I was convinced the paper business had no boundaries. I could purchase a trust deed in Arizona as easily as one in New York. I told him I could, and I was interested.

He had a fully amortized twenty-year first trust deed for $15,500, with monthly payments of $150. He'd taken back this paper on a single-family, owner-occupied home. The buyers had put down $6,000 cash. He had just finished building the house, and the buyers were about to move in. He asked what I'd pay for the paper.

I did some calculations. The note was for 240 payments (20 years × 12 payments per year) of $150 each. After I went through all the calculations and considerations I use to determine the value of the paper, I told him the best I could offer would be $9,000.

He asked me if that was the best I could do.

I said, "Hang on a minute. I'll check." I was a one-man shop, sitting there alone in the office, and didn't have anyone to check with. I simply held the phone for about two to three minutes, cupped to my hand. I didn't do anything, but I know he thought I was checking with a committee or asking a partner for advice.

When I came back on the phone I said, "I'm sorry, that's the best I can do. But since you're in Arizona, you'll have to pay the closing costs on this deal."

He was surprised. He said, "I didn't know I had to do that."

And I thought, neither did I. Remember, each deal is a fully negotiable situation. He and I can make any deal any way we want. He didn't legally have to pay the closing costs, a negotiable expense, but I was telling him that paying the costs was a condition of my buying his paper.

I needed to explain the costs to him because he was not sure how much he would have to pay. He was familiar with closing costs on the sale of real estate, but not on the sale of a trust deed. I explained that closing costs are all costs associated with the transfer of the cash-flow rights from him to me, and that most of them are similar to costs he was familiar with from real estate closings.

First, there's a credit check on the person making the payments to establish that they are indeed creditworthy and can actually afford to make the monthly payments. Next is a current market-value appraisal. There's a title search to see if the lien is really a first trust deed and all real estate taxes are current. There must be title insurance. Finally an assignment is prepared and the title company charges a small fee to actually perform the transfer of ownership and record the assignment from the developer to myself. No appraisal was necessary because of the recent sale of the property.

On a deal of this size, I told him, the total costs should not exceed $300. I had purchased real estate in Arizona, so I was familiar with the costs there.

Then I repeated that the price was the best I could offer. I told him that my offer was subject to everything checking out. He agreed to the price, and asked how long it would take to close and get him his money.

I explained it would take two to three weeks, depending on how quickly he could get me the paperwork and how fast we could put the whole deal together.

He said, "Okay, fine, where do I send the paperwork?" I gave him my office address and everything was off and running.

At this point, had I bought anything yet? Of course not. All I'd done was make an offer to pay $9,000 for twenty years of $150.00 per month.

I got on the phone and called Bob, a friend of mine who liked to buy this type of paper. I offered him exactly the same deal I had been offered by the developer not two minutes earlier. I asked if he was interested in buying twenty years of $150 a month payments secured by an owner-occupied home in Arizona.

He asked me the same questions I asked the developer: where the house was located, what were the terms of the trust deed, etc. Then he thought a moment and said, "John, I'd like to make you a creative offer on this trust deed. What I'd like to do is give you $9,000 for the first ten years of payments."

This was the first time someone offered me a partial, so I had to have him explain it. Bob said he was offering to give me $9,000 for the next 120 of the 240 payments. I'd own the remaining 120 payments.

I told him I'd have to think about it.

The deal looked like the following chart:

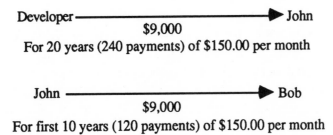

Developer ────────────────────▶ John
$9,000
For 20 years (240 payments) of $150.00 per month

John ────────────────────▶ Bob
$9,000
For first 10 years (120 payments) of $150.00 per month

What each would get:

DEVELOPER	**BOB**	**JOHN**
$9,000 in cash minus closing costs	120 payments of $150 per month on a 1st Trust Deed for $9,000	Takes a moratorium on 1st 10 years, gets remaining 10 years for NOTHING!

The way this deal works is that Bob will wire-transfer $9,000 into the title company in Arizona. The title company will assign, from the developer to me, 240 payments for that $9,000. I simultaneously assign to Bob, for the $9,000 that he put up, the first ten years of payments of $150.

The developer pays the closing costs for the entire deal. Bob gets the first 120 payments of $150 a month secured by a house worth $21,500 ($15,500 plus $6,000 down). I get the back ten years for absolutely nothing whatsoever out of my pocket.

After I hung up the phone, I started to think about the offer. I knew Bob only wanted to buy the first ten years because he was trying to limit his financial exposure and risk. At the time we negotiated this deal, Arizona real estate prices were extremely flat (a fact that may have motivated the developer to sell in the first place). Prices weren't going up or down; they just weren't doing anything. He wanted to be protected in case they got worse.

Bob knew what real estate was doing in Arizona because he's a smart paper buyer. Paper buyers must understand real estate values in any market where they buy, because the value of property there determines the value of their collateral.

Bob knew that if he had to foreclose and take back the real estate, he'd have to sell it. He wanted to make sure he could sell for what he put into it. He was protecting himself and his investment by offering to buy a partial. He realized that if he wanted to buy the entire trust deed it would cost him more than $9,000. He didn't want to invest that much in it, because it would put him at higher risk.

Bob was looking at the prices of real estate and the state of the current economy. He was worried that if he bought the entire trust deed and the value of the property dropped, he could find himself in a trust deed over basis—that is, the property would be worth less than the loans against it. That had already happened to investors in Houston and Denver in the early '80s. If that happened, he wouldn't be able to sell the property for enough to get his money back.

All Bob's thinking was predicated on the fact that there could be a problem.

Usually there's no problem whatsoever. The person who lives in the property makes the payments, and the person who buys the mortgage enjoys the payments.

But, as I've said before (and can't really say too often), you always want to look at the worst-case scenario so you can protect yourself. Investment, whether in paper or anything else, is not a place to play Pollyanna and assume everything is always going to be just wonderful, merely because it ought to.

Bob does not want to hold the entire trust deed because the property was a new home and had just sold. With new property there's sometimes an immediate drop in value, not unlike an automobile being worth less than you paid for it the instant you drive off the dealer's lot. Add that to generally flat prices in the area at the time of purchase, and Bob had a need to be cautious and protect his investment. By owning only part of the payments, he secured himself in case of default.

He knew, of course, that the value was there. Real estate prices may rise and fall, but he, and we as investors, are protected because we have wisely determined that the LTV does not exceed 72 percent. (I'll explain LTV in the next chapter.) The value of the house would have to drop dramatically for him to get burned. The worst thing that could happen to him is that he'd have to hold on to the house until values rose again—which they would.

What about my security in this deal?

Well, I didn't invest any money at all. How *could* I lose?

CHAPTER 13

Protecting Your Investment: LTV

Bob's concerns rely upon a concept of value everyone buying or selling paper must understand: the loan-to-value ratio (LTV).

LTV is an equation that relates debt to equity on any piece of real estate. The result of calculating the equation is a percentage, and so we speak of LTV as such: "The property has an LTV of 70 percent," for example.

LTV is defined as the ratio of the total amount of liens against the property to the current value of the property, expressed as a percent. To put this into a simple equation:

$$\text{LTV} = \frac{\textit{Sum of all the liens on the property}}{\textit{Current Value of That Property}} \times 100 \text{ percent}$$

This means that you divide the current value of the property, determined by an appraisal or by a sale within the last year, into the total of everything owed on the property—*not just the loan you are buying*, if there are more than one.

In our ongoing example, when Mary sold her house to Bill for $130,000, with a $50,000 down payment and an $80,000 loan, we divide $80,000 (the total of all loans) by $130,000 (the value of the property) to arrive at an LTV of 61.54 percent. When Bill sold the house to Harold for $160,000, he owed Mary $78,361.47. The LTV at that time had improved, because the loan had been paid down, even if only a little, and the value of the house had gone up by $30,000. At that point, the LTV was about 48.98 percent.

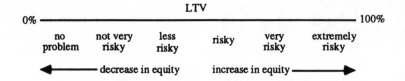

You can perform this calculation on a calculator, or with pencil and paper.

When a bank lends money on a house, it always looks at LTV. It wants the down payment to provide a comfort zone between what the buyer pays for the property (purchase price) and the amount of money owed against the property (lien or liens). The comfort zone is the equity. The more equity in the property, the safer a bank feels about lending money on it. The lower the equity, the riskier the deal looks.

A high LTV (closer to 100 percent) is very risky and a low LTV (closer to zero percent) is very safe.

Let's look at the LTV that Bob sees in the Arizona deal.

The house sold for $21,500, and the loan is $15,500. That's an LTV of about 72 percent. As we'll see in a moment, a 75 percent LTV on a single-family home is as high as I recommend a paper buyer go, so 72 percent is getting close to the limit.

Bob would like to see the LTV of his purchase look better than that, as would any paper buyer. He makes his offer based on an LTV using the present value of future cash flow.

When Bob buys 120 payments of $150 at about 10 percent, the value of his cash flow today is $11,331.18. He is discounting this amount by buying for $9,000.

He divides $11,331.18 by $21,500, to get a 52.7 percent LTV, which should be safe even if values fall drastically. This is why Bob wanted to do a partial. He bought a very safe investment.

Since the house just sold, he can use the sale price without asking for a new appraisal. (In some cases, if it seems as if the sale price was high for the area, you might want an appraisal anyway.)

The chart shows the relationship of LTV to risk.

The chart illustrates the range of risk involved in paper. As we leave 100 percent LTV and see more equity in the property, we feel better as paper buyers because there is more at risk (equity) for the property owner. The more equity there is in the property, the less likely it is to go into foreclosure, and the less likely it is that the person who owns the property will not pay on their paper.

LTV and Different Kinds of Property

The acceptable LTV ratio depends on the type of real estate used as collateral.

A single-family, owner-occupied home is the safest deal and commands the highest acceptable LTV of 75 percent.

A piece of land is the riskiest type of collateral, because there are no improvements on the property, so a 50 percent LTV is the maximum.

The owner of a single-family home lives on the property. He or she is strongly motivated to make payments rather than risk losing the home where the owner's family lives. But this is not a perfect world. Homeowners may encounter any of a number of possible financial problems, like loss of income, severe illness, or other major expenses. Since there's always a chance the owner may not pay, we use 75 percent as the maximum LTV for owner-occupied, single-family homes. The LTV decreases from there, depending on the type of property, as listed in the chart below.

In this chart, I give the *maximum* LTVs you should consider. The specific circumstances of any individual property may reduce these figures, sometimes drastically, or may make a mortgage something you wouldn't buy on a bet.

I was recently offered a mortgage that looked good until the appraisal came in, which noted that the property was a block away from a street known for prostitution and drug dealing and was in the path of an airport redevelopment project. I wouldn't have taken that one if they gave it to me!

LTV AND PROPERTY TYPE

Type of Property	LTV%
Owner-occupied, single-family	75
Single-family, rental property	70
Commercial property	60
Land and special-use properties	50

In order to fully understand loan-to-value and why we're so concerned with it, consider what happens when you lend money.

I don't recommend that you lend money, but let's say you do. If I want to borrow $10,000, you'll want answers to two questions: What security do I offer for the money I want to borrow, and how long will it take for me to repay your money?

If we could agree on a time to repay, like a year, a month, three weeks, or whatever, the collateral becomes a very important issue. Ten thousand dollars is really a lot of money. You need some sort of collateral.

Suppose you asked for collateral and I said I could offer either a piece of land in the middle of New Mexico or the home I live in.

You'd ask for the home that I live in without a second thought (assuming I have adequate equity in both pieces of real estate, of course). My home is where I live, not only physically but emotionally. It's where I go, it's what I do. It's important to the security and peace of mind of me and my family. I'd be far more likely to let go of a piece of land in the middle of New Mexico. It's only a piece of land, not a home.

I have nothing against New Mexico, of course, but I know they have lots of land available in the wide-open desert.

If the New Mexico land had a rental house on it, it still wouldn't be where I live, but it would be a place where I *could* live if I had to, so I'd be less likely to let go of it than a piece of undeveloped land, although I wouldn't hang on to it the way I'd try to hang onto my personal residence.

You can see that the home has a far higher security value to someone lending money or buying a mortgage secured than does a piece of land. As you decrease from single-family to raw land, real estate continues to offer good security for your investment, but you need to have more equity in the property to protect yourself in the event of foreclosure.

When we look at different types of property, we have to adjust the LTV to reflect the degree of security offered.

Types of Property

In the LTV chart above, we listed four kinds of property. It would be possible to break property down into narrower definitions, but these will suffice for paper buyers in most situations. If you find something that doesn't seem to quite fit one of these categories, seek expert advice about the particular property.

We begin with single-family, owner-occupied homes, which everyone understands. Single-family rental property is almost equally self-explanatory. The LTV is lower because the owner doesn't have the emotional investment of actually living there, and there is more risk that a rental occupant may trash the place or just not take as good care of it as if he or she owned it.

Commercial property, special-use property, and raw land cause the most questions and are the source of the greatest misunderstanding.

Commercial property includes anything over four units, all apartment buildings, and all real estate that is rented per square foot, right up to properties like megastore shopping malls and the World Trade Center.

Special-use properties create a very interesting situation. We see these fairly often. In some (extreme) cases, I think they should be a separate category with an even lower acceptable LTV than raw land.

"Special-use" is a real estate code word for any building that has only one or a very limited number of uses, like a car wash or an industrial building that can only be used to make one product.

Because the property has limited use, it's harder to resell if you have to take it back through foreclosure.

A car wash can only be sold to someone who wants to use it as a car wash—unless you sell it to someone who will tear it down and build something else on the land.

The possibility that you'll have to sell to someone who would have to tear down and rebuild is why, in some cases, special-use buildings should be considered to be worth less than raw land. If the buyer can't use the existing building, he or she will have the expense of tearing it down. Their purchase offer will reflect that cost. (Of course, if the car wash happens to be on a prime downtown corner, the property may be worth much more with the car wash demolished and an office building built in its place.)

If I hold a mortgage on a car wash on an ordinary business lot, the loan is secured by the real estate, not by the business. This may not be evident from past sale prices. You must be careful about all business properties where the sale price, and even the appraised value, may include the equipment and goodwill of the business as well as the land and building, but you must be even more careful about special-use business properties.

Another example of special use we encountered was a property that had a crane right in the middle of the building.

It was a particular type of industrial building in which the owners were manufacturing something that required that big crane. This limited the building's use to businesses that made things and needed that type of crane to do so. Anyone else buying the building would either have to set up their equipment around the crane, losing the utility of part of the building, or pay to have the crane removed, either of which would reduce what they could offer.

Real estate such as a car wash or the building with the crane or any similar property requires a particular type of buyer, is harder to sell, and often brings a lower price. You're looking for a specific person who has a specific use for that piece of real estate that matches the building's specific existing function.

It will take longer to find a buyer when you have to sell a limited-use building, often much longer. There's higher risk on your money, so you have to have more equity. If you had to drop the price to sell the property faster, you'd want a higher-equity position to protect your investment. You'd look for a lower loan-to-value position.

Back to Arizona

Let's go back to the Arizona deal.

The deal sounded pretty good. The more I thought about it, the more I knew I was going to take Bob's offer.

Think about it for a moment. I gave up the first ten years of payments, but I still owned the remaining ten years. How much did it cost me to do this deal?

Let's consider the mechanics.

Bob paid me $9,000, which covered the $9,000 it cost me to buy the deal in a simultaneous close.

The back 120 payments of $150 per month cost me nothing. I paid the developer $9,000 for the deal and received $9,000 from Bob simultaneously.

I got ten years of cash flow for absolutely nothing! A free deal! A no-money-down deal!

That sounded good to me, so I went for it.

Arizona and Infinity

The only thing I didn't like was that I wouldn't get any money for ten years.

Then I realized there was a good chance the real estate market in Arizona would turn around and the property would be sold during the first ten years.

Bob and I entered into an agreement just like David and Mary. We set up an amortization schedule to consider who was going to be paid if the property was sold early. Eventually all real estate does go up in value, and I was sure the property would also increase in value. We wanted to have everything spelled out, so when the sale took place we'd both be comfortable with what to do or who got what amount of money.

Bob and I were paid simultaneously at closing, just as David and Mary were.

But is this a good deal for me?

I didn't have any money in the deal. What was my rate of return going to be? You might think it's 100 percent, but it's not. A 100 percent return is when I give someone a dollar and they give me back two. In this case, I'm not giving the person any money for the deal, but I'll be getting money back. How can you figure the rate of return? You can't. It's an infinite rate of return. The rate of return is so high you can't even calculate it. How can you calculate a return on your money when you put no money into the deal?

When you realize what an infinite rate of return is, you'll look at deals a lot differently.

Think about people who do one of these mega-transactions where they borrow from the bank, then borrow from investors and take on partners, who put up more money. Some of the shrewdest business-people on Wall Street put deals together all the time, often in the millions, sometimes billions of dollars, and never use one penny of their own money.

That's an infinite rate of return.

It can be done on a very small scale, like with the Arizona deal, or it can be done on a very large scale, like a leveraged buyout of a company worth a couple of billion dollars that you buy with a very creative formula requiring no money out of pocket. Either way, it's the same infinite rate of return.

Going Higher Than Infinity with a Keogh Plan

I've talked about the choices you have when you buy any mortgage—sell to another investor at once, keep for your own portfolio, or keep and sell later—and the many reasons why you would choose one alternative or another.

Now I'd like to offer an additional alternative, which happens to fit exceptionally well with a deferred-profit purchase like the Arizona deal.

If you're already self-employed, you're probably familiar with Keogh plans. They're a tax-deferment investment option designed to benefit self-employed entrepreneurs, which is what you are when you become a paper investor.

A Keogh plan allows you to tax defer up to $30,000 of income in any one year (depending on your income), by putting it in the plan. You can invest that money, keeping the profits in the plan, and the profits are also tax-deferred. Check with your accountant or financial adviser for full details.

The Keogh is set up through a bank. The Keogh can then buy investments with the cash in the account, or you can let it collect nominal bank or CD interest. If you want to invest, you can buy stocks and bonds, or you can buy paper. You can invest the money you put into the plan in almost anything you choose. The profits of the investments are added to your Keogh plan account but are not considered part of the $30,000 annual limit. The investment income is considered similar to the interest income you earn on an IRA account. It isn't taxed until you withdraw it.

Remember, when you buy paper, you're not matching dollar for dollar. Each cash dollar in the Keogh does not buy you a dollar's worth of paper, because you buy paper at a discount. Every dollar you spend may bring you two dollars' worth of paper. That means your $30,000 in the Keogh plan could perhaps be used to buy $60,000 worth of paper.

The only drawback is that you can't touch the money without tax penalties until the age of fifty-nine and a half.

Have you seen where this is going yet?

Early in this book I talked about my panic at realizing that my wonderful corporate retirement plan would only pay me $1,600 a month at age sixty-five. If you thought I'd forgotten all about retirement in my excitement over all the money I could make in paper, think again!

A mistake many people make is to assume that someone who makes a lot of money doesn't need to worry about retirement income, because of course he or she has made all this money, and that will provide all that's needed.

Wrong!

Sure, if the money is left in bank accounts or put in conservative, low-yielding investments, it will be there—*but it will have been taxed when it was earned, and the interest on it will also be taxed.* There will be a lot less money available than if tax-deferred investments had been made.

I hope you can see why you should establish a Keogh plan as soon as possible, no matter how much money you're making.

It's simple to make a direct cash contribution to a Keogh, and that's what you'll be doing until you've made enough money to buy paper for yourself. Once you're buying and holding paper, the question becomes how to decide which notes to put in the Keogh and which to keep as regular income.

That's usually a matter of judgment. It doesn't matter what happens to the paper for Keogh purposes. Whatever money it makes is available for reinvestment into more Keogh paper. I'd tend to put the paper I considered safest into my Keogh, but you might feel differently. A logical argument could be made in the other direction, that if you put riskier notes into your Keogh, delinquent paper, for example, you have less risk of having problems in your day-to-day cash flow, and over the period of the Keogh the risks will even out.

Now let's look at how paper like the Arizona deal is custom made for your Keogh.

For openers, how much of my $30,000 annual Keogh contribution did the Arizona note eat up?

None! None at all! I got those last ten years of payments for nothing, remember? If I got the note for nothing, it goes into the plan with a value of zero. When the profits come in, whether from an early sale or the actual last ten years of payments, the income is treated as profit on an investment, not as part of an annual contribution to the Keogh!

Then, consider that while I paid nothing for the paper, I've also deferred taxes on any income from it.

The paper doesn't exist today as far as my current day-to-day cash flow is concerned, and won't give me any spendable cash for ten years, unless paid off sooner. Since the profit is already deferred for ten years, why not defer it the rest of the way to retirement, when it will be worth even more than it is at payoff?

Your paper will make more in your Keogh than it would if you held it personally and took its profits as current income. You'll be making an infinite rate of return, and can anything be better than that?

I had two really good reasons to put the Arizona deal in a Keogh. There's another reason.

Consider the keep-or-sell choices, and take a close look at the sell option.

The problem with selling the remaining ten years to another investor is that it's the back ten years. You have to discount it to today's value. The investor has to wait ten years (or until the note is paid off) for any return on his or her money. A smart investor won't pay much for that kind of investment. So while you could try to sell it for cash, you won't find a lot of investors who would buy it.

There are some who will buy that type of cash flow, but they want a very hefty return on their investment. They won't pay much for it today, probably no more than a couple of thousand dollars, if that.

You'd have to need cash very badly to sell the back 120 payments of $150 for so little, but if *you* were the investor, you wouldn't pay more for it, either. You'd have to protect yourself not only against a need to foreclose but against the possibility that the trust deed will be paid off early and you won't get those payments.

What would happen if I'd already put $30,000 (or the maximum my income permits) into the Keogh, and then I bought the Arizona deal? My Keogh account is full for this year. I can't put any more in until next year. Would I have to wait until the next April 15 before I could put an Arizona-type deal into the Keogh?

Or could I put this deal into my Keogh plan because I didn't pay anything for it?

This sounded like a great idea, but I thought I'd better ask my tax attorney if I could do this. Since I'm not personally paying anything for this deal (zero cash) and my Keogh isn't paying anything for this deal, I wanted to make sure I could put it into my account and allow my Keogh to hold it until I was fifty-nine and a half, deferring all the taxes due.

He told me I could, so I did.

Making Your Keogh Dollars Go Even Farther

You can see that because the Arizona deal is in my Keogh, any taxes I would have paid are now deferred to age fifty-nine and a half. In effect, that raised my rate of return from infinity to something even higher than infinity.

Even if your Keogh plan is full, with no room for any more money that year, you can still buy paper for it if you can orchestrate a deal where you buy the paper with none of your own money.

Now, let's take this idea a little farther. The fact that an investor wouldn't pay much for those payments was one of the reasons why I put it in the Keogh. But suppose I'm the investor and I'm looking for just that kind of paper? Instead of merely looking and waiting for a deal that requires no money, why not take the initiative and buy *tails of mortgages*—the end payments of a mortgage?

Suddenly, the fact that neither I nor any other investor will pay much for tails of notes becomes an advantage. Though I didn't want to sell the Arizona deal, many paper investors are quite happy to get rid of the last payments on their paper. They know these payments aren't worth much, so they're willing to sell for a small amount of money.

If you look for tails of mortgages, you can buy them all day long. You may find small mortgages where you buy the last three years of payments, or last ten years, as in the Arizona deal. You may buy a balloon payment due five or ten years from now. There are all kinds of opportunities. All that matters is that the paper is sound, like any other paper you buy, and the price is right.

Tails of mortgages are ideal for Keogh-plan purchases. You can make your retirement dollars go a lot further by using relatively small amounts of money to purchase paper that will pay off in the future. You're not worried about current payoff because the Keogh plan is for the long term anyway. The date of payoff doesn't matter!

If I spend $2,000 to buy payments that are going to give me $150 a month for ten years between ten and twenty years from now, I profit whether the paper goes to term or whether it's paid off early. No matter what happens, I'm not taxed on the money until I withdraw it after the age of fifty-nine and a half.

Paper profits put into a Keogh plan seem to be (and legally are) tax-deferred, but those profits are really tax-free money because the investment profits, plus compound interest on the money that stays in the bank over the time the Keogh account is in existence, will actually pay the taxes. If your profits and interest pay the tax, you get effectively tax-free money when you withdraw it anytime after the age of fifty-nine and a half.

You can see the advantage of spending the fewest possible dollars for the most possible deals for your Keogh. You can spread that investment of up to $30,000 a year over a lot of little deals that produce very high rates of return.

With the Stefanchik Method, you can get high rates of return by working your money through your Keogh plan. When you work your money through the Keogh, you separate yourself from almost everyone else. Most people have their money collecting low interest from a bank, or losing it in the stock market. You're getting phenomenally high rates of return, even infinite rates of return, tax-free!

What could be better than that?

Any type of retirement account could be used in this manner. An IRA (Individual Retirement Account) or even a 401k pension plan will work. I suggest that you explore your own personal situation with your tax adviser to see what best fits your needs.

It doesn't matter which way you look at it. I think there isn't anyone reading this book who couldn't scrape up enough nothing to purchase a deal like the Arizona one and put it in their retirement account.

Aren't you glad you have this book and can start to make these kinds of deals? Believe me, you'll find deals just like this one, and others even better, out there just waiting for you.

CHAPTER 14

The Combination-of-Ingredients Deal

We've looked at a simple example of a deal (Bill, Mary, etc.) and another example of how a partial can be purchased.

Now I'd like to show you how a number of paper-finding and paper-buying techniques can be combined in one deal.

This deal came to me from a contractor, another excellent source of paper. In this case, it's called _home improvement paper._

The contractor may do a major job for a homeowner, like putting in a swimming pool, building a deck, remodeling a kitchen, adding a room, or anything else you can imagine. If the job is big enough, the homeowner may ask the contractor to carry part of the cost, perhaps a large part.

The contractor may agree for a number of reasons. If he has good cash reserves, a portfolio of liens that pay each month may provide good cash flow stability for the business. More often, however, the contractor is like the builder in the Arizona deal. He or she needs to keep the crew working, and needs both jobs and cash to do so.

The homeowner may say something like, "I want a new swimming pool, and I have $5,000 to put down on it. Can you carry the balance as a lien against my house?"

The lien is a mortgage (paper) secured by the property, and so it's just as valuable to a paper buyer. The only difference is that no sale of the property has taken place.

The contractor needs the job, so he agrees. If the issue of the paper is brought up before the contractor quotes a price, he may quote a higher price to cover the costs of selling the paper. The contractor knows the only way to get cash is to sell the paper, which won't sell for its face value. If the paper issue comes up after a price has been quoted, the contractor may point out that if he has to carry a note, the price will have to be higher.

In this deal, a homeowner had paid $5,000 down on a $30,000 swimming pool project, giving the contractor a $25,000 second mortgage.

Obviously, it cost the contractor a lot more than $5,000 for the materials and labor to do all the work of putting in the pool. He needed his money as soon as possible, so he set up the mortgage to be attractive to a paper buyer. He also protected himself in the event he couldn't find a buyer. The mortgage he accepted was amortized over fifteen years, with payments of $275 per month, but with a balloon payment of $20,454.11 due at the end of five years. That meant sixty payments of $275 (five years until the balloon) and then the balloon, so the mortgage really had two parts; the cash flow of the payments and the lump sum of the balloon.

The contractor came to me wondering whether I'd buy the note. He was concerned about the same two things most contractors selling notes will be: He wanted to know how much I would pay, and how fast we could close.

As I've said earlier, closing usually takes two to three weeks, unless there are problems or some party to the deal is slow in getting the right information and documents to the title company. I've closed in four days, and I've seen deals take six weeks. In Hawaii, where things seem to get done on "aloha time," (and there's only one title company—no competition), things always seem to take longer.

Since this was a local deal, and I knew both the contractor and the title company, I was able to assure him that we could close in three weeks, and that I'd do everything I could to close sooner. It helps to have direct knowledge of the area and the people you'll be working with when you want to close a deal quickly.

I looked at the loan-to-value ratio and other factors, and it fit my guidelines with room to spare. This deal was good.

I negotiated with the contractor, and after the usual dickering back and forth we agreed on a price of $15,000. I told him he'd have to pay the closing costs, but he objected. That's a negotiable expense, so after more dickering we agreed to split the closing costs. On this deal, closing costs didn't run very much—about $600 total, so $300 for each of us.

I can hear you saying how great this is, but there was only one problem. This deal came to me when I was just starting, and I didn't have $15,000!

I had a few thousand available, but no way to come up with the rest of the cash from my own accounts.

By now, you know that the logical solution to my problem was to find an investor who would buy the deal, so I started contacting as many investors as I could. Some were friends or relatives; most were people I'd located through my mortgage dealings who said they'd be interested in buying paper if I offered them a good enough deal with a good enough yield.

I saw the possibility of being creative here, so I asked each investor, "What would you pay for sixty payments of $275 a month?" Since there were two parts to the mortgage, I wanted to see whether I could sell the five years of cash flow as a partial and keep the balloon for myself.

I was working on the time value of money principle I've talked about throughout the book, which in this case meant that the first five years would be worth more than the balloon payment to the investor because the money would come sooner.

When I called my potential investors, the best price I could get for the first part (the sixty payments of $275) was $12,000.

That meant I had to find the balance of $3,000 to give the contractor the $15,000 we'd agreed to, plus my share of the closing costs. As in other deals we've discussed, the contractor doesn't care where the money comes from as long as he walks away from closing with $15,000 in his pocket, less his share of the closing costs.

I had that much cash available, so we closed the deal. At closing, the contractor assigned the paper to me, and I assigned the first sixty payments to the investor.

What had I achieved? For $3,000 plus about $300 in closing costs out of pocket, I'd purchased a balloon payment of $20,454.11 due in five years!

You can see the progress of this deal in the first two steps of the following chart.

Contractor Deal

$25,000 2nd Mortgage at $275.00 a month on a 15 year amortization with a 5 year balloon.

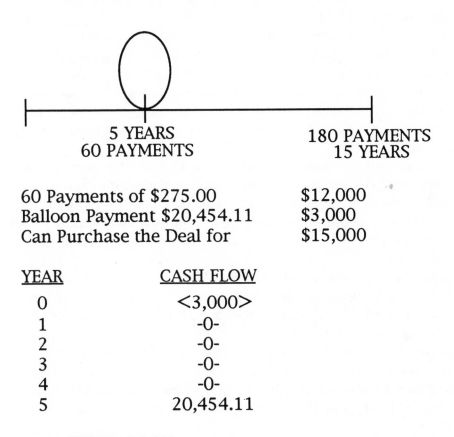

5 YEARS 60 PAYMENTS	180 PAYMENTS 15 YEARS

60 Payments of $275.00	$12,000
Balloon Payment $20,454.11	$3,000
Can Purchase the Deal for	$15,000

YEAR	CASH FLOW
0	<3,000>
1	-0-
2	-0-
3	-0-
4	-0-
5	20,454.11

YIELD 39.0%

How Sweet Is This Deal?

In step three of the chart above, you can see the effect of my investment on my cash flow.

I show this by making two columns, one with the year and the other with the cash flow.

Year zero is the year I took $3,000 out of my pocket to start the deal, and invested it in the purchase of the balloon payment. The brackets around the $3,000 show that it was an expense, not income.

Year zero is not a calendar year but the date the money was invested. Year one is the calendar year following that date. No money comes in that year, so for year one I had a cash flow of zero, and no yield on my investment.

There's no income in year two, either, nor in year three, four, or until the end of year five. My money isn't doing a thing for me during that time. I can't spend it, and it isn't producing income.

But at the end of the fifth year I receive $20,454.11 in one lump-sum payment, which is the balloon I purchased five years ago. When you calculate the rate of return, I get a 39 percent yield on my money.

Thirty-nine percent represents taking $3,000 out of my pocket and looking at what it produces over a five-year period. It's a time-related return, which means it's not calculated based on what $3,000 grows to. This calculation must take into account the fact that the $3,000 grossed $20,454.11 over five years with no money coming to me during the term.

A 39 percent rate of return is excellent! Compare it to bank interest, for example, or even excellently performing stocks, bonds, or mutual funds! Even zero-coupon bonds, which may pay 10 or 11 percent, tax-deferred, aren't even close.

Rates of return like the one in this example are where the value lies in the Stefanchik Method. It's so exciting to consider that you can pick up deals like this for a little bit of money. Your $3,000 grows to $20,454.11 while you sit there and wait for that balloon payment to burst.

If the loan is paid off early, you get your share according to the amortization table you put in the agreement.

As you can see, this is a very sweet deal.

What If I Didn't Have the $3,000?

You can recognize that there may often be times you'll find a deal like this when you're short of cash. Maybe you've been finding a lot of great deals and used your last $3,000 on another good deal just last week. The simple fact of being a paper buyer and making lots of money doesn't mean you'll always have cash available to buy the deal that comes in today.

Would you have to turn this deal down? Would you have to go back to the contractor and say, "I'm sorry, I can't do it?"

Is there any way you could do the deal and keep a piece of the action? Keeping a piece of the action is an important part of the Stefanchik Method. Keeping a piece of the action is where you get seriously wealthy.

Obviously, when you find someone like the contractor who may bring you more deals, and may bring his friends to you if he's happy with what you can do for him, you don't want to send him looking for someone else or leave him holding a mortgage he doesn't want. One of the ways you build your paper business is by making sure you take care of potential and repeat customers.

Less obviously, one of the ways the Stefanchik Method creates your financial security is by building a base of investments that don't cost much now but pay off handsomely in the future. The value of future payoff is what I was talking about when I showed how the Arizona deal was perfect to put in a Keogh account.

This deal, because of its low cost and deferred profit, is also perfect for a Keogh investment.

Now, is there a way I can buy it without that extra $3,000 I haven't got?

Well, I bought the Arizona deal without any money, didn't I?

Here We Go: Let's Get Creative

I need another investor.

But, can I bring two investors into one deal?

Sure, if the deal will support both their interests and give you a profit, too. You'll make less money, of course, but you'll make it with no money out of pocket, so you're getting that infinite rate of return I talked about in the Arizona deal.

I should point out that even when you're getting an infinite rate of return, you also need to be sure you're making enough actual dollars to support the work you do to complete the deal and cover whatever level of risk you decide it involves.

Where can I find another investor? I don't need someone with a lot of money, as I would if I were David, trying to buy Mary's mortgage for $50,000 and make a profit.

Let's try cousin Ernie. (See Step Four in the chart on page 171.)

Ernie has always told me at every holiday gathering or any time he's seen me, "Boy, I'd like to get a good solid rate of return on my money! Anytime you find a deal you think can do that for me, I wish you'd let me know."

I call cousin Ernie and say, "Ernie, I've got a deal for you that I think is going to work just great."

He says, "Okay, fine. What is it?"

Ernie is not a professional investor. He hasn't studied how paper works or any of the other ways he could invest. He just has a little money he'd like to put to work. I have to take the time to explain how the deal works and what his risks and benefits will be. He has to know what's expected of him, when he can expect to see his profits, and what happens if the mortgage is paid off early. Because he's family, I want to take extra good care of him.

I tell him, "A contractor brought me a deal the other day. It's a $25,000 second mortgage that we can buy for $15,000." I explain the deal: the first sixty payments of $275 will be bought by an investor, who put up $12,000 and will get a nice rate of return on his money. "But, Ernie, he's not going to get as good a rate of return as you will," I say.

Ernie replies, "What's a good rate of return, and how does that work? Why do I get more?"

Because Ernie isn't an investor and doesn't understand rates of return as I do, I have to tell him how it works, as I've explained above. Before I can tell him the rate of return he'll get, he has to know what it is and what the figures mean. Like a lot of people, Ernie gets distracted by yield and doesn't really understand what the value of a yield is.

I tell him, "Ernie there are two things you should be concerned with whenever you get into an investment. Any investment."

Ernie says, "Okay, what are they?"

"The first thing, of course, is yield, which I'll get to in a minute. The second thing is security on your money."

Ernie says, "Okay, what's my security?" That's easier for him to understand, so he asks about that first.

I say, "It's a piece of property."

Ernie says, "All right. Tell me about it. Is it a good property?"

I say, "Instead of telling you about it, I'll show it to you. I'd like you to drive by the property with me. You can kick the bricks; take a look around and see the type of property that we're dealing with when we talk about a safe return on your investment. The safety of your money lies in the property, so I want you to see the security for this mortgage we're buying. If anything happens to the payments, we'd share the responsibility of foreclosing so we could get our money back. There's adequate equity in the house." I quote the numbers and explain LTV while we drive to the property.

Ernie sees it and says, "This is great. You mean if something goes wrong we can foreclose and get that house?"

I say, "We could, Ernie, but there's so much equity that they're not likely to let us get the house. Unless they're really dumb or panic, they'll sell it and pay us off."

Ernie says, "Well, that's fine with me. It looks like that means my money is safe, whatever happens. Now tell me about yield."

I say, "Ernie, I'd like to offer you something that will make you feel really good about doing business with me."

Ernie says, "All right."

I say, "How about 22.17 percent on your money?"

Ernie says, "Twenty-two percent on my money? My God! I can't get that anywhere!"

I say, "That's right! Let me explain how this is going to work. You're going to take three thousand dollars out of your pocket. We're going to do the deal together. We'll create a simple partnership agreement that states how much I'm going to get and how much you're going to get, and what happens if the loan is paid off early."

Ernie says, "Fine. How does that work?"

"It's a bit like a zero-coupon bond, except that the yield is a lot higher. You take $3,000 out of your pocket today and get it back, plus your profit, in five years. You have to wait five years with absolutely no money coming in, but then you get a lump-sum payment back giving you 22 percent on your money. And the nice thing is that it's secured by real estate."

He says, "All right fine, but how many dollars does that yield mean to me?"

"Well, you're going to put in $3,000 and I'm going to give you

$9,000 back at the end of the five-year term when the balloon pays off."

Ernie says, "Let me get this straight. I'm going to put in $3,000 and I'm going to get back $9,000. I'm going to triple my money! I'm going to get 22 percent on my money and it's secured by real estate. When do I sign up?"

Ernie is very excited about the deal. He's going to get 22 percent on his money and triple his investment in five years. It's a secure deal, and he doesn't even know what he's doing!

The real-life Ernies you encounter may ask smarter or dumber questions than I've used here. One common question will be why he triples his money but the yield is only 22 percent, not 300 percent. You explain that this is a time-related return, based on the time value of money.

What This Deal Means to You

As nice a deal as Ernie gets, what happens for you is even nicer.

You're about to do the deal with absolutely no money. You don't have to take much money out of your pocket, except maybe the closing costs of $300. Ernie puts up the money, but he doesn't mind. He's getting a secure rate of return on an investment he had no idea he could make.

You'll make $11,454.11 on little money invested. (The difference between the $20,454.11 balloon payment and the $9,000 you must give Ernie.) You're entitled to more than Ernie (if he asks) because you found the deal, you have the knowledge of paper, and you're doing all the work.

You've made about as close to an infinite rate of return as you can imagine.

Now here's the beauty of the Stefanchik Method. You put no money into the deal and make $11,454.11!

You should be glad you didn't have $3,000 to invest. Why? It's real simple. If you had money and put in $3,000 you would have gotten $20,454.11, but you would have made only 39 percent on your money. Since you don't have money and bring cousin Ernie into the deal, you're making close to an infinite rate of return on very little money invested.

I want you to look at this deal for the specific techniques used, of course. But, more important, I want you to see the degree of flexibility and creativity which are possible with the Stefanchik Method.

I've used this deal to bring a lot of things together to show some alternatives you can use. It illustrates the partial, working with investors, bringing in a second investor, and the infinite rate of return.

Whenever you look at doing a deal, *any* deal, there are so many ways you can do it that you can take your choice and custom-tailor each deal to whatever your needs and financial situation are at the moment. That's what's so powerful about the Stefanchik Method.

In my seminars I found that people could really relate to this deal.

A lot of people would say, "Gee, I don't have the money. Where would I get the money?" That's almost always their first thought and the biggest obstacle to getting started. People are always worried about the money.

These students could always sell the deals to my office, but what would happen if they found a deal that I couldn't buy or couldn't buy fast enough?

Someone always asks, "What other alternatives do we have?"

Standing Naked In Front of an Audience

I was giving a seminar in Baltimore. I was right in the middle of my presentation, which was going very well. The crowd was really excited. They were feeling really good about the deal with Ernie. I was working them up to the spot where I could say to them, "Now look at this! You put in very little money, cousin Ernie puts up the $3,000, and everybody wins. Ernie gets $9,000 in five years, with a 22 percent yield. You get $11,454.11 with little money invested of your own!" The crowd was really with me. They were going crazy, cheering like any seminar speaker's dream.

But—about five rows in on the left side of the room sat a woman. She yelled, "Hey!" Her tone was sharp and high pitched, the kind of sound that gets attention. I wasn't sure who she was talking to, so I kept on going, but she said, "Hey, hey, hey, hey!" That got my attention and everyone else's. She said, "I have something to say!"

The crowd stopped, the excitement level dropped, and I turned to her and I said, "What's the problem?"

She stood up and said, "What happens if Ernie finds out what you're doing?"

I looked at her and said, "What do you mean, what I'm doing?"

She said, "What happens when Ernie finds out you have no money in the deal?"

I had just said that I make a point to tell Ernie that I don't have any money in the deal, but for some reason she didn't grasp that concept. She didn't like the fact that I was putting no money in the deal and thought there was something wrong with that.

I went through it all again. I said, "I found the deal. I'm putting the deal together and doing all the work. I educated myself to do the deal. Ernie couldn't do it by himself. I don't understand what the problem is. I could put up the money if I had it, but I don't. I'm asking Ernie whether he'd like to make an investment with a great return. I'm offering him a return he couldn't get anywhere else. The whole deal is based on return on investment. That's why I'm in it, why the investor who bought the first sixty payments is in it, and why Ernie will accept my offer."

She paused for a moment and then said, "Okay. What happens if Ernie wants his money back?"

You could have heard a pin drop in that big room. She was trying to expose me, and I was beginning to feel naked in front of this live seminar group.

She was asking what happens if, in about a year or so, Ernie discusses this with his accountant. What if the accountant doesn't like it or something else happens? Ernie realizes you have no money in the deal, and says he wants his money back.

She said, "Suppose Ernie confronts you with this and says, 'I want my money back. I don't want it in the deal anymore. Give me my money back.' What are you going to do?"

The woman had an interesting point.

The crowd could have turned on me at that point, but because of the power of the Stefanchik Method, I showed everyone why this was no problem.

When you're dealing with people who are not professional, experienced investors, it's possible that some of them may get scared after they've made the investment and want their money back. Legally, you don't have to give it back. You've got a valid, signed contract that does not have any such escape clause.

As a practical matter, though, you want people who do business with you to be happy. You don't want them going around telling all their friends and anyone else who'll listen what a nasty, inconsiderate person you are. Bad word, true or false, travels fast. And, in this example, Ernie's part of the family. You certainly don't want bad feelings in the family!

So I turned to the woman in the fifth row and said, "Let me get this straight. Let's say that in a year Ernie wants his money back. What am I going to do?" I explained the issues of legality and good will. "There are a number of choices available to anyone who works in paper using the Stefanchik Method. You can pay him; just give back his $3,000. He may say, 'Wait a minute, where's the money I earned in this year?'

"I'd say, 'Hold it. If you put your money in a CD with a bank or invested in some type of bond, lets say a zero-coupon bond, when you pull out early you get hit with a penalty for early withdrawal. You're lucky I'm not going to hit you with a penalty. I'm bigger than that, so I'll give you your full $3,000 back because I never expected you to leave the deal in the first place.'

"So I hand him $3,000. I can give him his money back with my own cash. When investing it paper, you have cash available more often than not. That would solve the problem. And, $3,000 is not $30,000 or $3,000,000. It's a relatively small amount of money.

"But suppose I still don't have the money. What can I do?

"I'd tell Ernie, 'Okay, I'll give you your money, but I didn't plan on having you pull out, so you'll have to give me a couple of days to get the money together. Then I'll give you your money and you'll be out of the deal.'

"Ernie says, 'Okay, fine.' He can't really say anything else, because I've explained that he doesn't have a legal right to demand his money back, and I'm doing him a favor."

Cousin Fred to the Rescue

I need to find $3,000, fast. Is this a problem? Have I had a problem locating money before? No.

I can approach cousin Fred, or anyone else who might have money and an interest in a good yield. Cousin Fred is glad for the opportunity and comes into this deal one year later with his $3,000.

We look at Step Five, the year zero. It's year one before Fred comes in. Originally, Ernie put out $3,000, would wait five years, and get $9,000—22 percent on his money. When he pulls out, that becomes meaningless.

If he wants his money back a year later, it doesn't matter where I get the $3,000 from.

The woman agreed. "Fine, just so long as you can pay him back."

I said, "Okay, I can pay him back out of my own pocket. Does everyone in the room agree with that?"

The whole seminar group said fine, sure, I could take money out of my own pocket. I wanted to take the woman's worries and the point of her question and totally turn it around. I said, "Okay, let's say I bring my cousin Fred in on this deal and I say, "Fred, I've got a deal for you. You put $3,000 into a deal and in *four* years' time I will—" And then I paused. I looked at the group and I said, "Folks, I have a choice of two things I can do, just to really show you the power of the Stefanchik Method. I'll let you choose which one you'd prefer."

The crowd agreed.

I said, "I can ask for Fred's $3,000, and in four years give him $9,000 back, just like I was going to do for Ernie. I'd be tripling his money in less time. The time value of money says the faster money comes to you, the more it's worth, so what have I just done for Fred if I give him $9,000?"

A few people said, correctly, that I'd increase his yield.

"Right," I said. "If Fred puts up $3,000 and gets $9,000 back in four years, his rate of return increases to a 27.7 percent return on his investment. I can offer Fred a higher return on investment to give him an incentive to come into the deal."

Everyone in the group started getting very excited. They realized that's a really powerful tool to use when you need an investor, fast. Then I said, "Now wait a minute, folks. I'm not done."

The woman in the fifth row started to get a little smile on her face.

You know, some people at a seminar want to get you. They want to ask the question you can't answer or don't know, and make you look foolish in front of the group, but I think this woman was sincere. She was trying to understand what would happen if this happened to her. She'd put herself in the situation, seen a problem, got scared, and wanted an answer. She wanted to know whether the Stefanchik Method would allow her the flexibility to solve the problem if something like this happened.

When I said, "Wait a minute I'm not done yet," she looked at me expectantly, and the crowd looked at me, and I said, "What if I offer Fred the same rate of return I was going to give Ernie? Remember, the money is coming to him sooner. What happens if I kept his rate of return at 22 percent? What would I have to do?"

The group was stunned. They didn't know what to say. The woman was almost ready to give the answer. She was very bright and could see what was happening.

I said, "Folks think about this. If I asked him to put in $3,000 and offered to give him $9,000, his rate of return went up. What happens if I offer him the same rate of return I was going to give to Ernie? If I say I will give him 22 percent on his money in four years, according to the time value of money, what do I have to offer him?"

The group finally yelled out the right answer: "You have to offer him less money!"

It works out that I'd have to offer him $7,224.67. To drive the point home and to work the crowd into a real cheer, I said, "Now folks, just look at what happened. What did the Stefanchik Method do? It gave Ernie his money. He's got his $3,000 and he's off into some lower-yielding deal. Fred comes into the same deal one year later, and I could either give him the same *amount* of money I was offering Ernie, or the same *yield* I was offering. I can offer whatever I choose.

"If I keep the yield the same as I was going to give Ernie, I give Fred less money. That means I pocket more money. I now would make $13,229.44 on almost no money invested."

The crowd went into a roar. The woman in the fifth row started to clap as well. She realized that either way she'd win.

Either way, it's going to work out. The faster money comes to you, the more it's worth. That's the time value of money. The example above was not done with smoke and mirrors but with a simple return on investment that anyone could understand.

Everyone in that room went crazy that day, because they realized this is a really powerful method.

But that is what the Stefanchik Method does. All it's based on is return on investment. Everybody wins, because everybody gets a good, solid return on investment.

Everybody is in a situation where their investment is secured by real estate, they're getting paid off, and the yield is high. Even if something goes wrong and someone needs their money back, the paper is there and the yield is there to return the money, find another investor, and give everyone involved their return on investment.

CHAPTER 15

What Happens When They Don't Pay?

Paper is the only investment I know of where you can get your money back when someone stops paying you. Try that with the stock market. If your broker invests money for you and your stock loses, what can you do about it? Cry, scream, fire your broker? You can't get your money back. It's history. In paper this is not the case. You have the power and the legal right to foreclose on the property.

Everything we've discussed about paper so far is based on the premise that the payor, like Bill in our example, makes payments to you regularly. If you bought and sold the mortgage, as David sold Mary's mortgage to John, you're out of it. You never know (and don't care) whether payments are being made. It's not your problem.

But if you kept the paper for your own investment and the payments stopped, what happens?

As I've said earlier, your right to foreclose is your protection against losing your investment. All our discussions of LTV and the other factors involved in judging whether to purchase paper and how much we can pay for it are based on assuring that if we have to foreclose, we will, at worst, recover our investment. At best, we'll earn our expected profit or more.

The down side of foreclosure is that it takes time, and you may wind up owning and managing real estate. You got into paper because you didn't want to own property. Still, you're far better off owning the property than losing your money, right?

Right, and that's why one of my fundamental rules is that I never buy a mortgage on a property I wouldn't want to own.

Foreclosure doesn't happen often, but it does happen. You have to assume that any mortgage or trust deed, no matter how good it looks when you buy it, may go into default at some time in the future.

Your first protection in paper is careful evaluation of the value of the property and the financial history of the payor. Your second and ultimate protection is your right to foreclose.

Afraid to Foreclose?

Don't let the word *foreclosure* scare you.

Some people hear that word and immediately picture some Simon Legree slumlord gleefully throwing a family out of their house and into the snow.

Believe me, it's not like that at all.

As I've said, foreclosure is your legal right to get your money back. This legal right is why you have a mortgage or trust deed and a promissory note. You wouldn't invest in paper without it.

There's a distinction between foreclosure and eviction. When you own rental property, whether it's a single-family home or a multi-unit building, eviction laws protect your right to collect rent. If someone's not paying the rent, you can then evict them from the property.

The difference between eviction and foreclosure is that when you evict a renter you have to find a new tenant. You may find that when one headache leaves, another headache comes in. When you foreclose, you take back control of the property or get paid off. The simple distinction is that eviction leaves you with no money, while foreclosure gives you your money back.

Why do payors stop making payments? There can be a variety of reasons, only rarely involving outright fraud or intent to deprive the mortgage holder of income.

Foreclosure forces the hand of the person who is not making payments.

No one really wants to lose their property, but under extreme financial pressure, from whatever source, some people simply freeze.

It really doesn't matter (to you) what has happened. All you know is that for some reason you aren't getting your payments.

You don't start foreclosure proceedings if they miss one payment. You should let them know you didn't get it and are concerned. But when they fall three or four months behind you know there's a problem. Now you have to do something about it. Legally, you could start foreclosure after the first missed payment, in most cases, but that's rarely done, and then only in cases with special circumstances.

When people get that far behind, an interesting phenomenon occurs. They get paralysis of analysis. They're so far behind, usually on more than their mortgage payments, that all they do is worry about how they are going to get out of it. They worry and analyze, but they don't do anything about it. They've paralyzed themselves with fear. Perfectly intelligent, capable people just freeze.

Yet they usually have a number of viable options readily available. All is not lost, but they have to do something. If they just sit there, they'll lose their property.

Someone who is about to lose their property usually goes through predictable phases. Panic and worry come first, and from them comes paralysis of analysis. They really don't know what to do. They're facing an action of doom that they don't want to have happen, but they got themselves into this mess and aren't doing anything to get out of it. They get farther and farther behind.

At that point, the person may freeze completely and go into denial (this can't happen to me, so it can't be happening, and it won't happen if I just ignore it).

Or the person may realize that they can't solve the problem alone.

You can't do much for the person who has gone into denial. All you can do is foreclose, because they'll probably reject or ignore anything you or anyone else offers as a solution.

If, however, they realize they need help, you may protect your own interests while helping them to the best possible resolution of their problem.

Most people are not really familiar with the foreclosure process. If you send a letter advising that they're behind on their payments, many people won't make the connection with the possibility of losing their property.

What they normally think is, "Oh, yeah, I'll pay it when I have the money." As if their good intentions are all that matter, and you should read their minds and know that they're good people and will take care of it when they can. It's not at all unusual to get no response to the letter that advises them that they're a month behind, then two months, going on three.

As I do it, the third letter is sent near the end of the second month, just before the third missing payment would be due. The third letter is followed by a letter from my attorney, on his letterhead, stating that foreclosure is a legal remedy for failure to make payments. The letter advises them to check the paragraph in their mortgage document that provides that right, and identifies the paragraph. The letter states that we have the legal right to foreclosure against them, and not only will foreclosure ruin their credit, but they will also lose their house and all the equity in it. The letter makes it clear that it's time to start talking to us about what we can do to solve the problem, because we have the legal remedy of foreclosure if the problem is not solved.

If the person is not into total denial, they'll respond.

There is also the possibility that when the person realizes that they face a problem they can't solve alone, they may go to an attorney or a credit counseling service and ask for help and advice.

They may go to their attorney, explain the problem, and say, "I'd like to solve this."

The attorney may say, "Well, what are you going to do? You're not paying, right? You did sign this mortgage and promissory note, right? You have to pay and that's all there is to it."

Now let me add a note about lawyers. They're specialists, and they know the kind of law they practice, but rarely *all* the law. To appreciate why this is so, all you have to do is look at a law library in an average attorney's office. It's huge! No one could possibly know, or even read, everything that's in there, much less be fully versed on all the implications.

The result is that our payor who goes to an attorney for advice may get differing advice, depending on the attorney he or she picks out of the phone book, goes to because some family member or friend made a recommendation, knew from church, or whatever.

A bankruptcy attorney who needs business may suggest filing for bankruptcy. The attorney who did their divorce may give the "Well, you have to pay," advice without suggesting other alternatives. A real estate attorney will know the alternatives and lay them out. Any attorney, of course, may (and should) know the alternatives and possible solutions, but many don't, apparently. If they did, I think we'd see fewer foreclosures.

Alternatives for the Payor Who Can't Pay

You might think you don't need to know what the payor can do, because, after all, *you* are not facing foreclosure. But remember, you don't want to foreclose.

You may be able to help the unfortunate payor either directly or through your attorney. Normally I'd suggest that your attorney contact the payor and say, in effect, "Look, you've clearly got a problem because you aren't making the payments. My client has no interest in taking your house through foreclosure, but that's the only remedy available if you don't solve the problem. There are alternatives between paying at once and losing your home and credit through foreclosure. I can tell you what they are, in my view, but because I'm the attorney for the person who holds your mortgage (or trust deed), I'd advise that you consult your own attorney before taking action on any of them. I'd also advise that you consult a real estate specialist who will be familiar with these alternatives. Both my client and I would like to see you work something out that doesn't require foreclosure."

Some of the alternatives the attorney, or a knowledgeable attorney for the payor, would suggest are:

1. Sell the house quickly, at a below-market price, and pay off the mortgages. The payor will save some equity and avoid having a foreclosure on his or her credit record. A quick sale doesn't always work, but for the kind of paper we're buying, there's enough equity in the property that it will be rare that a property can't be sold for enough to pay off the mortgages. If the payor is trying to sell the property and is asking a reasonable price, you might be willing to wait a little longer before beginning foreclosure proceedings. You're better off if the property is sold and your mortgage or trust deed is paid off than if you have to proceed to foreclosure.
2. Sell the house to a foreclosure investor. The payor may get

a quick sale, but will get less for the property. Foreclosure investors typically want to buy the property for 30 percent or more below market value. You can find them through realtors or at foreclosure sales. Either the payor's attorney or your attorney may know of such investors.

3. Refinance and pay off all existing liens. Refinancing may be a problem if the payor is out of work, but lenders are sometimes understanding if the probability of reemployment is high, the past record is good, and there's plenty of equity. That's great for you, because you're paid off and you don't have to worry about any future problems the payor may have.

4. Consult a credit counseling service and work out a plan to restructure their debt so their monthly income can handle it. If this happens, they may come to you and ask to change the terms of the mortgage so they can, for example, make lower payments over a longer term, or make lower payments for the same term, but add a balloon payment at the end.

5. Sign the property over to you. Giving up title to the property in exchange for avoiding foreclosure is called giving a *deed in lieu of foreclosure.* Offer this solution if the payor has not been able to sell the property. In this case, the payor loses his or her equity in the property, but avoids a foreclosure on his or her credit record. It's not good to lose all the equity, but it's a lot better than putting a foreclosure or bankruptcy on your credit record. A good attorney will point this out to the payor. I've had people offer me this option before I or my attorney ever suggested it. I even had one person turn around and ask to buy the property back from me *after* the foreclosure!

6. Declare bankruptcy. Sometimes this is the only solution for a person who has really messed up his or her finances. It ruins their credit. Bankruptcies stay on a credit record for ten years. You want to try to help the payor avoid this, but if it happens you're still protected. You'll just wait longer to get your money back.

7. Let the property go to foreclosure. That's what both you and the payor want to avoid. Foreclosure will happen

when the payor freezes into denial and refuses to accept help.

What If the Payor Declares Bankruptcy?

Some payors think, wait a minute, why not declare bankruptcy? That will get us around this problem. We'll get to keep our house.

No, no, no! These payors don't understand how bankruptcy works. A knowledgeable attorney will advise them against it.

Declaring bankruptcy to get around foreclosure doesn't work. Many people have a major misconception about declaring bankruptcy. They think that if you declare personal bankruptcy, you can keep your house and live there free. They think everything will work out. That's *not* the case! Some states have homestead laws that protect part of the homeowner's equity, but those laws don't stop foreclosure.

A bankruptcy will delay foreclosure for a short time, depending on the state's laws, but will not cure it. The problem will not go away.

Foreclosure will take place, even if delayed a few months.

Will They Trash the Property?

Many investors worry that a payor who has lost a property through foreclosure and/or bankruptcy will be so upset and feel so unfairly treated that they'll trash the place before leaving, thus vastly reducing its value, and resulting in costly repair and renovation work.

Yes, that happens, occasionally. More often, they don't leave it wonderfully clean, or have deferred normal maintenance. You can expect to do painting, carpet cleaning, and other cosmetic work, perhaps more than you'd expect to do between tenants in a rental, but it's rare that someone is so angry that they trash the house. And, if they do, you can prosecute them for vandalizing your property, if it was done after the foreclosure, or for violating the loan provision that requires them to keep the property in good repair if the damage was done before foreclosure.

Don't hesitate to foreclose because of a fear that they'll trash the property. If they're the type who'd do that, it won't matter whether you foreclose at once or put it off hoping they'll start paying again.

You Can Benefit from Foreclosure

If you stop to think about it, foreclosing on someone can increase your yield. You don't want to do this to someone just to improve your profits, of course. But, when it happens, you're accelerating the time in which the money is repaid to you.

Remember when I talked about the time value of money and how your yield increases the quicker you get paid? That's what happens in foreclosure. You're getting your money sooner than expected, so your yield increases. Remember, the faster money comes back to you, the more it's worth.

Heidi's Deal

This story is kind of embarrassing, but it illustrates how a problem deal can turn out well.

Before we got married, my wife, Heidi, came to me and said she had $10,000 and wanted to put it into paper. I figured this was a chance for me to earn money for her. She knew how deeply I was involved with paper. I realized she must have faith in me if she was asking me to help her. I also thought that if I could make a good deal for her, it would be easier to work together investing in paper after we were married. I started looking for a good deal in which to place her $10,000.

It didn't take very long to find the deal—paper on a property in southern New Jersey. I bought her a third mortgage for $10,000, and everything was fine.

I've stressed that when you buy a mortgage, you can negotiate the price. I got Heidi a good yield. But remember that the terms of the mortgage itself are already fixed and you're buying them as they exist. On this deal there were no payments during the first six months but, starting with the seventh month, Heidi was to receive $510 a month until the mortgage was fully paid off. It was a good deal with a nice yield and an acceptable LTV, even though there were two loans in front of hers.

Heidi waited patiently for those six months to end so she could start collecting her money. Month seven came and went, and she received no money.

She said to me, "Great. What happened? Aren't they supposed to pay me $510 this month?"

I said I'd find out. (You can see me starting to sweat a little, here.) I called the payor. He said he had forgotten what month it was and would send a check right away.

We waited and waited, and still no money. I called him again and, finally, he sent the check. Heidi deposited the check and it bounced.

You can imagine this situation was getting more than a little embarrassing for me. Heidi was starting to get upset about the whole situation.

I called the payor again. He told me he'd forgotten to put money in his checking account. Heidi could redeposit the check and it would clear. Heidi redeposited the check and it finally cleared.

Next month, no check—again.

When the payor finally sent *that* check, it, too, bounced.

Now Heidi was more than just a little mad. I can still remember what she said. "What are we going to do about this? I thought you told me paper was so great. You said it was just so fantastic. You're always so excited about paper and look what happens to me on my first deal!"

I also remember what I said to her: "Now, don't let this come between us." (I had visions of my future marriage going down the tubes). "We do have a remedy. We can foreclose if there's really a problem. Let's just see what happens."

We were about ten months into the deal by now. Heidi got a letter from an attorney. In it was a check made out to her for $15,189.89. I called the attorney and asked what happened. He said the guy who wasn't paying Heidi had sold the property and this was Heidi's payment in full!

Do you realize what happened to Heidi's return on investment? Within ten months she got back her original $10,000, plus an additional $5,189.89. All this on a deal that wasn't even paying her like it was supposed to!

Now, not every deal is going to work out like this, but again it shows the flexibility of paper, even on a bad deal.

There is almost always something you can do to get a debtor to work with you. When they get behind on their payments they usually don't know what to do and any direction you can give them is usually appreciated, if they haven't frozen into denial.

They can sell the property, refinance the property, or even borrow short-term money from somewhere else to help them get past the tough time. You may offer them the option of rewriting the mortgage with you if it would help the situation—but only with your approval.

Losing property to foreclosure should be a very last resort and only after one has tried everything else.

When the Last Resort Is Your Only Option

As we've seen, there are a lot of alternatives to foreclosure that are far better for the payor, and also better for you.

When you begin foreclosure, your first question will be how long it will take. You're getting no income from the mortgage during the foreclosure process.

The length of time before you can begin foreclosure, and the time it takes to complete foreclosure once it has begun, differs from state to state.

Most mortgages give the paper holder the right to begin foreclosure if one payment is missed, but in practice it's rare to begin foreclosure before two or three payments are past due. This practice gives both the mortgage holder and the payor time to correct the problem or work out a mutually acceptable solution less drastic than foreclosure.

Once foreclosure proceedings have been started, they can take from 120 days to over a year, depending on the state. In general, foreclosure is faster in trust-deed states and longer in mortgage states.

The reason is that in mortgage states foreclosure is a judicial proceeding. The mortgage holder must go before a judge and prove that payments haven't been made and/or that other terms of the mortgage agreement have been violated. It's normally a routine proceeding—a defaulted payor has no legal argument against foreclosure—but it takes time to go through all the steps, schedule a court date, notify everyone, and so on. This is called *judicial foreclosure*.

In trust deed states, the promissory note specifically gives the trustee, the neutral third party who holds the note in trust for the payor and the paper holder, the right to foreclose without further court action. This is called *non-judicial foreclosure*.

In either case, the length of the proceedings varies on a state-by-state basis.

Trust deed states work out much better for foreclosure than mortgage states, because the process is faster. For example, in California there is a twenty-one day period of notification that foreclosure is about to take place (a *notice of default*), followed by ninety days for the actual foreclosure process. If the payor has not redeemed the trust deed by then (brought it current and paid all foreclosure expenses and penalties), the property is sold.

In a mortgage state it takes longer to get your money back, but you get accrued interest and the legal fees are taken care of.

In either system, if problems come up that can stall the foreclosure, it can be delayed. Foreclosure can't be stalled indefinitely, and it's harder to delay foreclosure in a trust deed state, but even there it can be stalled for a time.

How long the process takes in a mortgage state is really a matter of how efficient your attorney is and how efficient the judicial system is in the state where the property is located.

Wherever you buy paper, you should know the foreclosure system of that state and know about how long the process will take. You should also know how long it will take under worst-case circumstances, as when a bankruptcy is involved.

Should you buy paper only in states where you live? You may want to do that, especially at first. Should you always buy paper in the states where the foreclosure laws are favorable? Yes, that's true, especially if you buy with borrowed money or use an unknowledgeable partner like cousin Ernie. But, if a good deal comes along you may want to take advantage of it even if the foreclosure laws are not that great.

It doesn't matter what state it is—foreclosure laws are there to protect you and your investment.

The Steps of Foreclosure

If nothing you've tried works or the payors simply aren't willing to save the deal, then you have no option but to go ahead with the foreclosure. What are the steps you must take?

First, you're not the one handling the foreclosure. You're going to have an attorney take care of it. Attorneys know what needs to be done and they take care of all the paperwork and filings that are necessary. They know the requirements in their state and will advise you on how long it will take and what you can do to help speed the process, if anything. Then, when you receive your money, the attorney's fee is included in the proceeds. You don't lose money on attorney fees.

You should become familiar with the steps that the attorney takes during the foreclosure process.

These are the seven basic steps that take place during the foreclosure process in a mortgage state. In a trust-deed state, the steps are similar, but less complex or legally involved.

1. Both you and the person behind on payments need to be aware that a default in the mortgage has taken place. That you both should be aware of the default may sound obvious, but sometimes it's not. You should have notified the payor that they're in default after the first missed payment. If you didn't, your attorney will. Make sure he or she did. In trust-deed states, notify the trustee. If everyone isn't notified, there can be no legal grounds for foreclosure.

2. You have tried to overcome the payor's problem of not paying. You've looked for solutions to the situation. You and/or your attorney have given them some options that will help them overcome the nonpayment problem. They chose none of the options. From this point on, every time I say "you" do something, I mean that your attorney does it in your name (on your behalf).

3. You file a *lis pendens*, literally, "suit pending," a legal notification that a foreclosure proceeding has been begun against the payor. Filing a *lis pendens* establishes the juris-

dictional power and control that the court acquires over the property in suit pending action until a final judgment is reached. The person is now on notice, through public record, that there is a problem with their property and a suit is pending against them.

4. A summons and complaint is filed with the court system.

5. The defendants, the payors who are behind in their payments, are served the summons, complaint, and *lis pendens*. In addition, the state, the county, the town, and the holders of any liens in front or behind yours are notified of the suit. Everyone who is or might possibly be involved is notified about what is occurring. Except for the main defendant, the defaulting payor, everyone will respond with a notice of appearance. The main defendant may not respond, because, by this time, they may be ignoring everything they receive. If they respond, it may be to attempt to correct the default, which would make everyone happy— but by this point in the proceedings that rarely happens. Everyone has been notified and understands they should appear at the sale.

6. If by this point the payor has not responded to the suit by correcting the problem, they are legally in default. You make a motion for a default judgment and ask the judge to appoint a referee. The referee is an independent third party appointed by the court, and his responsibility is to discover the value of the property and place all the ads in the newspaper when the time comes. The referee's job usually takes about sixty days. At this point you're about 150 days into the foreclosure process; sixty days for the default, plus thirty days to respond and sixty days for the referee.

7. The foreclosure sale takes place, with the sheriff conducting the sale "on the courthouse steps." This may be literally true, but today in many jurisdictions the actual sale takes place in a room in the courthouse. All monies realized from the sale go to pay your lien, plus accrued interest and legal fees, including the referee's fees. If there was a lien ahead of yours, it gets paid first. Liens behind yours are paid after you are paid. Any money over the amounts paid

to the lien holder(s) goes to the payor, who owned the
property that was just sold.

Once you see the process spelled out like this, I hope you realize
it really isn't all that hard to go through a foreclosure against a defaulting payor.

The foreclosure process in a mortgage state, on average, with de-
lays, should take less than eight or nine months, even if there are
additional problems.

In a trust deed state, the trustee handles most of the work done
by the judge, referee, and attorney in a mortgage state, but the steps
are similar. The process may take four months or so.

If the defaulting payor is also declaring bankruptcy, it will take a
little longer to receive your money. The risk that bankruptcy will
accompany a foreclosure is why you always want to do a credit
check on the person making the payments before you actually make
the deal and buy the paper. Remember that when you buy paper
you usually can't do many of the things lenders do before making a
loan, like check employment, bank account balances, and other assets. The credit report is your prime indicator of the financial health
of the payor.

If the credit report shows that the payors are behind on all their
credit cards and monthly bills, you should be aware that they may
be headed for bankruptcy. Stay away from these types of payors.

You can still recover your money in a bankruptcy because you
are a *secured creditor*. That is, your debt is secured by an asset that
will be sold to satisfy your debt. *Unsecured creditors* are paid, if at
all, from whatever is left after secured creditors have been paid.
However, getting your money back will take longer.

Different areas of the country have different laws regarding bankruptcy, and some of these laws slow the process even more.

Every state in the Union and Canada has a foreclosure law. There
is not a single area of the country where you can't use the power of
foreclosure.

Don't forget, you aren't going to be handling the foreclosure. Your
attorney is. You should get progress reports, and agree to sign any
relevant papers and appear in court when needed, but that's the limit
of your involvement. If you don't get progress reports, or if they

report that the procedure is going too slowly, call the attorney and ask why.

What If the Sheriff Holds an Auction and Nobody Comes?

If no one shows up, and therefore no one bids, the property is yours. If no one bids a price equal to at least your remaining balance plus interest, plus attorney fees (plus the remaining balance on any lien ahead of yours), you simply get the property.

If there are no bids, the foreclosure auction takes about fifteen seconds. The property is awarded to you.

If someone holding a lien behind yours files for foreclosure, they have to pay you or assume responsibility for your mortgage before they take possession of the property. If someone, a bank, for example, holds a lien ahead of yours, they will expect you to take over their loan or pay it off with a new loan. They'll usually be happy to accommodate you rather than add the property to their REO (real estate owned) list. It pays to talk to them before the auction so that your taking over their mortgage is arranged in advance.

There are now no liens against the property, save any that were ahead of yours. You own the property.

Even if no one shows up at the auction, you win by getting the property. If someone does show up, they need to outbid your remaining balance on the mortgage, plus accrued interest, plus attorney's fees in order for them to get the property.

While sometimes there are few or no bidders at an auction, there are usually plenty.

We recently had a property in Riverside, California that went to a trustee sale (the form used in trust-deed states). It sold within ten minutes. The bidding went very fast. There were a number of serious buyers, and the usual people who seem to show up to watch. A person outbid our remaining balance (and, of course, the balance of the first) and we were paid off.

Remember that people come to bid at foreclosure auctions in the expectation of getting the property at a significant discount from market value. As with investors who buy before the foreclosure, they usually want to get it for at least 25 percent to 30 percent under market value, and prefer to get it below that. They've normally had no opportunity to inspect the property except from the outside, so they're taking the risk that there may be a lot of work to do inside before they can put it on the market for sale.

Do You Want the Property?

What happens if you take a property under foreclosure back?

You own the property, which is not the worst thing that can happen. You have several choices, all of them good:

1. Clean up the property and resell it. You may make much more than your mortgage would have paid. A quick resale is the standard choice of paper investors.
2. Clean up the property and rent it for a positive cash flow. If you can't get significant positive cash flow, you shouldn't rent it, unless real estate sales are flat and you anticipate that it will take time to sell, even at a below-market price.
3. Clean up the property and rent it until property values rise. Remember that even if you use a property manager (who costs money) you're going to be dealing with property-management hassles. The manager may manage the property, but you have to manage the manager.

If you make the decision to sell the property, remember that it may take a few months to get the price you require. You will either leave it vacant and keep making payments on other loans, or rent it out.

I always want to collect some money while I am waiting for a property to sell (unless, of course, it's vacant land). So there will be some management involved, or you may have to carry a mortgage you assumed, but you can keep these problems to a minimum by offering to sell the real estate for a really good (low) cash offer.

The closer to market value you ask for the property, the more likely you'll be in the management business for some time. There may be times this is desirable, but to avoid delay, offer a "fast-cash" or "quick-sale" price and sell it immediately.

There are basically three rules for real property that you must know. These are simple and straightforward, but I learned them from the management school of hard knocks.

Rule One.

Never purchase a mortgage on a piece of real estate you would not want to own yourself. If this property is so bad, or is so special-use, that it does not fit into something you could take over and manage, then don't buy the paper. Most mortgage notes will *not* go bad, but when buying paper you have to assume that every mortgage you buy *could.*

If you follow this rule and wind up with the property, there's no need to worry whether it's property you feel comfortable with.

For example, suppose a building is in an area full of druglords and teen gangs, or even in an area that is considered to be not very good, but the yield on the mortgage is really high. Unless you feel you have the personality necessary to collect rents in that area, then *don't* purchase the mortgage! If you don't know that an area is okay, check!

Don't *ever* let a great yield sway you into purchasing a mortgage on a building you would not want to own. If you assume that you'll foreclose on every mortgage you purchase, you're not likely to buy paper on a property you wouldn't want to own. Buildings you would not want to own include much more than areas where you might get shot while collecting the rent.

Once I was offered a really good discounted mortgage in Montana. The numbers looked great, but once I was told about the collateral, I turned the deal down.

The collateral was a small building with a bar and restaurant on the first floor and an apartment upstairs, where the owner of the bar/restaurant lived. The mortgage was secured by the real estate and the liquor license owned by the bar. Liquor licenses are a premium in Montana, I'm told, and command a good price.

I turned down the deal because I don't want to become a long-distance bartender. I was a bartender back in college. I don't want to regress if I have to take back the property. The real estate alone was not enough to support the mortgage, so the liquor license had been used to add value to the collateral.

Therefore, if I took the property back and waited to sell it, I would have to become a bartender until I found a buyer. As a manager of the property, or a manager of the property manager I hired, I'd be working by phone and fax until the property was sold. That can take a lot of time. I could spend that time more profitably buying and selling paper, which I do much better than tending bar by fax and phone.

You have to recognize that if this property is going to take time to sell and you want to collect something from the property, you'll probably have to keep the bar open.

The Montana bar is an obvious example, but similar things happen in all sorts of commercial situations. The more specialized the building, the longer it takes to sell. You will probably need more time to find the individual who wants to run that bar, that car wash, that industrial building with a crane in the middle, etc., than you would need for other kinds of property. You don't want to sit there without any money coming in during this time.

The reason I turned the Montana deal down was not because it was a bar and restaurant, but because the value was not just in the real estate. The value was in the real estate plus the liquor license. The liquor license doesn't mean anything if we're going to foreclose. We can't foreclose on the liquor license; we can only foreclose on the real estate.

Rule Two.

This is called the 1 percent rule. The 1 percent rule is a technique in which you calculate 1 percent of the purchase price of the property to determine what you need to get in rent to break even. If you know that the property, for example, is a single family home worth $150,000, then to rent it out and break even on cash flow, you should get $1,500 per month (1 percent of $150,000 or 0.01 ×

$150,000 = $1,500). If you can't get the $1,500, you will wind up spending dollars out of pocket just to break even. Remember, that's a negative cash flow—more money going out than coming in. The 1 percent rule is simple and broad-based, but strict adherence to it will lead to few mistakes, which means avoiding the awful fate of negative cash flow.

But, I can hear you saying, what if I bought the paper with a good LTV and don't owe the full $150,000?

Good question!

As a practical matter, negative cash flow is based on what you owe—the cash you have to spend each month to hold the property.

Now suppose I'd bought a $30,000 second mortgage on that $150,000 house, and there was a bank loan ahead of it with a $70,000 remaining balance. When I foreclosed, I'd have to assume or refinance the $70,000. So, let's say my second was at 11 percent for twenty years, which would mean a monthly payment of $309.66. The bank didn't want the house, so it gave me a new loan for $70,000 at 1993 rates, 7.5 percent for thirty years, fixed. The monthly payment would be $489.45. Taxes and insurance would vary according to the location of the house. For this example, let's say they're another $300 per month. That means we have total expenses of $1,099.11. I'd probably better add another $75 a month for a property manager (that will also vary with location), and maybe I should allow $50 a month for maintenance, which might be a low estimate. I'm up to $1,250 a month on a property with a 66.6 percent LTV ($30,000 plus $70,000 in loans, divided by a current property value of $150,000). Even if I decide I can forgo the income from my second mortgage, I still have to cover more than $900 a month.

A payment of $900 a month is less than $1,500, true, but you can see why it might be better to sell this property as quickly as possible. If I sell it, even way below market, say for $130,000, I make $30,000, less sales costs—right now, not in twenty years.

Rule Three.

Real estate is only worth what someone is willing to pay for it.

It doesn't matter what you think the real estate is worth, or what you want it to be worth; the property is worth what someone is actually willing to pay to own it.

I guess the most flagrant recent example of not adhering to this rule is Donald Trump. The Donald rode high for many years by simply overpaying for real estate and getting away with it because when a property took on his name it went up in apparent value.

The apparent value may have been real during the roaring '80s, when real estate prices were soaring and people were paying higher prices for real estate with The Donald's name on it. Today, in the realistic '90's, prices have dropped considerably.

Real estate values are cyclical; they move through highs and lows. The Donald is now left with a negative net worth because he owes more money on the real estate than the property will bring on the open market. He was dropped from the Forbes 400 in 1992 thanks to one downward turn in the cycle of real estate prices, all because he ignored this simple rule of price versus value. Today, you only hear of him when he does yet another restructuring of his debt, or one of the ladies in his life makes news.

What I want to do with these three rules is to give you a good feel for real property. It's the third entity of paper, and it's crucial to your success. If we adhere to the three simple rules I have outlined, then entity number three is a moneymaker.

CHAPTER 17

Can I Buy Paper That Is Already Bad and Make Money? The Risks and Benefits of Delinquent Paper

The chapter title may seem a bit misleading: If something is bad, how can you make it good?

Actually, the last several chapters should give you a pretty good idea of the answer. I talked about how you could profit even when the payor missed payments, as in Heidi's deal, or defaulted and let the property go to foreclosure. You saw that this could result in major, sometimes unexpected profits, and in you getting your money back sooner so you can reinvest it.

What if you could intentionally buy a mortgage on a property where the people are not making their payments? Then, unless they surprise you and bring the loan current, they either sell the property and pay you off, or you foreclose and get your money back.

What happens to your yield?

Remember the time value of money. Your yield just increased dramatically, as it did for Heidi.

Such mortgages and trust deeds are called *delinquent paper*. These mortgages carry higher risk than the good paper I've been talking about, but the potential yield is dramatically higher.

Notice that I said *potential* yield.

Because the risk is greater, you should not try this technique until you have done enough safe paper deals to feel fully confident in your skills and ability to judge property and paper. Once you have those skills and that confidence, you may want to try delinquent paper.

To understand delinquent paper and what we are trying to accomplish in buying it, let's go back to our example with Bill, Mary, and David.

Let's say that David had money and was buying mortgages and trust deeds for his own portfolio and does not intend to flip the paper. As before, he gets a call from Mary.

Mary says, "I'd like to sell my mortgage."

David says, "Okay, give me some information."

Mary says, "I sold my house to a guy named Bill. It's been a year and I'd like to sell the mortgage."

So David says, "Okay, fine. Has he made all twelve payments on time?"

And Mary says, "Yes, he's made all three."

David scratches his head and says, "Wait a second. If the property was sold a year ago how come he's only make three payments?"

She says, "Well, he's made three but he's behind nine payments. He still owes nine payments. He's way behind on his mortgage, and I'm tired of dealing with it."

Under the conditions and criteria for buying, selling, and holding paper that we've been talking about, a statement like that would be a red flag, a real warning that this paper is not very safe. But if David *plans* to profit from delinquent paper, it's another matter entirely.

When Mary offered David good, secure paper, he offered her $50,000. Will he offer the same for delinquent paper? Of course not. If he has to buy good paper at a discount, he has to buy bad paper at a much deeper discount.

His offer will be fully dependent on what he thinks about the deal, how much risk he thinks is involved, how long he thinks it will take to get his money back, and how much potential profit he can see.

After considering these and other factors, he offers $30,000. That is not an unrealistic offer, considering Mary has a rather severe problem she can't handle, and David is buying that problem away from her.

Why is David going to buy it? He's looked at the numbers and the property, and he can see that, at worst, he'll get back his investment. At best, he'll get an awesome return on his money.

But why doesn't Mary just foreclose on Bill? There could be many reasons, most relating in some way to her lack of knowledge about real estate, foreclosure, and paper. Perhaps she's moved out of state. Perhaps she doesn't have money to hire an attorney. Perhaps she doesn't want to get involved in foreclosure because she doesn't understand how relatively easy it is, once you get an attorney to work with you. Perhaps she has a fear of what can happen with foreclosure, like Bill trashing the property before leaving. Perhaps she doesn't want to do the foreclosure herself.

David is not concerned with *why* she wants to sell. His only concern, once he's determined that he wants this deal and what price he can pay, is whether she'll accept his offer.

If she declines, he doesn't worry about it. There's always more delinquent paper than investors willing to buy it.

So David offers $30,000, a price that is fully negotiable. Mary can take it or leave it, but there's an offer on the table of $30,000, in cash, for her to walk away from her problem entirely.

To continue our example, we'll say Mary answers, "Fine. I'll take it."

The sale and assignment process is the same as it would be for good paper. When the deal closes, David owns the mortgage and Mary has no further interest or concern in what happens.

Bill, who owed Mary money and is not paying, now owes David money and is still not paying. What does David do? He looks at the various ways to get his money back and make his profit.

David Becomes the Heavy

The first and simplest thing David can do is contact Bill and ask why he hasn't paid and what he plans to do about it.

Bill can either take a positive or negative attitude toward the problem. It really *is* that simple.

The positive solution to Bill's problem is for him to respond, "David, can we work something out? Is there something we can do?"

There are some possible solutions. Bill might ask David to extend the mortgage for a longer term. He might ask to make the monthly payments lower or ask to change the interest rate. He might ask whether David will allow him to sell the property and then collect the past-due monthly payments when the property sells. He might ask whether he can just give David the property and avoid a foreclosure on his credit record. As we discussed, there are many things Bill can do to remedy the situation.

If Bill doesn't suggest them, David can list the alternatives and suggest Bill check with his attorney or financial adviser for help in deciding which one is best for him.

Bill may choose to do absolutely nothing. He may refuse to even talk to David, or may say, "If you want to foreclose, go ahead." That's short-sighted of Bill, but it isn't David's problem. If Bill chooses to mess up his life and credit report, that's his business.

David will hire an attorney. The attorney will file the papers and follow through to foreclosure unless Bill corrects the problem. David will either get the property or be paid off at the foreclosure auction.

David has put himself in a position where, for $30,000, he either buys a house that at one time not too long ago sold for $130,000, or he is paid the balance due on the loan, almost $80,000.

Can you imagine the situation if he goes to the foreclosure and the worst possible thing happens? No one shows up. David gets the property. He now owns, free and clear, a $130,000 piece of real estate that he purchased by buying the delinquent mortgage for $30,000. He's paid some attorney's fees and had some other collection hassles and costs, but he's bought himself one heck of a bargain.

David can sell it, rent it out, or move into it. He can do anything he wants with that property. No matter what happens, he wins big.

Delinquent paper stands head and shoulders above any other technique for buying real estate at a really serious discount.

Another Use for Delinquent Paper

Many times, my students ask me how they can buy a piece of real estate. They don't have much money, but would love to have their family in a house instead of living in an apartment.

While buying real estate isn't really what the Stefanchik Method is all about, delinquent paper can provide a way to get a nice house at a serious discount—far less than market value.

Remember my earlier advice that, even in good paper, you should never buy a mortgage or trust deed on any property you wouldn't want to own? In delinquent paper, you can take this a step farther and buy paper on a house you might want to live in.

If you want to acquire real estate, look over the properties securing the available delinquent paper and pick one you might like to live in. If you get paid off, you've got a lot of money you could use to buy a house; if you foreclose and get the house, you fix it up and move in. If you get paid off on your first choice, pick another. If it takes several delinquent paper deals before you get a house, you're making major money in the meantime.

How I Learned About Delinquent Paper

I first heard about delinquent paper when I got a call from a Wall Street attorney a number of years ago.

He knew I bought paper, but asked whether I bought delinquent paper. I didn't even know what it was. He explained that it was mortgages where the people were slightly behind on their payments. I could buy them at a good discount. "All these deals have really good collateral," he said. "Are you interested, John?"

I still had no idea what he was talking about, but I figured it wouldn't hurt to have him send some information, so I gave him my address. That wasn't what he wanted though; he wanted to fax the information to me immediately. I gave him my fax number and sat back and waited for a couple of pages to come in.

Each deal was on one page. After I had received four or five pages I figured the faxes would stop. Boy, was I wrong! Pretty soon I was up to thirty pages and was trying to get the fax machine to quit, but it just kept spitting out page after page.

I quickly called the attorney and told him to stop. What he said surprised me. "But John, I've barely started. These are just the deals from Long Island. I still have the five boroughs of New York to send you!"

I told him thanks but no thanks; I already had enough to consider.

I've related this story for a couple of reasons. First, this experience is how I got introduced to delinquent paper. Second, the length of the list of delinquent paper the attorney faxed me opened my eyes, in a big way, to just how much delinquent paper there is out there. There's an endless supply available.

Back to Delinquency

Let me say again that delinquent paper is not for the beginner. It's an advanced form of paper. You're purchasing paper where the people are already behind on their payments. You have to take some sort of action to get your money. When you're comfortable working with regular paper and want to try to increase your yield dramatically, give delinquent paper a try. Don't start with it.

While there's a lot of delinquent paper available, there are very few interested buyers. The supply and demand ratio is really skewed. Most paper buyers figure, why bother with this type of deal when there are so many good deals out there? But I want you to understand the opportunity that delinquent paper offers. You have to know about it in order to decide whether (and when) you want to try it.

How do you make money on these kind of deals? There are quite a few ways to make these deals profitable. All depend on careful, accurate assessment of the deal and the property.

Let's review the methods I've described and add one more:

1. Foreclose on the property. You purchase the paper and foreclose on it. That's all you do. I've already explained the foreclosure process, so you just put it into motion. You need to be the right kind of investor to consistently be involved in foreclosures, but it's a way to get paid faster than usual and increase your yield.
2. Negotiate with the payors. Let them know you're going to foreclose unless they can work something out with you. The threat of foreclosure followed by negotiation applies to all the remaining techniques.
3. Change the payment terms, if that will help. Offer a longer term, lower payments, temporarily lower payments with a balloon, lower interest, etc.
4. Allow them time to sell and pay you all the back payments plus the principal on closing.
5. Ask them to deed the property over to you with a deed in lieu of foreclosure. I have actually had this happen to me. Look at Breakthrough Deal Three at the back of this book

and you'll see one of the finest deals I've ever done, one where I wound up getting the property back because the person didn't want me to foreclose on them.

6. You can take the deed in lieu of foreclosure one step farther.

Tell the payors that in exchange for giving you a deed in lieu of foreclosure, you will give them either a one-year *lease option agreement,* or a one-year *option to purchase.*

The sixth technique is an idea I haven't talked about before, because it's a way of buying and selling real estate, while we've been concerned with paper. With delinquent paper, however, you become involved with real estate, and must use real estate techniques to sell or hold any property you acquire.

A lease option and an option to purchase are two quite different agreements, but their effect on your end of a delinquent paper deal can be similar.

In a standard lease option, the person makes a non-refundable cash deposit, called the *option consideration,* which will apply toward a down payment if they purchase the property for an agreed-upon price within an agreed-upon period of time. Usually, the lease payments are divided into two parts; one is the rent and the other adds to the option consideration. The lease payments are usually higher than market rent.

In normal real estate practice, lease options are a somewhat tricky and risky technique. Investors may use lease options when they can't sell a property in a slow market and can't get enough rent for positive cash flow. Buyers who lack a down payment or who have shaky credit may use a lease option as a way to buy a house they otherwise couldn't qualify for. The investor risks that the buyer won't keep up the payments, but keeps the option consideration if the buyer doesn't complete the purchase. The buyer risks not being able to complete the purchase and losing his or her option consideration.

In a delinquent paper deal, in which the object is to give the payor time to become financially healthy, you might offer a lease option in which they are required to pay at least enough to cover your costs of carrying the property. They have the opportunity to pay the delinquent payments and resume the regular payment schedule at any time up to the end of the year.

To do this, they must first give you title to the property with a deed in lieu of foreclosure. You now own the property. They sign the lease option agreement. You are being kind to them by giving them one more chance to keep their home. They are able to remain in the home while solving their financial difficulties.

If they succeed, they bring everything current and get title back at the end of the year. If they fail, then at the end of the year the property is yours and they must leave. You have no need to go through foreclosure. You own the property. You shouldn't need formal eviction proceedings, because you've worked with them and given them their extra chance.

A year is only a few months longer than the average time foreclosure takes in mortgage states, so you traded some time to avoid the expense and hassle of foreclosure. You've received income from their lease payments, rather than receiving no income during the foreclosure process.

An option to purchase differs from a lease option in that in exchange for the deed in lieu of foreclosure, you simply give them the right to buy the property back for an agreed-upon price in one year. They must leave the property, which you can then rent for a year. If they fail to buy it back at the end of the year, no further action is needed on your part. You own the property. The agreement is dead, because its terms—purchase in one year—were not met.

If you use this technique, have the option agreement reviewed by a real estate attorney. The agreement is simple, but you want to be certain that all possibilities are covered and that you comply with the laws of your state.

These are just a few of the ways to make money with delinquent paper. There are many others. You can be as creative as you want when you buy one of these mortgages or trust deeds.

Delinquent Paper Fundamentals

In this chapter I can't go into every bit of detail of working with delinquent paper. That's a full book in its own right, and I've written one for my students.

As I've suggested, you should learn and practice the fundamentals of regular, good, solid paper before you start investing your own money or working with an investor's money to buy delinquent paper.

If you're interested in purchasing a home, as I mentioned earlier, start with good, solid paper first. Work with my office, make some money, and then gradually get into delinquent paper. Buying delinquent paper before you've learned how to do good paper is a little like trying to run before you learn to crawl, much less walk.

These are some fundamentals:

Fundamental Number One

Don't waste your money advertising for delinquent paper. You don't need to put ads in the newspaper for this. Probably one of the best places to find delinquent paper is through local attorneys who represent banks or individuals who may own delinquent paper.

Attorneys are a great source of both delinquent paper and good paper. Attorneys are always a good referral source. They come in contact with problems when someone can't pay, or when someone wants to sell their mortgage, or any other situation involving problem paper. When working with attorneys, make contact on a face-to-face basis. Don't send a letter to an attorney and expect a response. They usually don't have time to bother. It's better to target one or two attorneys, arrange to meet them, give them your business card, talk with them, tell them what you're interested in, and work from there.

Fundamental Number Two

Make sure you understand that the missed payments that have made this mortgage delinquent paper have a major effect on LTV. Every time a payor misses a payment, the principal balance increases by the amount of the payment. A few months of missed payments can add several thousand dollars to the principal. You need to take that into consideration when you're considering the value of the property. (*Always* calculate the LTV!)

You have to consider the impact on LTV if the total of missed payments is high. In our running example, if Bill missed nine $775 payments, he's added $6,975 to the $80,000 principal, less the small amount of principal paid off by the three payments he actually made. David now must calculate an LTV based on about $86,975. He must also estimate the number of payments he'll miss before he can foreclose, and add those to the principal. That leaves still less equity in the property. David may also use a lower acceptable LTV ratio than he would for good paper.

David must consider a couple of other things. Taxes may be in arrears. Back taxes often occur before the payor actually gets behind on mortgage payments. The payor is more worried about the lender coming after him than the county, so taxes are often ignored before mortgage payments stop. A person not paying on a mortgage may also be behind in paying income taxes, and may have had a court judgment filed against the property as a lien. When the property is sold at the foreclosure auction, the IRS gets the first bite, then property taxes, then judgments and certain other liens, then the mortgage lien, then the interest, and any other fees accompanying the foreclosure such as attorney fees. You can see that you need to know about all these liens before making an offer for the paper.

It's vital, when you calculate the LTV, that you have a good, solid estimate of value for the property itself, particularly guarding against the possibility that the property hasn't held value.

I hope you understand the importance of working with accurate numbers in all paper deals, but in delinquent paper it is even more important to have everything absolutely right. The need to be even more certain than usual that you have everything correct is the greatest reason I advise that you stay away from delinquent paper until you're confident about doing good paper. If you make a mistake in the numbers on good paper, you've usually got enough safety built in to at least avoid losing money. If you make a mistake in the numbers on delinquent paper, you can really get hurt.

Fundamental Number Three

Have a complete understanding of the property—not just the actual value of the property, but the type of property, where it's located, whether it's commercial or residential, everything you can find out about it. You may very well end up owning the property. It had better be a property you can do something with quickly. If it's not, skip the deal and go on to the next one.

I cannot overemphasize or overstate the importance of knowing the property. One of the first things that I do when considering a delinquent mortgage is to drive by the property. Yes, you can buy delinquent paper all over the country, but I'm suggesting that you buy delinquent paper close to where you live. That way, if there's a problem before you buy, you can spot it and drop the deal. After you buy, you can personally deal with anything that comes up.

You probably know values in your own area better than you know values across the country. Since it's so vital to find and establish those values, you're giving yourself an advantage by dealing where you're familiar with value. You'll find lots of delinquent paper in your own area, so why buy elsewhere?

If you get big enough to run out of local delinquent paper, you'll have gained the expertise to deal with out-of-area opportunities.

Select the types of delinquent paper you want to work with. You may decide you'll do no paper on commercial property, or that you'll only do single-family, owner-occupied homes. Perhaps you only want to do properties on the west side of town. You can pick and choose the type of delinquent paper you want. You can decide that you'll only work with first liens, or firsts and seconds. I suggest just working with firsts on owner-occupied, single-family homes. You can be very selective because there's so much to choose from.

Fundamental Number Four

Have a title search done, or do one yourself. The title search may be the single most important step when dealing with delinquent paper. You want to be certain there won't be any title problems. If you don't do a search you're asking for trouble.

Once, I was buying a delinquent mortgage and the sellers said they'd give me clear title. I thought I was buying a second mortgage and everything looked good. I had a title search done, as I always do. The paper wasn't a second but a *fifth* mortgage! A fifth mortgage is so far back in the line of payment that the possibility that I would be paid off in a foreclosure was very slim. I could say I was lucky to pass on that deal, but it wasn't luck. I passed because the title search told me I was being lied to, and the apparently good deal I planned to buy was a really terrible deal.

Earlier I mentioned taxes, judgments, and other liens. The title search is how you find out about them. Be sure you look for any unpaid back property taxes. Property taxes are an interesting type of lien, because they will come in front of your lien. When taxes are owed, they are always a first lien. You won't get paid until the tax obligation has been met. The title search will let you know what position you actually hold in terms of the paper.

Either have a title search done or do it yourself. It's not hard to do, and doing it yourself, in the beginning, will save you time and money. Doing it yourself will also give you a thorough understanding of what a title report says and means once you get big enough that you no longer have time to do it yourself.

I'm *not* recommending that you buy either delinquent or good paper without a title search and title insurance by the title company. You would be extremely foolish to buy without title insurance. The reason for doing the title search yourself is to eliminate the costs of doing a title search when it's not necessary. You may have half a dozen potential pieces of delinquent paper you could buy, but you only want to buy one of them. Do you want to pay for six title searches to decide which to take? No! If you do your own title search on each of them, you can eliminate the ones that have problems you weren't told about and select the ones that look best for your final decision.

All you need is the legal description (lot and block number of the property). Go to the county recorder's office and look up the information on public record. Remember, it isn't a secret.

Once you've determined that there appears to be nothing against the title to deter you from buying the mortgage or trust deed, you can request that the person who's selling you the delinquent paper pay for the title search and title insurance. You could also ask that the person selling the paper pay for the title search and not do it yourself, but I prefer, because it is so simple and easy, to take the initiative and do it myself. My doing the title search saves me from asking people to pay for a title search on paper I may not buy.

Fundamental Number Five

Make sure you buy at a steep discount. There's no reason you should get just a normal discount when you buy delinquent paper. You should be getting a 40 or 50 percent, sometimes in excess of 60 percent, return on your money. The potential of such large returns is how the serious money is made in delinquent paper. You're buying paper no one else wants, so you get it at a huge discount. There's no real market for delinquent paper and you can dictate the terms under which you are willing to buy it.

It's unlikely that you'll ever get into a bidding war over delinquent paper, but it can happen occasionally. Don't let yourself be talked into overbidding. If you can't buy the paper for your price, don't buy it.

Double It at 72

I was out running along a wooded trail one day, and it was beautiful; just me and the scenery.

All of a sudden I had an amazing idea. It had to do with delinquent paper and the "Rule of 72."

You may have heard of the term and think it's some part of esoteric bankers' gobbledygook. It's actually quite simple and very useful.

The Rule of 72 states that if you divide 72 by the interest rate you're currently receiving on your money, the result will tell you how long it will take to double your money. Can you get much simpler than that?

$$\text{Rule of 72} = \frac{72}{\substack{\text{current interest rate} \\ \text{money is earning}}} = \substack{\text{Number of years to} \\ \text{double your money}}$$

For example, if you are getting a 10 percent return on your money, divide 72 by 10 percent. The answer is 7.2 years.

Thus, it will take you 7.2 years to double your money.

The Rule of 72 works for any interest rate and is especially true and useful for paper deals.

If you buy delinquent paper and get your money in less than a year, your rate of return will depend on the deal, but it will be quite high. While running, I suddenly wondered what would happen if I could get a 72 percent return on my money. I'd double my money each year!

To get a 72 percent return would mean that I would have to buy a seriously discounted mortgage. But such mortgages *do* exist! If I get a large enough discount, it doesn't really matter whether I get my 72 percent return by foreclosing, working with the payor, or whatever. If I get my money back in a year with a return of at least 72 percent, I double my money!

Doubling my money sounded like one heck of a plan.

Think about this a little bit. If you started with only $1,000 and bought just one delinquent mortgage a year, what would you have at the end of the first year? If you got your 72 percent, you'd have $2,000, right? How about the end of the second year? $4,000, then $8,000, then $16,000, then $32,000 and on and on. The numbers really start to get large when you get past the eleventh, twelfth years, as seen below.

Year	Amount of Money
0	$ 1,000
1	$ 2,000
2	$ 4,000
3	$ 8,000
4	$ 16,000
5	$ 32,000
6	$ 64,000
7	$ 128,000
8	$ 256,000
9	$ 512,000
10	$ 1,024,000
11	$ 2,048,000
12	$ 4,096,000
13	$ 8,192,000
14	$16,384,000
15	$32,768,000

Turn $1,000 into almost $33 million in fifteen years?

Yes, it's certainly possible. The only thing is that as the numbers got larger, you'd have to either do bigger deals or more deals, all the deals would have to work right and yield 72 percent, and you'd start needing a company with a staff, a payroll, and other business expenses . . . but then, if you have a company going, you've got other people out there multiplying your efforts.

If it seems like the numbers I've used are just a little too large, and you may be scared at the prospect of needing your own company just to handle it all, consider that this only represents doing one deal a year for the first few years. It merely assumes that you make sure you select the right deal, get a 72 percent return, recover your money in one year or less, and reinvest your profit at the same rate.

The point is not that you could literally turn $1,000 into $33

million in fifteen years, but the tremendous potential of delinquent paper.

With this kind of potential, why only do one deal a year? Why not
do three, five, or ten a year? Doing a lot of delinquent paper deals
in one year sounds like a great idea, but will it work?

Yes, (but). There is so much delinquent paper out there that you
can pick only the best of all the available deals. You only buy the
deals that make sense to you. You're not forced to take anything you
don't want, and you only need to do just one at 72 percent.

The "but" is a big one—you have to work at it, and delinquent
paper involves more time than good paper does. You have to do even
more checking before you buy, you have to deal with negotiations
with the defaulting payor, you may have to foreclose, renovate, and
resell, and so on. You might find that you're taking time away from
good paper to deal with your delinquent deal.

On the other hand, you may find that you want to become a specialist in delinquent paper. Another possibility, once you're big
enough to have an office with a staff, is to find one person who is
good with the details of delinquent paper and have him or her do
all the day-to-day work involved, leaving you free to evaluate the
paper and make buying decisions.

You can see that doing one or two small delinquent deals in the
first year wouldn't be hard. But it's obvious that doubling your
money gets increasingly difficult after the eighth and ninth years,
because now you're dealing with large amounts of money.

Yes, at that point you'd need your own company, with a good staff
and specialists in various kinds of paper. Is that a scary idea to you?
It shouldn't be. It's something that will grow naturally as you buy
more and more paper.

If you only buy good paper, you'll still probably find that, as you
learn how to do it and become successful, you need help. You won't
do it all yourself unless you choose to limit yourself to your own
efforts. As you grow, you will quite naturally develop the company
and the staff, as well as the expertise, to do more and more paper
and larger and larger deals.

To double your money after the ninth and tenth years, you'll have
to buy a lot of delinquent paper. You'd have to buy packages of
delinquent mortgages or trust deeds—but you'd have the staff and
financial resources to do so.

If you choose not to grow that big, you can still pursue delinquent paper on the side, on the theory that you could double your money (or at least make a nice yield).

Doing a little delinquent paper on the side is another way to look at your retirement income whether or not you put any or all of your delinquent paper in a Keogh plan. You're not doing anything more than putting your money back out to earn more money once you get it in from each deal, and continuing to do that.

You may not work up to the $33-million mark (that would take some doing!), but you really can generate a lot of money in a very short time by turning over your delinquent paper money as fast as possible.

Delinquent paper could actually provide you with the greatest retirement program you have ever heard of. Do you think you can buy delinquent paper and put it into your Keogh plan? Sure, why not? There are a lot of money-making things you can do with delinquent paper. Don't ignore this aspect of the paper business. But remember—delinquent paper is for an advanced investor, not a beginner.

Integrating Delinquent Paper into Your Paper Business

You can see where my thoughts about delinquent paper are heading. You may decide you don't want to ever touch delinquent paper and just stick to good paper. That's fine; most paper investors do. For those want to make delinquent paper profits a part of their business, let me repeat—*don't* start with it.

Start working with entity number one. Buy and sell good paper. Turn some deals and see how it all works.

Then get into entity number two and reinvest your money in good paper and hold on to these mortgages and trust deeds for cash flow. Get comfortable doing paper deals. After you've gained enough experience, try a delinquent paper deal.

If you're paid off, you have a large chunk of cash to reinvest.

If you get the property back through foreclosure, you're into entity number three. You have a property you can rent out, refinance, or turn around and sell. You'll find that it really doesn't matter how you want to make money in the paper business; the important thing

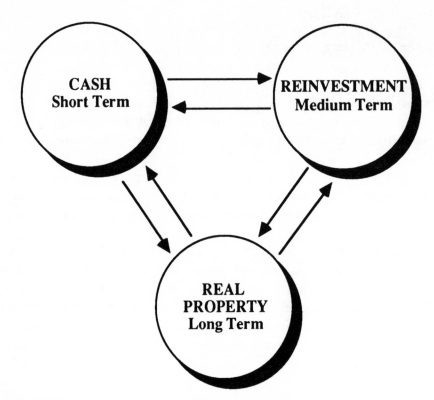

is to know what you are doing and make sure you are doing it profitably.

Once you've done both good and delinquent paper, make a decision on how much of your time and energy will be devoted to each. Make your plan, set your goals, and achieve them. Here's the chart with the three-entity approach to remind you that all three entities must work together when dealing with both paper and delinquent paper.

CHAPTER 18

Having It All Make Sense

To pull everything together and help you see how easy it really is to get started, let's return to my story. My real estate ventures had left me with a negative cash flow, and it looked like paper might be the answer. I knew less about paper than you know from reading this book, but I had to do something, so I did.

The first paper deal I ever put together was in Yonkers, New York. I agreed to buy a mortgage for $36,000.

Of course, not only did I not have $36,000, I was in a negative cash-flow situation. How to solve the problem? I ran an ad in *The New York Times* that said, "Mortgage For Sale, call John" (with my phone number).

Within two weeks I received thirty-nine phone calls.

Not every caller was interested in buying the mortgage, but quite a few were. Nine calls were from investors who wanted to bid. The best offer from the investors was for $42,000. Did I take it? You bet I took it!

I was able to orchestrate this deal with no money because I was buying and selling the deal at the same time. I used a simultaneous close where everything came together at the title company. The simultaneous close allowed me to orchestrate the deal in such a way that neither the seller of the mortgage nor the buyer of the mortgage knew I had no money to put into this deal. Not that it mattered, of course, but because this was my first deal and I felt insecure and worried about running into problems, I wanted to make sure everybody was kept separate from the other parts of the deal.

Orchestrating it this way allowed me to do the deal with no money and everybody got what they were supposed to get. The person selling the mortgage got $36,000. The person purchasing the mortgage got it for $42,000. And I made $6,000 on the deal!

I had to subtract the closing costs, which I had to pay. You see, when you orchestrate a deal in this fashion, and you control it the way I did, you have to cover the closing costs. For a deal of that size, that ran about $600, so I wound up making $5,400 on my first deal.

I'll tell you, I was very excited! I wanted to try that again! It may not sound like a lot of money, but to me $5,400 felt like a million dollars. It gave me the money I needed to do what I was trying to do: pay off my debt.

But it made me think. All I need to do is repeat this whole process all over again. And again!

And that's exactly what I did. I set out to repeat the process, which was to find somebody who wanted to sell a mortgage and somebody else who wanted to buy the mortgage and put them together so I could collect the difference between what the seller of the mortgage was willing to accept and the buyer of the mortgage was willing to pay.

I kept going back to county recorders' offices to find names and addresses of people who were holding mortgages. Every spare minute I had, I went to the recorders' office. I spent my vacation days in the courthouse because I figured every name I found was a potential deal. I learned that the recorders' office I was working opened at 7:00 A.M., not the advertised time of 9:00 A.M. Now I was searching the records from 7:00 to 8:30, then getting to work by 9:00.

I spent weekends sending out letters to potential mortgage sellers. I was so excited about making money that it didn't bother me to work as hard as I was to make it, because I'd seen the potential of what I could do through my first deal.

But the $5,400 I made in the first deal was not the driving force behind my desire to do my second deal. I realized that I'd stumbled upon something that was going to make me cash each and every time I utilized this technique. I saw a way to not only pull myself out of the financial hole I'd dug for myself, but at the same time get into something I liked that could help me reach the goals I'd tried to reach through real estate.

I liked paper because I knew I could make money. I knew I could control my own destiny. Every time I went to the recorder's office, I realized what a wealth of information was there that most people didn't know about.

I felt really great and very fortunate to have discovered paper.

I was working very hard. I don't want to scare you by saying it was difficult work, but if you're afraid of work you won't succeed in paper or anything else.

There are two kinds of hard work: that which you have to do and don't like, and that which you love. It's very hard to succeed doing something you don't like. If you love what you're doing, you can work like I did, which was to live, eat, and breathe paper just about every waking moment I wasn't working at my job.

I tend to be impatient, and I want things to happen right away, so I worked hard, for long hours. You don't have to do that. That's the beauty of the Stefanchik Method!

I pushed myself much harder than I had to, because I loved what I was doing. If you're motivated, you'll work hard at whatever you want to do. If you're not as highly motivated as I was, or if you have less time or less energy, you can work less intensely at paper, or at anything else. You won't do as much in any given period of time, but if you do it consistently, you'll achieve success.

A friend told me a story that illustrates this persistent, consistent work ethic quite well. A woman wanted to write a novel, but she had small children, a full-time job, and her husband worked two jobs just to make ends meet. She read, enviously, interviews with famous writers who talked about having a certain time during which they would go into their study and write, undisturbed, for some number of hours every day. She felt lucky to have the peace of a couple of ten-minute breaks at work. But then she heard what the famous writers were really saying: They wrote *every* day. Consistency.

I suppose she went through a process similar to my time-crisis, when I blocked out my week on paper and saw that I really did have time for everything I wanted to do. She started her novel, in long-hand on a steno pad, during her breaks at work; she learned to write while riding the bus, wrote at the kitchen table while supper cooked, wrote between changing diapers, and trained herself to think about her novel in any little bit of time available. Sometimes she only wrote a line or two a day, but three years later her novel was finished.

Then she started on her next one.

Consistency and repetition, just like the secret of success in paper. And, by doing it the first time, she knew she could keep doing it over and over, no matter what else happened in her life.

Motivation is important, energy is important, making time available is important, but *consistency* is the most important thing of all. You may do a lot in a short time, as I did, or you may do it over a longer time. The important thing is to keep doing it.

In my seminars, when I talk about how hard I worked, I'm repeatedly asked, "What motivates you?"

When you work that hard, your motivation can't be just money. Mine isn't. That first $5,400 was gone as fast as I could collect the check and put it in the bank. I had debts I had to pay off, so the cash was gone almost before the ink was dry on my deposit slip.

As I made more and more money, I realized that cash wasn't my motivation. It was the challenge of doing more. The challenge of being in a position where I could make things happen. The challenge of being my own boss. The challenge of being financially independent. The challenge of traveling, lecturing, and doing what I wanted to do when I wanted to do it.

That challenge was and is my motivation.

We all need a challenge, and we need to understand what it really is—it will be different for each of us—and how to focus our energy on meeting our challenge. When we do that, we succeed.

That's why I created a set of materials, *The 100% Solution: How to Succeed to the Maximum.*

In thinking about what I've done over the years, and how I could teach people to motivate themselves and keep themselves motivated, I realized that there are seven steps to success, and based the workbook and video on them. Those seven steps will provide you success in whatever you decide to do.

I've directed myself toward making money in paper because I just absolutely love it and think it's wonderful. But for anything you want to do, anything at all, I've found that there are always those seven steps to success.

My *100% Solution* workbook and the video and cassette tapes that go with it take you through the seven steps one at a time. *The 100% Solution* includes exercises to help you orient yourself to succeed.

I won't go into the seven steps here, because a meaningful and useful discussion is an entire book.

Are You On Track to Success?

You may have asked yourself, "Am I the type of person who is on track to succeed?"

Most of us have doubts, or look at our success and think we should be doing more or getting better results. We all know people who were at the top of their class in high school or college, but now are just achieving ordinary success in ordinary jobs. They may go from job to job, gaining neither success nor happiness. They may have achieved a success or two in the past, which they may talk of fondly but seem unable to repeat.

You probably know people who showed no promise whatsoever, but who now live in mansions, drive Mercedes sedans, and vacation in places we know only from travel ads.

What makes the difference?

A few successes scattered through your life does not mean you are a success; it just means you've had *some* successes.

Success is an *attitude*. If you expect to succeed at whatever you try, you probably will. Consistency and repetition, again, are the keys. If you consistently expect to succeed, and repeat the things that made you successful, you can expect to succeed at whatever you try.

Now, the interesting thing is that we've all had success in something in our lives, often far more success than we give ourselves credit for. For some reason, many of us learn how to feel bad when we don't achieve what we expected (or someone expected of us), but not how to feel good when we do succeed. This often means we may overlook a success that wasn't quite as successful as we expected, or as great as someone else expected of us. (We may even fall into the trap of letting someone else define what "success" should mean for us!)

Stop a moment and think of the successes in your life. Don't fall into the trap of judging yourself by unrealistic expectations.

Now think of what you did to achieve those successes. Yes, think about each one of them. Do you see a pattern? Something you did each time you succeeded that perhaps you didn't do other times? If you do, you're looking at *your* secret of success. The chances are, one of the things you identified was a challenge.

Challenge, and the recognition of it, is one of the keys to success. When you understand what challenge means, you can sustain the motivation to attack a goal and keep driving through, even when you get a NO, or when life throws you a curve ball. When you understand the power that meeting a challenge gives you, you will consistently work at what you're doing, so you can keep going and going until you've achieved your goal.

I Really Didn't Know What I Was Doing, But Succeeded Anyway

The funny part of this whole thing was I really didn't know what I was doing. I didn't know anything about the seven steps to success or the importance of meeting challenges, or any of that, any more than I knew about paper in the beginning.

I was learning as I went. There wasn't a book like this or a seminar to tell me what to do. I did what seemed to make sense and hoped for the best. With each deal I learned a little more.

I made numerous mistakes, but I only made them once. That's another key. If you don't learn from your mistakes, you've got a problem. I learned from them and never made the same mistake again.

After I completed six successful deals, I'd made a pretty good sum of money. My excitement about the paper business was growing every day, and with it my desire to quit my job and get into paper full-time.

Quitting my job really wasn't a hard decision. I'd really started to hate that job. It was keeping me from working in paper, where I was making more money in my free time than I could ever make at my job.

Yet when it came right down to it, it was hard to walk away from the safety of a salary. I mean, I knew how much I would be making each week, and there's security in that. But I made the decision to quit. I was on my own now.

The nice thing about that decision was that was I had hit my first long-range goal. Remember, I'd set quitting my job as a goal after my first paper deal.

I wanted to quit my job for a number of reasons. I wanted to explore financial independence. I wanted to work for myself. I wanted to set my own hours and make my own money. And I just didn't want anybody telling me what to do, where to be, and how much I could make.

Your life is basically dictated by how much you make per month. That's the way most people live. If I make $1,000 per month, I have a $1,000 life-style. If I make $4,000 per month, I have a $4,000 life-style. Almost anyone you know fits that pattern.

I wanted to make so much money that it couldn't dictate my life-style. With enough money, I could choose whatever life-style I wished.

I didn't want to say I had a $1,000-a-month life-style or a $5,000-a-month life-style or a $10,000-a-month life-style. What I wanted to do was say I could choose any life-style I want. If I had $30,000 a month coming in and I chose to live a $5,000-a-month life-style, that was *my* choice.

Either way, I controlled what I wanted to do and how I wanted to live. I made my own time and my own future. That's one of the basic driving forces that makes me work so hard.

As you've read my story, you've been able to see that my business grew by small, logical steps from having too much real estate and not enough money and a desperate need to do something about it to where it is today.

With each deal, and later with each seminar and each set of teaching materials, I learned a little more, and my students made more.

You'll find the same will happen for you. You're beginning with a lot more knowledge than I had, but if you don't feel like you're learning and growing with each deal, take a moment and look at what you've been doing and how you're evaluating each deal. It's easy to fall into the trap of not recognizing what we're learning; but if we don't learn, we're going to repeat mistakes along with successes.

Remember what I said earlier about making a lot of mistakes in the beginning, but never making the same one twice. I did that by learning from each deal, and never forgetting the lessons. If I'd kept working my nine-to-five job, it would have taken me years to learn what I learned in a few months. With each deal I learned something that helped me on the next.

You'll find that it does take time and dedication to your business to really make paper work. But you'll also find that paper isn't is a complex business, but it is one that requires patience and the ability to focus on the overall plan (the three-entity approach) at all times.

Looking back at what I have learned, I've compiled a list of things I call:

IF I HAD TO DO IT ALL OVER AGAIN, I WOULD—

- Not chase down deals with high LTVs or in really bad areas.
- Keep current on real estate prices and rents in my area.
- Go to a variety of county recorders' offices, as often as time permits, and keep good records of responses.
- Keep current on my investors' criteria (which can change without notice).
- Always follow up each mailing one week later with a phone call to discuss quotes as well as to get marketing feedback.
- Remail to names obtained at the county recorders' office sooner (once every three months).
- Never mail bulk rate; always use first class. Bulk rate may never get there, and you cannot accurately track either your response time or response rate. Also, people are more likely to throw out bulk rate mail without reading it. (Don't you?)
- Take out more ads in secondary, not primary newspapers. The cost is cheaper and return on investment is higher.
- Use remnant-space classified advertising. It's cheap and highly effective.
- Never mail around Christmas or tax time.
- Never be afraid to ask the question, "What do you need the money for?"
- Always follow up each closing one month later to ask the person who sold you the paper how everything is going. Follow-up can lead to repeat and/or referral business.
- Never get boxed into the situation where I try to close too fast and end up blowing the deal because of unrealistic promises.
- Never assume anything about the seller. Whenever I assume, I always lose.
- Always remember: The person with the gold makes the rules. Maintain control of the deal at all times.

Moving On Up

Since I came out of the South Bronx, you can understand the feeling of success and security I gained as I began to accumulate more and more mortgages for my personal portfolio, gaining a cash flow of $214.20 from this one, $445.60 from that one, and so on.

When you begin to acquire mortgages, you, too, will start to add up these payments until you have a nice solid cash flow each month. All you have to do is get the checks to the bank for deposit.

I had to ask myself the question you'll probably eventually ask yourself. How much cash flow do I really need to live on?

If I'm spending all I'm making to live, I might as well stay at my job. I have to make more than enough to live, or I'll never reinvest. *The key to making paper work for you is to only spend the interest and reinvest the principal.* Reinvesting principal is critical to your financial success.

Each payment you receive is usually made up of both interest and principal. (It could be interest only—it's very rarely principal only.)

Split it up when it comes to you and you'll never go wrong. Put the interest in one account and the principal in another, ready for reinvestment. You'll always have a base to work with if you do it this way. If you need more money to live on, buy more paper, but don't mess with the principal. Be sure you understand the importance of keeping your principal intact and making it grow, which is critical to your financial success.

As you grow, you'll want to invest part of your interest, too, so you'll have a larger base of principal to invest.

Let me give you a good example of what can happen when you spend your principal. Say you went to the casino because you enjoy gambling. You're not addicted to gambling, which is something else entirely, but you enjoy it now and then. You brought $500; after that was gone, you planned to stop gambling.

You started to play and lost, as is usual in a casino, but all of a sudden you started to win. Your winnings soon reached $1,000. You'd doubled your money!

Now you can either leave or say to yourself, "This is neat, but

I don't want to lose more than I came with." You can do one of two things. You can decide you have $1,000 to play with (because you'd expected to lose the $500 you came with) and gamble until it's gone (the casino will love you for it), or you can decide you've made a profit of $500 and still have your original $500 to play with.

If you think your luck is running strong and you want to continue playing, treat the original $500 like your investment principal. Of course, "investing" in the roulette wheel is a true high-risk investment, but the principle is the same. You want to try your keep your principal intact and working for you (which is much easier in paper than at a casino).

I'm using the gambling example because a lot of people go to the casinos and enjoy it, but sometimes they bring the gambling mentality to investment, which is a mistake. The casino is recreation. Investment is business.

Protect that principal and add to it!

You never want to get into the position of eating into your principal when you're buying paper. You're definitely not rolling the dice in a casino. You have more control. You're not worried about what the turn of the cards will do to you. You're worried about making sure that your principal stays intact, keeps working for you, and grows. And it should. There's no reason things should ever get out of control in paper.

The other day I was visiting a friend who knows how much I'm into paper. He asked me, "John, when you get these checks in the mail, how much of that money do you really get to keep?"

He asked this because he's a landlord. When his tenants pay him $500 for rent, he has to make his mortgage payment from that. He also has to pay property taxes, insurance, make repairs on the property, and all sorts of things. In the end he may keep $150 of that $500, and that only on a building with very good cash flow.

I probably never should have told him how much I kept, because he nearly had a heart attack.

I said, "A hundred percent." I explained to him that I didn't own the property. "All I own," I said, "is a lien on the property. If something breaks, I don't pay to have it fixed. The owner does. The property is the collateral, but someone else owns it. I don't have a landlord's problems and worries. When my check comes to me, it's all mine. All I have to do is take it to the bank. I can handle that kind of work pressure. I'd guess you could, too."

He said. "Yes! How do I get started?"

I told him, of course.

CHAPTER 19

Heading Up to the Great White North: Doing Paper in Canada

Buying paper in Canada is about 85 percent like buying paper in the United States.

The 15 percent that is different, however, is one of the reasons Canada turned out to be a wonderful, wide-open market.

I hadn't really given Canada much thought. I'd been so busy giving seminars in the U.S. that I had no need to look north. I'd give seminars in Los Angeles and buy mortgages in Los Angeles, give seminars in Chicago, Seattle, or wherever, and buy mortgages there. I was more than busy enough finding plenty of opportunities to buy paper in the U.S.

Then an interesting thing happened to me at a couple of seminars.

I was giving a talk in Buffalo, which is right at the U.S.–Canada border and very close to Toronto. At the end of my talk, a group of people came to the back of the room to buy my materials. They asked if they could talk to me in private for a moment.

I said, "Sure."

They asked, "Does your company buy mortgages in Canada?"

I said, "No, we don't. You're from Canada?"

They said, "Yes. We heard about the seminar and came to see whether you buy Canadian mortgages."

I said, "No, I don't, but I appreciate your interest." We talked a little more and they left.

A couple of months later I was giving a talk in Detroit, which is right across the river from Windsor, Canada, and the same thing happened. I gave the talk and a group of people asked me the same question, "Do you buy paper in Canada?"

Again, I said, "No, I don't, but you're the second group who's asked me, so I'm going to look into it."

I promised I'd get back to them. I realized I was missing an opportunity. I knew Canadian real estate laws were similar to those in the U.S., but I also knew there was just enough difference to make it hard to make U.S.–style creative real estate buying techniques work across the border.

I decided to investigate the Canadian system to see whether the Stefanchik Method would work there. I was very busy, so I didn't prioritize it as something I had to do right away. I looked at it as something I'd get to someday.

Three months later I was giving a seminar in Seattle, which is close to the Canadian border and Vancouver, British Columbia. Of course, you can guess what happened.

All of a sudden I had a large group of people asking me the same questions. Can we use this system in Canada? Do you buy paper in Canada?

I decided I had to take Canadian paper off the back burner and do something about it. I had to at least tell my Canadian students whether or not my system would work in their country.

Just about that time, I got a call from Charles Furnivall, a very bright, successful investor from Toronto, who had taken my course some time ago.

Charles and his wife, Vivian, were looking for an opportunity to set up a business that could make major money for them. Charles said he was interested in making the Stefanchik Method work in Canada. (Talk about good timing!)

He said, "John, you have to come up here and check the Canadian market out."

I went up to Toronto and met Charles. We talked to people who were in the business—attorneys, title people, investors, even mortgage brokers.

We asked them what they thought about the paper market. We learned two interesting and exciting things.

Canadian real estate is a wide-open market. There's a lot of paper and very few buyers. To our knowledge, at that time no one bought paper all across Canada like I bought paper all across the U.S. We also started asking Canadian attorneys about partials. We got strange looks.

They said, "What do you mean by partials?" When we explained, they said they didn't do anything like that.

I asked, "Why?"

They said, "That's a good question. I don't know."

We asked more questions and learned that the reason they didn't do partials was because they didn't have a legal document to execute a contract for a partial purchase of a mortgage! They didn't have anything that spelled out the details and terms of a fractional assignment of interest. It wasn't illegal or anything; it was just that no one had done it, so the legal paperwork didn't exist.

Can you imagine me passing up such an incredible opportunity? Of course not! We developed the legal documents and got the approval of Canadian attorneys.

Charles and I formed the S.E.S. Funding Corporation of Canada. Charles runs the operation, Vivian works there, and we have a wonderful operation that buys paper throughout Canada, just like S.E.S. Funding does in the United States.

Since we opened our doors, we've been buying paper all across Canada. Canada is such a wonderful place; aside from the paper market, the country is beautiful and the people are great. Buying and selling paper has been just as wonderful an opportunity for us as it appeared to be. It's the same opportunity the Stefanchik Method offers people in the United States. The potential for profits in paper exists throughout North America, not just in the U.S.

What About the Other 15 Percent?

To the books and tapes I created to show how to buy and sell paper in the United States I added important new information aimed at the Canadian market. The materials are 85 percent the same as the U.S. materials. We've added the Canadian Addendum, which provides the 15 percent difference.

The addendum is based on Ontario law, which applies, with some variation, throughout Canada, except for Quebec, whose legal code is based on the Napoleonic Code (as is Louisiana's in the United States).

To deal in mortgages there one must be a licensed mortgage broker. However, you can still act as a finder of mortgages and be paid a fee for that service. This arrangement is fundamentally the same as finding and flipping mortgages in the U.S.

One major difference between the two systems is that Canadian mortgages are structured differently. The fully amortized mortgage is almost unheard of in Canada, and the loan terms are usually shorter. Twenty-five years is standard, and ten years is not uncommon.

The usual structure of a loan is to set the payments based on an amortization period, but to set a much shorter "term" of anywhere from six months to five years. The usual Canadian loan is structured similarly to a balloon-payment mortgage in the U.S., except that it is routine to continue the mortgage for another term with another balloon, usually with the interest rate current at the time the balloon came due. In effect, a Canadian mortgage is a type of adjustable-rate mortgage.

Effective interest rates, on which a paper buyer computes yield, are different because interest on Canadian mortgages compounds half-yearly, not monthly, as in the U.S. A Canadian paper investor will have to convert the interest values unless his or her calculator is set for Canadian values. This conversion is not hard once you've practiced a little. For a further explanation, see the conversion table in the appendix.

You will find fewer high loan-to-value mortgages in Canada. Seventy-five percent is the normal maximum, but loans to 90 percent are permitted with mortgage insurance. You'll probably find more mortgages with an LTV acceptable for paper purchases.

Institutional loans are easily available, so most personally held paper will be for second mortgages. In Canada, this is called a *vendor take-back* loan (VTB). The term *vendor* is used commonly instead of *seller*.

Like the U.S., Canada has two systems for recording title. One system is based on the Torrens Title system, first developed in England as a system for ship registry. Torrens was also the basis for some U.S. title recordation (for example, a Torrens system was once used in parts of California, where you may find Torrens registry records in old titles). The specifics of searching for mortgages in Canada are different.

The next place that I'd like to research is Great Britain, a market of fifty-six million people, eight million of whom live in London. The British could really take advantage of this system. I think it would work because the Canadian system came from British law (so does a lot of U.S. law, for that matter). Australian law also is derived from British law, so that's the next frontier.

Accumulating and Protecting Your Wealth

As I've said a number of times throughout this book, making money means nothing if you don't build and protect your wealth.

Entity number one, cash, is necessary to get you started, to support your life-style, and to create new investment capital.

Entity number two, investment and reinvestment, is necessary to increase your cash and investment capital.

Entity number three, real estate, secures your investments and can become an investment itself.

To rise beyond the level of scrambling for enough cash to live on, which is no better (and may be less secure) than having a salaried job, you must move to the level of entity number two. If you don't, you'll never build wealth. If you don't build wealth, you have none to protect.

Building wealth in paper can take a number of forms. Here are just some of the possibilities.

Building Wealth

The first source of wealth-building is, of course, the cash you make from your first deals.

What you do with that cash makes the difference between building wealth and always needing more cash than you can make.

You can spend everything you make from entities one and two,

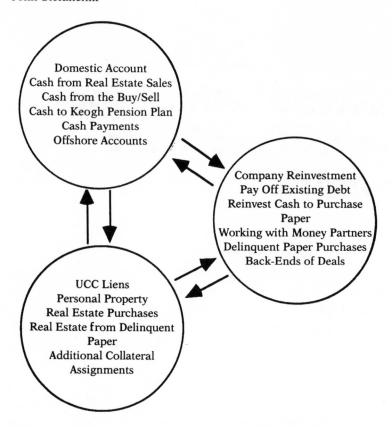

of course. You'll have a great time and enjoy what you can buy with it.

But remember what I told you about *always* reinvesting your principal? If you make enough to invest, but then spend both principal and interest, you've *lost* money.

If you plan to make your wealth grow, you should not only always reinvest your principal, but also take as much of your profit as possible and add it to your principal for more investment and reinvestment.

In your goal-planning, decide on a certain percentage of your profit, say, 25 percent, that will *always* be added to your investment principal no matter what. If you don't set this minimum, you're only too likely to always find a reason why, this time, you really need the cash for something else.

A basic truth about cash is that it will spend itself unless you stop it.

I had a friend who faced, and eventually went through, bankruptcy. His attitude was that his money was always spent before it came in. He spent his principal and never invested his profits. He couldn't rearrange his income to always separate his money into both current expense and investment accounts.

Setting a minimum amount of profit to reinvest can be a trap of its own. If you never reinvest more than the minimum, you'll grow, but you'll grow more slowly—and if you're even a little like me, you'll begin to get frustrated and impatient, wondering why your business isn't growing faster. Your second goal should be to add a larger percentage of your cash profit to your investment capital—at least 50 percent. Make a list of emergencies or other needs that might be a reason to spend part of that second-level cash for current expenses. Make it a short list. Medical or similar emergency expenses might be a reason. Setting up an office and buying business equipment might be a reason *if you really need it.*

The larger the minimum percentage of reinvested profit, the faster you'll build wealth. Remember my goal of having enough money to choose any life-style I wanted—This is your goal. Until you reach it, decide on the cost of your lifestyle and stick to it until you've made enough so that the level of your life-style is truly optional. Then decide how you want to live—and stick to that level while your money continues to make more money.

I can't stress too strongly the dangers of letting your life-style run away with your profits.

The Third Entity

Real estate is the third entity because it secures your investment. I've talked of the pros and cons of actually owning it as an investment.

My personal choice has been to avoid long-term ownership. I feel that management problems, especially on out-of-area property, are just too great. Also, the percentage of return is much less than it is from paper. There are exceptions, of course, but normally when I get property back in foreclosure I sell it as quickly as possible. I want to get my investment capital back to reinvest.

For some investors, and you may be one of them, a combination of paper and ownership of real estate is the best (or the most comfortable) solution to their problems, and the best way to reach the goals they've set. If you're such a person, keep only the very best deals. Sell the rest.

Protecting Your Wealth

The best, the ultimate, protection of your wealth is to keep your money working.

If it's sitting in a bank account at a few percent interest, it may be "safe" and "protected," but it isn't working. The only way you can make it work is to keep it going out and coming in on high-yield paper investments, then going out again.

Perhaps it's because I fly so much, but I'd like you to think of your future in paper as an airport.

If the airplanes landed and the airport kept them on the ground, what would happen? Airplanes that needed to land would keep circling until they had to go off to some other airport—which wouldn't be long. Airplanes don't have unlimited fuel and pilots don't have unlimited patience. The airplanes on the ground wouldn't be producing anything for their owners, because airplanes make money by flying. The airport wouldn't make money because it would get no landing fees. Passengers who wanted to take off on the planes that couldn't land would leave, angry, and either go to the next airport, drive, or take Amtrak.

In paper investments, you're the airport. You bring the airplanes (money and deals) in. You turn the money around and send it out to make more money and come back again, not unlike a flight that leaves New York for San Francisco, then returns to New York. If the constant turnaround ever stops, the whole system grinds to a halt—whether it's the airline industry or your paper business.

When you make your first paper deal, you're like the pilot who's just soloed. If that pilot is satisfied because he or she flew a plane alone once, there will be no flying career for that person.

When you make a lot of paper deals, you're like an airline. You're making a lot of flights and you're taking a lot of people along with you. When you grow enough to buy and hold your own deals, you become like the airport, directing the action and giving everyone involved destinations, schedules, and a place to land when they come back. Your steady cash flow from deals you've bought are like the landing fees airlines pay for the use of airports.

You'll always need to have a certain amount of cash available to buy deals. How much will depend on the size and scope of your paper business at any point in its growth. If you develop your business to the point where you buy, say, fifteen deals in a year and keep three of them, you'll need less cash on hand than if you did two or three times that number, or if you grew to the size of S.E.S. Funding. Just remember that cash sitting in the bank is making less money than money invested in paper.

You'll need at least two accounts, one for your principal, and one for current expenses.

As soon as you've done a few deals, I recommend splitting the current expense into two accounts, one for your personal expenses and one for the expenses of the business. One way to do this would be to decide what you needed to earn as a salary and put that into your personal account. In effect, you're paying yourself for the work you've done for your company. Check with your accountant for how to handle this for maximum tax benefits. The remaining profit would go into a company account.

Does it sound like you should incorporate?

Yes—as soon as you're big enough to justify the step. Your state laws on incorporation will determine when this becomes beneficial for you. It's essential to consult with your accountant and/or attorney. You don't want to incorporate before you need to, and you certainly don't want to miss the benefits when they apply.

Once you have your own company, you may want to consider having both a domestic and an offshore account. Offshore accounts are far beyond the scope of this book, but I want to introduce you to the idea that such accounts are not taxable (according to current law) and anything you do to limit your tax liability will put more dollars in your pocket, which you can invest to make even more dollars.

I've talked at some length, earlier in the book, about protecting your investment through putting money and deals into a Keogh retirement account. I won't repeat it here, except to remind you that retirement planning is essential, and the Keogh offers a fine way to shelter income for that purpose.

Because tax laws and retirement benefits change, always consult your accountant for the best current information on how to shelter your wealth.

Starting Your Own Company

I find that many people get a little scared of the prospect of running a company when I talk about it as if it is a natural progression from buying your first deal. And it is. If you keep growing (and to stop growing is to limit yourself needlessly), you'll need your own company.

You may feel that you have no talent at all for running a company. That may even be true—now.

Running a company is like anything else. Some people seem to be born with the ability, but even they have to learn how. The rest of us ordinary folks can learn, too, and running a business *is* something anyone can learn to do.

My advice is—*Don't worry about it!*

Don't let the prospect of running a company prevent you from doing your first deal. Your first deal is far more important than any other deal you'll ever make, because it's the one that will prove to you that you can do it, and that you can make money doing it. After that, everything follows naturally.

By the time you're ready to incorporate, you'll know enough about paper, and what a paper business needs, so that with good advice from your accountant and attorney—you'll have both by then, even if you don't have either now—setting up and running a business will be exciting, not scary.

You'll find you've worked into it in a series of steps, and that you've really been running a business since your first paper deal.

I began in a one-room apartment in the Bronx. I had no staff and no business equipment whatsoever. Just me, pen and paper, my telephone, and an address to receive mail. My parents lived around the corner, so I could go talk to them or do things with them anytime I wanted. When I went to courthouses, I wrote everything down in longhand, and then addressed the envelopes by hand, too.

I couldn't afford any business equipment, so I got along without it. You can, too.

I'm not saying that a fax machine, a computer to handle the mailings and keep track of the responses, and a laptop computer to take to the courthouse aren't great tools for the paper investor. They are, and I use them all now. My point is that they are *not* essential to success.

If you already have an office in your home or outside it, use the office. But, don't feel you have to have these things to start up. Don't feel you can justify buying them until you've made the money to afford them out of what will by then be your company account, whether you've actually incorporated or not. Avoid spending before earning. Overspending before earning is what drove my friend to bankruptcy. This is a very dangerous habit to get into before you've even made your first paper deal.

You can send faxes from almost any copy shop, print shop, office-supply store, and many drugstores (but shop for prices; some are quite high). If your letter doesn't have to be there instantly, services like Federal Express, UPS, DHL, and others offer next-morning delivery. Even the U.S. Postal Service offers two-day service for $2.90.

Print shops, typing services, and many copy shops will help you create your letter. Copy and print shops will run off a few hundred copies for very little. Most will help you design a letterhead and business card.

If you need computer services, you can get those, too. Today, most "typing" services work on computers rather than on actual typewriters.

Again, in the beginning you *do not* have to own all the equipment of a business!

Make your first few deals, *then* worry about buying the equipment you don't have.

Equipping Your Company

Your first piece of company equipment is *you*. You're the business machine that goes down to the courthouse, looks up names, and sends out letters.

Your first office may be your kitchen table. Your first business phone may be your home phone.

Then you begin to build.

Ideally, you should have a room, or a part of a room, that you can dedicate to office space for your budding business. I didn't have that luxury in my one-room apartment, so if you don't have it, don't worry.

If you start like I did, you may move to a larger apartment where you can set aside office space, or you may rent a small office, as I eventually did in Manhattan. Don't do this until you've made enough money to pay the rent.

Your first office purchase should be a desk and office chair. You can often find these quite cheap at used office-furniture stores, or even garage sales if you keep your eyes open. If you make enough money, you may wish to wait a little longer and buy better office furniture, with the expectation that you'll be living with it for a while.

You'll find that a really good office chair, even if quite expensive, is a good investment. "Really good" doesn't mean covered in leather or some other luxury; it means one that is ergonomically sound and has enough adjustments that it can provide comfort no matter what you do or how long you're sitting in it. Good chairs are especially important when you begin to use a computer extensively.

You're likely to feel the most pressure to buy a fax. Most out-of-town investors, and many people in town, will ask you to fax them the mortgage worksheet and other paperwork. Since fax prices are rapidly coming down, this may be a good investment, but don't buy the cheapest models. They usually lack a paper cutter, have slow transmission speeds, and have a small document feeder. Do some shopping before you buy. Expect to pay at least between $300 and $500.

A typewriter for labels is another good, inexpensive investment, but you may find that it's more profitable to have someone else type the labels while you look for more names. An adequate typewriter can be found for less than $100.

You'll remember that when I started, I was doing everything in longhand, including addressing letters. Later (not much later) I hired my parents to do the labels, stuff the envelopes, and mail the letters.

Computers are much faster for letters and labels, but they cost more. The advantage is that once you've typed in the names, you can call them up at will for future mailings or to see how long an ad or letter took to get a response. You can do many things with computers that you can't do with any other tool, but you need to have done several profitable deals before considering a computer, unless you already own one. Expect to take some time to learn to use a computer (but once you learn, you'll wonder how you lived without it).

You can expect to pay at least $1,200 for an adequate computer and printer, plus the cost of software. This is not something you want to buy and spend the next year or two paying for.

A portable computer to take to the recorders' office is a real convenience, but should come after the basic office system. Some people have used a portable for both office and the recorder's office. The problem is that portables cost more for equivalent performance, and the keyboards are usually small and nonstandard.

An office copier might be the next priority. These start at about $400. You may want to wait until you can afford one of the more heavy-duty models, or check out leasing arrangements. Servicing on heavily used copiers can be quite important. If the machine quits, you want to know you can get it fixed *right now*.

If this much equipment sounds like you'll need staff to run it, you're right.

You may want to use family members, like your spouse, children, parents, or relatives at first, the way I used my parents. You're hiring people you know and who know you. You can get some beneficial tax results when hiring your children, but the rules are rather narrow. Check with your accountant to do it to best advantage.

Now can you see how, by the time you're ready to incorporate your company, you'll have learned a great deal about how to run a company, and have most of the equipment you'll need?

Money Partners

Let me reiterate my story about how I got to the point where I was able to reinvest. I'd bought and sold paper for a long time. Eventually I could buy for my own portfolio.

Once I started to buy my own paper, I bought in a number of different ways. First, I bought with my own money. Second, I bought using money partners.

Money partners are people who have money available at a cheap rate, say 8 to 14 percent. Bringing them into a deal and giving them part of the cash flow, while I kept the other part of the cash flow, produced a high return for me, because the bulk of the money was put up by the money partner. He or she got a good return on investment, and I got an even better return because I didn't have much of my money invested.

Everybody wins in that type of transaction. (For further details on a money-partner deal, please refer to Breakthrough Deal number five.)

The Arizona deal shows how an investor can put up the money on the front part of a mortgage while you keep the back part of the mortgage for free. This type of deal is perfect, as I described, to put into your Keogh or IRA account because it just sits there, deferring taxes until you retire. Deferred taxes mean dollars in your pocket, if you do proper tax planning.

If You Choose to Own Property

Last but not least, there's a lot of money to be made through entity number three, real property, if you choose to own it. It's not my choice, but it's a valid option.

You must remember the one fundamental law of property: Real estate is only worth what someone is willing to pay for it.

Why not purchase real estate with the cash that you may have available to you from the paper business?

I've gone over the pros and cons in previous chapters, but an interesting phenomenon often occurs when you run ads that say, "I Pay Cash for Mortgages."

That ad sends a message to people in the marketplace that says, "This person has money."

When you advertise, "I Pay Cash for Mortgages," the key word to most readers is "cash."

Ads to buy paper have instead produced offers to sell real property. People have called me and said, "Listen, I have to dump this property, quick. I'm willing to unload at this price. Do you want it?"

More often than not, I don't want to buy investment real estate. But if you are considering investment real estate, you may want to wait for some of these phone calls to come in and welcome them when they do.

Real estate purchasing can become one part of your investment program, adding to real estate you've taken back through delinquent paper.

When you get delinquent real estate back from a late payor, you normally want to sell it immediately, because that's when you maximize your return.

I don't feel that anyone will maximize their return by playing the property-management game. It takes too much time and too much effort to manage property, especially if it's out of state. If you sell the property as quickly as possible, you produce cash that goes back into entity number one, which can then be used to purchase more paper in entity number two, which keeps the whole cycle going.

Collateral Assignments

I haven't talked about this aspect of entity number three. You won't encounter it often, but it can sometimes present good opportunities.

Additional collateral assignments occur in situations where a person wants you to consider purchasing paper they create against real estate. In this case, the paper is not created due to a sale. The person is creating paper against real estate they own, and is selling it to you. Additional collateral assignments will sometimes be used by putting additional pieces of real estate into the deal to add collateral value.

You want to think about additional collateral assignments because it is part of entity number three. If it ever goes to foreclosure, you may wind up with some property. Don't always think of just one piece of real estate as collateral, but also consider additional collateral assignments, if you get into a situation where a mortgage is being created.

You always want to make sure that there's enough real estate to collateralize the debt. Money can be made if the paper does go bad. You now take back not just one piece of real estate, but a group of properties.

Collateral assignment is advanced paper investment and not recommended for your first deals.

UCC Liens

There's another kind of property that is very active in New York as well as other areas of the country: personal property liens or UCC (Universal Commercial Code) liens.

In New York City there are plenty of large apartment buildings, sixty-unit, hundred-unit, and larger properties where the residents have gotten together and purchased the building from the owner.

In making this purchase, the buyers create a corporation. The corporation buys the building. The entire building is liable for the mortgage and promissory note, and each person in the building becomes a shareholder in the corporation.

This produces a co-op instead of condominium ownership. In a co-op, you own shares in the corporation that backs the lien against the real estate.

This a little different for a paper buyer and as a means of holding title.

Can you buy this type of lien?

Yes, but you have to realize it's a different situation, because you're not buying the mortgage, you're buying a UCC lien, which has a whole different set of requirements.

I want to introduce this topic to you, so at least when you come across it, it won't scare you. Get advice from experts who have dealt with UCC liens before. Don't deal with one until you've done enough other deals to feel confident of your skills.

Other Personal Property Liens

You may be unfamiliar with the various types of personal property liens. These do not have the same security as real estate-backed mortgages and trust deeds.

Time-share paper as well as mobile homes are personal property. There are many forms of personal property you should know about, including accounts receivable held by a business. If you are ever asked to purchase this type of paper, you have to be aware that it is not a straightforward mortgage and note. The whole concept of security and the criteria you should look to check for are basically the same. Again, don't buy these kinds of liens without experience and expert advice.

Moving Forward

One final word before going on to some of my breakthrough deals.

Keep your money working. Leaving it sitting in the bank or in other low-yielding investments just doesn't make sense.

Keep your money moving. The faster you move through each entity, the better the result for you.

Paper is not a static system, it's a dynamic one. It should be turning over as fast as possible to work the money from entity number one through entity number two into entity number three, out of entity number two, back into entity number one, and so on.

That's why there are two arrows in my entity diagrams, one going toward an entity and one going away from an entity, interconnecting each one of these entities. They all work together. It's not something that works if you just work one entity.

You're working each of the entities with each of the others to maximize this system.

The faster you make this system work, the faster you'll get to wealth and financial freedom. There are very few programs that are a sure bet to financial security and financial independence. I know this is one of them.

It has taken me a long time to realize how powerful this program is. My primary message in this book is to urge you to get involved with paper.

Do it *now!*

Breakthrough Deals

In this section, I'll tell you about a few really good deals.

A breakthrough deal is one that breaks through the ordinary to earn special recognition as an outstanding achievement in paper. These are examples of what *can* happen in paper. They don't happen every day, but they happen because someone used the same basic principles and tactics used routinely in everyday deals and achieved an exceptional result.

I have three reasons for going through them with you. The first reason is to show how deals can be put together in different ways. The second is to show what you can get out of a deal, depending on how you orchestrate it. Third and last, these are exciting deals, and I want you to finish the book excited about what *you* can do in paper.

Each of these deals was the result of students of mine (or myself) actively working to put a paper deal together, recognizing an opportunity, and becoming creative. Being aware of and alert to the creative possibilities of paper deals, and taking advantage of those possibilities, means putting more money in your pocket.

Why are there great deals?

Because someone worked to create the deal, recognized the opportunities, and worked to take advantage of them.

Breakthrough Deal Number One

I was in Albuquerque for a seminar, but before going out to speak I did a radio call-in show for a station in Baltimore. I answered the listeners' questions by telephone from my room. The program host had told me the show had a two-hour time slot, but the interviews rarely lasted more than an hour. I had two hours before I was scheduled to go out and speak in Albuquerque, so I figured I'd have plenty of time to relax and go on stage fresh.

Well, interest in paper in the Baltimore area was so intense that we took the whole two hours!

Fortunately, I had a friend in the room with me to answer the door, bring me water, and make sure I was undisturbed and had whatever I needed.

About halfway through, someone slid a card under the door. It was a note on an index card from Ken, a student of mine in the Albuquerque area. He gave a testimonial about how the Stefanchik Method had worked for him and described a recent deal he'd done.

His note added, "I made a lot of money on this deal with only $100 at risk, and I'd be happy to tell anyone about it."

When I went out to give my seminar, I gave my usual introduction to paper and then asked Ken to stand up and tell everyone about his deal.

This deal is his story.

A person contacted him to sell a mortgage (they call them *real estate contracts* in New Mexico). After some negotiation, Ken agreed to a price of $115,000 to purchase the entire cash flow of a real estate contract with a face amount of $165,000.

Ken was in the same position I was when I found my first deal. He'd found this great mortgage, but he didn't have $115,000! He wanted to be sure the mortgage holder didn't change his mind or sell to someone else while he found the money, so he asked for an option to purchase the paper. The mortgage holder gave him a forty-five day option for $100!

We talked about two kinds of options in the chapter on foreclosure. Remember, you can give defaulting payors either a lease option or a one-year option to purchase their property back from you.

The kind of option Ken asked for and got was the kind commonly used in real estate, except that he got the option for purchase of a mortgage, not the property.

For a non-refundable amount, always negotiable, the person purchasing the option has the right to exercise a purchase contract for a certain period of time. If the option is exercised, the option money becomes part of the purchase price. If the option is not exercised, the person granting the option keeps the money and looks for someone else to buy the property. All the terms of the purchase contract, and the option consideration amount, are fully negotiable. Once the agreement is signed, the terms are fixed.

In Ken's case, he and the seller had agreed to price and other terms and conditions, and the seller gave him the forty-five day option.

Now, for his hundred dollars' option money (all he has at risk) Ken has the option to purchase this paper for $115,000. With this option in hand, Ken set out to find a person who wanted to buy the cash flow. He located a buyer, negotiated a purchase price of $140,000, and closed the deal in twenty-nine days!

The real beauty of the deal was that Ken did not sell the new buyer the actual real estate contract. Instead, Ken sold the new buyer the option to purchase the cash flow (not the cash flow itself), for $25,000, the difference between $115,000 and $140,000, so the new buyer could execute the option to purchase the paper for $115,000.

The result? Ken made $25,000 on one deal with only a pittance at risk. Very simply, Ken turned a hundred dollars into $25,000 in just under a month!

Why was Ken willing to share his story with my seminar attendees? Simple. He realized that by telling people from his own area of his success in that area, he might create a market for paper I might turn down. Local investors may turn to him because he is local, and may buy a deal I don't want because I'm not close enough to have local control of it.

Breakthrough Deal Number Two

Caven, a very creative student of mine in Kent, Ohio puts an interesting twist on the way he buys paper.

I met him before he became a student, because he worked with an attorney I knew. Caven was making money buying and selling real estate. He was very creative, approaching every deal in a well thought out manner. His goal in buying real estate was very much like my goal in paper. He wanted to buy at a discount, renovate if necessary, and sell as quickly as possible so he got his money and profit back to reinvest. (Does that sound familiar?)

He took it one step farther. He wrote all his purchase contracts so he could assign them to someone else before settlement and get a fee for doing so. That's what you can do when you write your name on a purchase contract and add "and/or assigns or assignee."

He might, for example, find a $100,000 property that he could buy for $75,000. With his "and/or assigns or assignee" purchase contract, he tied it up until he could find someone who wished to buy the contract for, say, $82,000. He'd make $7,000 on the deal quickly.

So when Caven learned about the Stefanchik Method and became one of my students, he already had experience and a thorough knowledge of real estate. He'd been doing it long enough that he had his own money with which to buy mortgages. He could flip mortgages any time he wished, just as he'd been flipping real estate, but when he wanted to or had to, he could use his own money. If he made money it was all his gain, and he usually gained big. If he lost money, which was rare, he had only himself to blame.

That experience and level of financial security gave him a strong, confident, creative outlook on life that he brought to all his deals. You'll feel that way, too, when you've made enough deals.

When he began buying paper, he found a way to get his money back faster, thus increasing his yield.

He told me of a deal in which he purchased a long-term mortgage secured by an owner-occupied home, with a remaining balance of $55,000, for $41,000. That was a really good discount.

Caven liked the property because it was a nice home, it appeared that the owners might live there for a long time, and it was right in Kent, where he lives.

As soon as he bought the paper, he went to the home where the people who were paying on the mortgage lived. He introduced himself as the new mortgage holder and told them that today was their lucky day.

They asked why.

He said, "According to the amortization schedule, the remaining balance owed on your loan is $55,000. If you would like to pay it off any time in the next two months, I'll let you pay only $48,000. You'll save $7,000."

The homeowners got all excited about saving $7,000, but they didn't know where they could go to get $48,000 to pay off Caven.

Caven pointed out that they had lived in the house for quite a few years and the house had appreciated in value. They could go to the bank and refinance the property.

That was why he gave them two months. If the bank dawdled and took longer, of course he'd have given them the extra time, but he didn't tell them that up front. He wanted to give them a deadline and a sense of urgency so they'd act and not wait.

Then he added that if they wanted, they could refinance the full $55,000 from the bank (the bank would have a new $55,000 first mortgage). Then they could pay Caven $48,000 and keep $7,000 cash from the new loan. With that cash, they could put in a swimming pool, build an addition, or take a well deserved vacation—anything they wanted.

But the real beauty for the homeowners is that borrowed money is not taxable. Therefore, they'd pull out $7,000 tax-free!

Now they were really excited.

They got the loan and paid off the mortgage Caven had purchased for $41,000.

Caven created about as ultimate a win-win situation as anyone could wish for. He bought the mortgage at a discount, giving the original mortgage holders the cash they needed. Then he split his $14,000 profit ($55,000 minus $41,000) with the homeowners. In exchange, he got back his principal and a $7,000 profit (in today's dollars; remember the time value of money) within two months. He received just under 100 percent yield (98.4 percent, to be exact) on his money.

Since he tied up his cash for only two months, Caven could now repeat the process.

He had a new deal to consider, because during the two months he was waiting to be paid off, he actively looked for paper.

Remember how the Rule of 72 stated that you could double your money in a year if you got 72 percent interest?

Imagine what would happen if every two months you could get

almost a 100 percent yield on your money! Would it take long to become very wealthy?

Caven is well on his way.

Breakthrough Deal Number Three

One day an attorney friend of mine, Jay, called and said, "John, I need $19,000."

I said, "For what?"

He said, "Trust me."

I said, "How can I? You're an attorney." (You can see that we're good friends.)

We had our laugh, and he said, "Let me explain this deal. The IRS is having a seized-property auction in Cleveland. Among other things, they're auctioning twenty-eight mortgages. I want to buy two of them. They're in Cleveland and I think we should make a nice profit."

I said, "Only two?"

"Trust me," he said again. He added, "I've checked. We should get them at a good price. We can create a partnership to own the deals."

I agreed, and we wire transferred the $19,000 to him.

A tax-seizure auction is where the IRS sells assets taken for back taxes to investors who come with cash. You can't buy on credit. That limits how many people can buy, and keeps prices down by limiting the bidding competition.

The assets to be auctioned are any kind of property seized by the IRS. The IRS can seize any asset available to pay back taxes: cars, boats, houses, planes, or even mortgages (where someone is receiving payments).

Jay headed off to the sale with our money. He bid on the first mortgage he wanted and got it. Then he bid on the second one he wanted and bought it as well. He'd spent $17,000 for both deals, so he had $2,000 left.

There were still quite a few deals to be auctioned. The auction proceeded very slowly. The IRS agent conducting the sale was starting to get anxious and looked at his watch. He announced to all bidders, "It's getting very close to lunchtime. I have two mortgages left. Anyone want them?"

Jay shouted, "Two thousand dollars!"

The agent replied, "Sold!" He headed off to lunch.

Jay called the next day to tell me that we did not merely purchase two deals with the $19,000, but four! The total remaining balances on our four mortgages was over $76,000, and we only paid $19,000!

What a productive day!

But it gets better.

Jay assembled all the paperwork and sent it to my office. Three weeks later we sold one of the mortgages for $21,300. That meant we got our original $19,000 back, plus a $2,300 profit, in just under a month.

We still had three mortgages left! These were just pure gravy (they were now free) because we'd already gotten back our original investment.

The only snag was that each of the three was delinquent and way behind on their payments. (No wonder those last two were still left and the agent was happy to dump them for $2,000!)

Since you read the chapters on discounted paper and foreclosure, you know that we weren't worried by that little problem. We had a number of ways to deal with it and make money.

Jay, since he's the attorney, wrote to each of the delinquent payors, informing them that we were the new owners of their mortgage, that they were way behind on their payments (as if they didn't know), and if they didn't bring their mortgages current or make other arrangements to solve the problem, we planned to foreclose.

That forced each property owner to consider the consequences:

1. Bring the note current with cash (which they didn't have).
2. Borrow money to bring the note current, but put themselves further in debt (assuming anyone would lend them anything at that point).
3. Allow us to foreclose against them, thereby ruining their credit rating for years.
4. Give us the property by a deed in lieu of foreclosure.

The delinquent payors opted for neither one, two, or three.

What each one did was quite unexpected to us. They each, independently, deeded the property to us to avoid foreclosure. Most property owners don't even know they can do this until you or their financial advisor tells them they can. We now owned three pieces of property free and clear in Cleveland, Ohio.

I have nothing against Cleveland. I have wonderful friends there, and my brother lives there (he also happens to be the local movie critic). But if I kept these properties, I'd be an out-of-state landlord. The problem with being an out-of-state landlord, as I've discussed earlier, is long-range property management.

We decided to sell each property separately, but quickly. When you sell quickly, you sell for a discount. We made only a $45,000 profit from the three sales. Add that to the $2,300 profit on the first deal and we had a net $47,300 profit.

Excellent!

Since we got our original $19,000 back so quickly, we had an almost infinite rate of return.

Breakthrough Deal Number Four

As I've mentioned, an ad we run in New York consistently reads:

WE BUY MORTGAGES
FULL AND PARTIAL

This ad brings us a lot of calls, but one day I got a call that was very different.

Usually, the caller wants to know what a partial means. Are we talking about partial payment, partial interest, partial amount, or partial something else? That's fine, because it gives us the opportunity to explain what a partial is, how it works, and how it can benefit a mortgage holder.

The woman who called was an astute, knowledgeable business-woman who knew exactly what a partial was. She wasted no time saying that she owned a mortgage and wanted to buy an existing business, a newspaper concession shop at a hotel on Long Island. She needed $30,000 and asked, "How many payments will I have to sell to net $30,000 cash? But before you give me a number," she added, "I must tell you the property is located in Harlem." She knew the need to disclose relevant facts, especially those that we'd learn anyway.

I said, "Let me look at the property tonight. I'll call you back."

That night, on the way downtown for dinner, Heidi and I drove past the property. I was pleasantly surprised to see a nice street in the northern section of Harlem, with a series of row houses (brownstones), all nicely kept. Almost in the middle of the block was the house that served as collateral for the woman's mortgage.

I called her back the next day and discussed the details. I told her we needed the next forty-eight payments in order to pay her $30,000, leaving her with seventy-seven payments remaining behind those we were buying. She agreed. Because she was knowledgeable, she knew we'd offered a fair price. We didn't have to negotiate much or waste time explaining why we offered that price.

The deal closed and everyone was happy.

About two months later we got another call from her. She said she'd seriously underestimated the startup costs of her new business. She needed more money and wanted to sell the remaining payments she held on the mortgage.

We offered her a price, to which she agreed. We set the closing for the following Monday morning.

At Monday, about nine A.M., we gave her the cash and now owned the entire mortgage. She left, happily, with her money.

Just an hour later, we were sitting around in our office having coffee and discussing a few matters when the phone rang.

It was a bank on the phone, telling us that the Harlem property on which we held a mortgage had just been sold. They wanted to know where we wanted the payoff check sent.

It took a few minutes to realize what had just occurred. Since we had purchased the rest of the mortgage from her not one hour before, we were now to receive the entire payoff amount, about a $30,000 profit instead of just part of it (if we owned the partial).

The morning was one to never forget because we had just made $30,000 in one hour. Life is just so unpredictable and fun when you're in the paper business.

If you're wondering why the woman, being knowledgeable, didn't complain, there are two reasons. First, she sold the mortgage and didn't know the property was being sold. She left with her money before word came to us. She had no further interest and probably never knew or cared what happened to the property that had secured her former mortgage.

Second, if she had learned of it, she might have been unhappy, disgusted with herself for selling, perhaps even used unprintable language in frustration, if that was her style, but she wouldn't have come to us to complain. She knew enough about the business to know that these things sometimes happen.

The key thing for her was that she made a business decision based on the best information available to her, and sold the mortgage for money she needed. She got her money and was happy.

We just happened to be in the right deal at the right time.

Breakthrough Deal Number Five

I got a call one day about a really good mortgage for sale.

The mortgage was for $110,000, with monthly payments of $1,078.12 and twenty-three years remaining (276 payments).

After an hour of intense negotiating, I offered $65,000 for the entire mortgage and it was accepted. The only concern the mortgage holder had was to get the money real fast. For this type of deal I said, "No problem!"

But, I *did* have a problem. It wasn't the time frame that concerned me—I didn't have $65,000! I really wanted to do this deal, but what could I do?

Since you've read about money partners earlier in the book, you know what I had to do. By this time I'd done enough deals to have confidence that I could find the money, so I had an easy time telling the mortgage holder, "No problem."

Just a few days before finding this deal, I was at a party where a wealthy friend of mine told me his wife was looking for a safe, high-yielding investment that she could control herself. I thought of her even as I negotiated the price for this deal. The only question was whether she'd found her investment in the meantime.

I called my friend to ask if she was still interested.

He said, "Yes, but call her directly. It's her deal."

I called her about the deal and told her it was a $65,000 deal at 14 percent interest, payable monthly.

She got excited about the deal, because it was high-yielding over a long period of time. Her only concern was collecting the payments herself.

I told her I'd collect the payment and forward a check to her each month.

She said, "Great! When do you want the money?"

I told her next week and she said, "Fine. You'll have it."

The only detail I'd overlooked was closing costs, about $651, which had to come out of my pocket. I definitely had that much cash, so we made the purchase.

At this point, you may think this sounds like an ordinary paper deal and wonder why I consider it a breakthrough deal. You should also be wondering what happens if the mortgage pays off early. Do I have to pay her 14 percent for 23 years? Wouldn't that eat up more than my profit? And what happens if the mortgage payments stop? Do I have to continue to pay her 14 percent until I foreclose? Good questions!

First, compute my rate of return. I've spent $651 and my time. Every month I collect a check for $1,078.12. I deposit the check in the bank and write a check to my money partner for $790.51, which is 14 percent on her $65,000. I keep $287.61 every month (the difference between $1,078.12 and $790.51) for 276 months with only $651.00 at risk. My rate of return is over 500 percent! (To be exact, 530.15 percent, if it goes to maturity.)

She's put up the $65,000 to buy the deal and I kicked in the closing costs of $651.00. She's thrilled to get a 14 percent secured return on her money, doesn't even have to worry about collecting the payments, and the payments go on for twenty-three years (276 payments).

That's a great deal for both of us.

Now, what happens if this note pays off early or we have to foreclose?

I'm very careful in my agreements with money partners, and you should be, too. This is covered in our partnership agreement or contract, and I covered it carefully in my discussions with her before she put up her money.

Few people become wealthy enough to have $65,000 to invest without understanding risk, but I made it a point to tell her that we were in this deal together. If the payments stopped, we would consider foreclosure and other options together. If we foreclosed, we'd do it together. I'd take care of all the details, but I'd consult with her, and we shared both the risks and profits. Protecting our investment was a mutual responsibility, covered in full detail in our agreement.

If the mortgage pays off early, she gets her money back and can invest it in something else. She doesn't get interest for payments not made because the loan paid off early. That, too, is covered in the agreement.

I *never* guarantee an investor the money. He or she knows the risks and realities of the marketplace, or I make sure that I've explained everything clearly and that the contract protects us both.

There's an interesting thing about working with money partners: If you take care of them, they'll be ready and happy to take care of you when the next deal comes along.

If this deal pays off early, or we have to foreclose and get our money back that way, I can either pay her the agreed-upon 14 percent, or I can pay her more. If I pay her more than the contract provides, do you think she'll be happy to do business with me again? You bet she will.

I shouldn't forget to add that, just as I need to make money, she needs to make money, too. When I find her a good deal and then make it better, I just about guarantee that she'll place her money with me again as soon as I can find her a deal she likes.

I just love working with money partners because everyone wins.

Breakthrough Deal Number Six

You might think by now that a breakthrough deal has to be one where someone made an unusually large profit, or got paid off early, or someone solved a problem creatively, or something else happened that made the deal a rarity.

Of course we all like to talk about the special and the exceptional, but most deals are ordinary deals for ordinary amounts of profit. Of course, in paper an "ordinary" profit is much larger than you'd find elsewhere.

Ordinary deals are special, too. You should get in the habit of treating each deal as if it were a breakthrough deal, because you'll often find it as necessary to be creative and flexible on a deal that makes a few thousand dollars as for one that makes $50,000. If you do that, two things will happen.

You'll make more ordinary deals than the next person, because you'll solve problems that would have stopped most people.

When you encounter a major breakthrough deal that requires every bit of knowledge and creativity you possess, you'll be far better prepared than any other person. You'll find it easier to treat the big one as just another deal.

Breakthrough Deal Number Six is the kind of ordinary deal that most people would have lost or given up on. The problem that would have killed the deal was simple, but appeared out of anyone's control.

My student took it upon himself to creatively solve the problem in a way most of us would never think of.

My student brought us a deal, presented the mortgage worksheet (which looked quite good), and we made a quote on it. The mortgage seller accepted the quote. We asked for the usual preliminary paperwork: copy of the promissory note, copy of the mortgage, copy of the closing statement, and some pictures of the property. All routine so far, just like any other deal that comes through our office.

Pictures, of course, can be worth a thousand words, or thousands of dollars. You remember the story I told earlier of the house that had been painted a different color on each side, with a graffiti-like mural on the garage door. You can really learn a lot from a picture.

We got the pictures of the property. It didn't look that good. The owner had not taken care of the property, at least the exterior, which is all we can judge when estimating value for paper buying purposes, because we do drive-by appraisals.

The student drove by to check it out, looked at the property, and called us back to say, "You know, you're right. It doesn't really look that good."

Still, the numbers were good enough for us to do an actual drive-by appraisal.

The student realized that in its present condition and appearance, the house would not appraise enough to make our deal work.

Now he faced the problem that would kill this deal for nine out of ten students, or maybe ninety-nine out of a hundred.

He, as a potential purchaser of the mortgage, has no legal right to either do, or ask the homeowner to do, anything about the appearance of the property. The mortgage holder has a technical legal right to require the homeowner to maintain the property in good condition, but such loan clauses are not invoked in practice, except sometimes during foreclosure proceedings.

The student said to us, "Hold off on the appraisal. Let me take care of this."

We said, "Great. Keep us informed."

The student went to the mortgage seller and said, "You know, I made you an offer on your mortgage, but I don't think we can meet that because of the appearance of the property."

The mortgage seller replied, "What do you want me to do? I don't own the house. I can't do anything."

The student said, "Let's try this. What would happen if I bought the paint and you went to the homeowner and told him that if he'll paint the house, you'll provide the paint?"

The mortgage holder agreed that this was worth trying. He went to the homeowner and said, "If you're willing to paint the house, I'll provide the paint."

The homeowner had never heard of anything like that, so he asked, "Why are you making this offer?"

The mortgage holder said, "I want to do some things with the cash flow from my mortgage. It's not going to affect you in any way, except that you'll get your house painted for no cost at all except the time it takes you. I think it will work for both our interests."

The homeowner saw this as an advantage to him and said, "Sure. I'll do it."

So the student provided the paint to the mortgage seller, the mortgage seller provided the paint to the homeowner, the homeowner painted the house, and our appraiser came by and appraised the house for *more* than we thought the property was going to be worth.

We bought the mortgage, the student made a few thousand dollars on the deal, minus the cost of the paint, the mortgage seller got his money, and the homeowner got his house painted. Everybody was happy.

You may wonder why the student didn't ask the mortgage seller to foot the bill for the paint.

My student was smart enough to know he was dealing with human nature. If the mortgage seller wasn't paying for the paint, he'd be more positive and more relaxed when he went to talk to the homeowner—he had everything to gain and nothing to lose. There would be no voice in the back of his head saying that if the homeowner didn't accept, at least he wouldn't be out the cost of paint. The student recognized that he was dealing with people's feelings and emotions. By sending the mortgage holder to the homeowner with motivation and a positive attitude, he'd improved the chances that the homeowner would accept the idea. The student realized that, for a few hundred dollars in paint, it is just not worth going back and forth about who's going to foot the bill.

The student paid for the paint and saved the deal.

I've seen students get in their own way and block a deal over concerns about pennies. They trip over pennies and wonder why they don't get to the dollars. That's not the way you should look at making money in paper.

You have to look at how you can solve the problem and make money on the deal. That's exactly what this student did, and that's exactly why I'm applauding him with the story of this breakthrough deal.

The creative use of your ability to solve problems can either make or break a deal.

Breakthrough Deal Number Seven

Four Years at Harvard for Only $7,000? Heidi and I were talking about college with our two girls the other evening. One of them is seventeen, and college is right around the corner for her. As she started mentioning the schools she was interested in, I realized they were all the expensive ones—Ivy League schools.

I started adding up what it was going to cost to send her to school and almost died. I don't know how parents do it today. I look back at the job I had. I was paid $30,000 a year; there would have been no way for me to send a child to college without going into major debt. I guess that's how most people do it, though. They get student loans and hope they or their child can pay them off.

Paper offers a better way (and this applies to much more than just college expenses).

At one of my recent boot camps, a deal came in from Seattle and we reviewed it as a class, looking at the numbers and doing all the normal calculations.

There were 362 payments, the interest rate was 10.5 percent, the present value was $70,000, and the monthly payments were $640, but it had a balloon payment due in 120 payments (ten years). The current balance on the balloon was $64,202.59. There were 107 payments (a month less than nine years) of $640 remaining.

My office offered 15 percent yield for the 107 payments without buying the balloon, because of the LTV. This worked out to $37,648.06. We then learned our student could buy the entire deal, including the balloon, for $45,000, which he did.

My student could use this note in a number of ways, as you might when doing a similar deal. He could put it in a Keogh, in an offshore bank account to defer taxes, or he might use it to put a child or two through a top-notch college.

Suppose you purchased the paper for $45,000 and sold the front end of this deal, 107 payments, to S.E.S. Funding for $37,648.06. The difference from the $45,000 you paid for the mortgage and the $37,648.06 you sold the front end to us for is $7,351.94. For a little over $7,000, you own a balloon payment of over $64,000, due in eight years, eleven months. You get nothing for your $7,000 until then (unless it pays off early), but if it goes the full term your yield works out to be a 24.55 percent return on your investment of $7,351.94.

If the trust deed pays off early, your return will be even greater. Now this is one heck of a return on your money. In just a little under nine years your money has compounded to about eight times your original cash investment.

Suppose you put a deal like this together when your child was eight years old. Do you think you could send him or her to four years of college, and maybe even some graduate school for $64,202? I think that would cover most of the major expenses you or I might face when paying for college. It would put a real good dent in the cost of the most expensive schools in the nation.

Of course the trick is to find deals like this, but they *are* out there. They will not come looking for you. You have to go out there and do the work necessary to find this kind of deal and put it together.

Then, when your child is attending Harvard and someone asks

how much that costs, you can smile and tell them it was only $7,000 for all four years.

They'll be amazed and probably ask if your child is on a scholarship.

Just say, "No, she's on paper."

Glossary of Paper and Real Estate Terms

You should be familiar with the basic vocabulary of real estate. In this short glossary, I give you definitions of some key terms. Whenever you don't understand a word, look here first.

You should read the entire glossary so you've at least heard of some of the terms you may encounter. Don't try to read the glossary like you've read the rest of this text. Read a page or two at a time, and come back to it. Use the glossary to get a general idea of terms and what they mean, and then keep it as a reference to go back to when you encounter a term you're not sure of.

A

Abstract of Title: A full summary of all conveyances, deeds, liens, judgments, marriages, divorces, deaths, wills, and so forth that affect the title to a specific parcel of real estate, in any manner, in an abbreviated form.

Accounting Rate of Return: The equation by which you determine the amount of money you made during the time you owned an investment (account for all cash flow during a period of ownership of either a property or a note).

Acceleration Clause: A clause in loan contracts that states that the entire amount is due and payable on the occurrence of a certain event, such as sale of the property, failure to make payments or pay interest, failure to pay taxes or insurance, assignment of the property, or the placing of an encumbrance on the property.

Adjustable-Rate Mortgage (ARM): Also called a "Variable-Rate Mortgage," this is a mortgage loan in which the interest rate may increase or decrease at specified intervals. It is usually based on an outside index, such as U.S. Treasury bills or the cost of funds in the local Federal Reserve District. There are other variations on this basic idea, each with its own name.

ALTA Policy: A type of title-insurance policy that insures the beneficiary against the widest range of possibilities. Never buy a note or a property without title insurance.

Amortization: The payment of a financial obligation over a period of time on an installment basis in equal payments, as in, "an amortized loan." In an amortized loan, the amount of the loan, the interest rate, and the total number of payments are used to determine what the monthly payments will be. The term also means the recovery over time of the cost or value of an investment.

Annual Debt Service: The amount of money paid in a twelve-month period toward a mortgage or trust deed. This total includes both principal (if any) and interest.

Appreciation: An increase in the value or worth of a property due to economic or other causes. The opposite of depreciation.

ARM (Adjustable-Rate Mortgage): An amortizing permanent long-term flexible loan in which the interest rate can be adjusted by the lender from time to time. Such adjustments are based on changes in a public index (e.g., treasury rates, consumer price index, etc.) to which the interest rate is "pegged."

Assignment: The transfer of rights, such as the rights in a mortgage, from one person to another. The person giving or transferring the rights is called the *Assignor*. The person receiving the rights is the *Assignee*. In our Bill and Mary example, Mary was the assignor and John, via David, was the assignee in the assignment of her mortgage.

Assumption of Mortgage: The taking of title to a property in which the grantee (the person being granted title) assumes personal liability for the payment of an existing mortgage against the property. The grantee also becomes a co-guarantor for payment of the mortgage or deed of trust note.

B

Balloon Payment: A large payment on a mortgage due at the end of a certain period of time. For example, a loan might be made for three years, "interest only." In that case, the borrower would pay only interest during the life of the loan and would be required to either pay off or refinance the full principal at the end of three years. Another (of many) forms of balloon payment will compute payments of principal and interest for fifteen or thirty years, or some other long period, but require the unpaid balance to be paid off or refinanced after a shorter period, often five years or less. Do not purchase a note with a balloon payment in a state that requires that a balloon be refinanced at the original rate. Do not purchase a balloon-payment mortgage originated in the state of Oklahoma.

Beneficiary: The person or entity receiving the benefit of something. Often used in insurance, where the beneficiary receives the benefit of any payments made under the policy. The beneficiary in a trust-deed transaction is the institution or individual receiving payments (benefits) from the note. In trust-deed states, the title to real property (real estate) is placed in trust for the benefit of the lending institution or person to secure the repayment of the debt.

Bond: Any interest-bearing or discounted government or corporate security that obligates the issuer to pay the bondholder a specified sum of money, usually at specific intervals, and to repay the principal amount of the loan at maturity.

Blanket Mortgage: A single loan secured by two or more parcels of real estate. A release clause is usually included in the mortgage so that parcels covered by the blanket mortgage may be released (sold) on an individual basis in return for payments to the lender according to a specified release schedule. For example, if you had two $100,000 parcels under a $200,000 blanket mortgage, the mortgage would not permit you to sell one of the parcels for $50,000 under the release clause.

Blended-Rate Mortgage: A loan-refinancing plan that combines the interest rate on an existing mortgage with the interest rate of a new mortgage on the same property to arrive at an averaged, "weighted" interest rate.

Bond: Any interest-bearing or discounted government or corporate security that obligates the issuer to pay the bondholder a specified sum of money, usually at specific intervals, and to repay the principal amount of the loan at maturity.

Broker: A person who buys and sells for another for a commission.

Buy-down: A cash payment up front to the lender to reduce the interest rate a borrower must pay on a new mortgage loan.

C

Capitalization: A mathematical process (formula) for estimating the value of a property using a proper rate of return for the investment and the annual net income expected to be produced by the property. The formula is:

$$\frac{Net\ Operating\ Income}{Capitalization\ Rate} = Value$$

Net operating income is obtained by subtracting fixed expenses and operating expenses from gross income.

Capitalization Rate (Cap Rate): The rate of return that is considered to be a reasonable return on an investment. It is used by investors in determining the value of a property based on its net income (the income after all expenses are paid). It can also be used to determine the yield that will attract the money of an average informed investor to an investment, which can apply to paper as well as property.

The formula for determining Cap Rate is:

$$\frac{Net\ Operating\ Income}{Purchase\ Price} \times 100\% = \frac{Overall\ Capitalization}{Rate}$$

Cash Flow: The net spendable income from an investment, determined by deducting all operating and fixed expenses from the gross income. If expenses exceed income, this results in a *negative cash flow* (you don't want to see this!). Income that exceeds expenses produces a positive cash flow, the desired result.

Cash Flow After Taxes: The net income from an investment after taking into consideration all tax ramifications as well as normal expenses.

Cash-flow Analysis: Methods of examining an investment through its cash flow.

Cash-on-cash Analysis: The return on the initial cash outlay that the investment yields during the time of possession expressed as a percentage. It can be used for the total time the investment is owned, or can be used for any selected period of time during ownership. The formula is:

$$Cash\text{-}on\text{-}cash = \frac{Net\ Operating\ Income\ Less\ Debt\ Service}{Down\ Payment} \times 100\%$$

Certificate of Title: A statement of opinion on the status of the title to a parcel of real property based on the examination of specified public records.

Chain of Title: The succession of conveyances from some accepted starting point whereby the present holder of real property derives his or her title.

Chattel Mortgage: A personal-property lien.

Closing Statement: A detailed cash accounting of a real estate transaction showing all cash received, all charges and credits made, and all cash paid out in the transaction.

Cloud on Title: Any claim, encumbrance, or condition that impairs the clear title to real property (real estate) until disproved or removed.

Compound Interest: Interest paid on accumulated interest as well as on the principal.

Comparables: Properties listed in an appraisal report that are essentially equivalent to the subject property.

Competitive Market Analysis: A comparison of the prices of recently sold homes that are similar to a listing seller's home in terms of style and location.

Construction Loan: A short-term loan made to a builder, developer, or owner to cover the construction costs of a house, building, or development project, in addition to other improvements to a property. The total loan is not paid out to the borrower in full but is paid out in periodic installments as the project reaches specific stages of completion.

Contract: A legally enforceable promise or set of promises that must be performed. If a breach of promise occurs, then legal remedy is provided by law.

Contract for Deed: Under the terms of the contract, the seller retains the legal title to the property and the buyer receives the equitable title and possession of the property while making payments. When the buyer pays off the seller in full and meets any other required conditions of the contract, the seller conveys title to the buyer.

Conventional Loan: A permanent long-term loan that is not insured by the Federal Housing Administration (FHA) or the Veterans' Administration. Conventional loans are made by institutional lenders, mortgage companies, and private individuals.

Covenant: A written agreement between two or more parties in which a party or parties pledges to perform specific acts with regard to property.

D

Deed: A written instrument (legal document) that, when executed and delivered, conveys title to or interest in real property.

Deed in Lieu of Foreclosure: A conveyance of title to real estate in which the borrower gives the lender a deed to the property instead of (in lieu of) the lender having to foreclose. The sole consideration on the part of the mortgagee (lender) is an agreement not to foreclose on the property. This allows the mortgagor (borrower) to maintain a clean credit record. It saves the lender the time and expense of foreclosure.

Deed of Trust: The instrument (legal document) used to create a mortgage lien by which the mortgagor (borrower) conveys his or her title to a trustee, a neutral third party who holds it in trust as security for the mortgagee (lender or note holder) for the benefit of the mortgagee. It is also called a *trust deed.*

Default: The omission or failure to perform or fulfill a legal duty, obligation, or promise. In real estate and lending, it is most often used in the context of payments that have not been made as contracted and promised, as in, "the mortgage is in default."

Depreciation: In real estate investment, an expense deduction for tax purposes taken over a period of ownership of income property. An artificial loss for tax purposes.

Discount: To sell a promissory note before maturity at a price less than the outstanding principal balance of the note at the time of sale. (This is what we do when dealing in discounted paper.) Also, an amount deducted in advance by a lender from the principal of a loan as a part of the cost to the borrower of obtaining the loan. (We talk of "points" in the cost of obtaining a loan, but "discount points" would be the full and correct term.)

Discount to Yield: Offering in cash a lesser amount than the face value (principal sum) of a lien, whereby the return on capital increases over the life of the lien above the stated interest rate on that lien.

Discounted Cash-flow Analysis: Accounting technique for expressing other opportunities in the marketplace versus real estate investment, through a number.

Down Payment: The amount of the selling price that is paid (usually in cash) at the beginning, and is not financed.

E

Easement: The legal right a person has in the limited enjoyment (use) of the real property of another. An electric company might have an easement to run power lines across a property owned by someone else. A property owner whose property does not have direct access to the street might have an easement for a driveway across the property of a neighbor who has street access. An easement is considered an interest in real property (real estate).

Encumbrance: Any claim, lien, charge, liability, encroachment, easement, etc., attaching to the title of real estate that may cloud the title and may affect the value of the property.

Equity: The value an owner has in his or her property over and above any mortgage or other lien or indebtedness.

Equity Rate of Return: A technique for assessing the rate of return on an investment that takes equity into account. The formula is:

$$Equity\ Rate\ of\ Return = \frac{Equity\ Cash\ Flow\ Value}{Initial\ Investment} \times 100\%$$

Escalator Clause: A clause in a mortgage allowing the lender to adjust the interest rate based on the occurrence of a certain event. You'll usually hear a phrase such as, "This mortgage adjusts every six months based on the 11th District Cost of Funds Index."

Escrow: The system by which money, documents, personal property, or real property (real estate) are held in trust for others by a disinterested third party until the terms and conditions of the escrow instructions, made by the parties to the escrow, are completed or otherwise terminated.

Estoppel Certificate: A legal document from the mortgagee and/or mortgagor stating the exact balance due on the loan at that point in time, and also stating the monthly payment amount and the interest rate. An estoppel is a bar or impediment that precludes allegation or denial of a certain fact or statement of facts. An estoppel letter is a notarized document upon which facts are sworn to by a party. The purpose of the letter is to prevent, or stop, the same party from later claiming facts contrary to those sworn to on the estoppel letter. Primarily used to verify the remaining balance on a mortgage before purchase.

F

Fee Simple: The maximum possible estate or right of ownership of real property, continuing forever.

FHA: The Federal Housing Administration, a government agency that insures FHA-approved conventional lenders against loss under any of a number of FHA loan programs.

FHA Loan: A loan insured by the Federal Housing Administration. Similar in principle to a VA loan.

Fiduciary Relationship: A relationship of trust and confidence, as between principal and agent or attorney and client.

Financial Rate of Return: A technique that takes into account all parameters, including negative cash flow, in order to determine what an investment is worth today for future cash flows. You must use a financial calculator, such as the Hewlett-Packard 12C, to compute this figure.

Financial Calculator Variables: The values you need in order to figure various equations on a financial calculator. You'll find keys on the HP-12C marked with these values. Usually, if you know any four of the five variables, the calculator can solve for the missing variable. The variables are:

n	*n*umber of payment periods remaining
i	Effective *i*nterest rate
PV	*P*resent *V*alue at the beginning of the holding period
PMT	*PayMenT* Amount
FV	*F*uture *V*alue at the end of the holding period

Fixed-Rate Mortgage: A mortgage loan in which the interest rate and payment amount remain the same throughout the life of the loan.

Foreclosure: A legal proceeding in court to enforce payment of a debt secured by a mortgage that is in default. The property is sold by court order to satisfy the debt in mortgage states. In trust deed states, the trustee has authority to sell the property in default after meeting certain legal requirements of notification and a waiting period.

Fraud: Deception intended to cause a person to give up lawful right to a property.

G

Grantee: A person who receives a conveyance of real property from the grantor.

Grantor: The person transferring title to or interest in real property to a grantee.

Gross Rent Multiplier: The relationship between the gross rents and the purchase price. A figure used to estimate the value of income property. The formula is:

$$\frac{Purchase\ Price}{Gross\ Rents} = Gross\ Rent\ Multiplier\ (GRM)$$

H

Homestead: Land that is occupied as the family home. In many states a portion of the value of the land is exempt from judgment for debts.

Hypothecation: The pledge of a lien (mortgage or trust deed) by a lien owner as collateral for a new loan.

I

Infinite Rate of Return: The inability to calculate return on capital when no money was put into a deal. The highest possible return on investment.

Interest: A charge made by a lender for the use of money.

Interest-Only Loan: As opposed to a self-liquidating loan, where some principal is paid down with each payment, this loan only charges interest and no principal is paid off during the loan, only at the end of the loan. Interest-only loans are balloon-payment loans.

Internal Rate of Return (IRR): A technique for analyzing cash flow that takes into account every dollar the investment earns per period; a measure of the worthiness of an investment. This is the discount rate that reduces all future cash flows to their present value. The HP-12C includes instructions for calculating IRR in its manual.

Investment: Money directed toward the purchase, improvement, and/or development of an asset in expectation of future income or profits.

J

Judgment: The formal decision of a court upon the respective rights and claims of the parties to a suit.

L

Land Contract: A contract for the sale of real property in which the seller retains title to the property until all or a specified portion of the purchase price has been paid. May also be called a "conditional sales contract" or "installment sales contract." The Statute of Frauds dictates that the contract must be in writing.

Lease: A written contract between a landlord (the lessor) and a tenant (the lessee) that transfers the right to exclusive possession and use of the landlord's real property to the lessee for a specific period of time and for a stated consideration (rent).

Letter of Credit: A guarantee issued by an entity guaranteeing a creditor satisfaction of a debt created by another party, should that other party fail to satisfy the debt. Most often issued by entities such as banks and other large lending institutions to guarantee payment for goods or real estate purchased on credit. It is used extensively in foreign transactions.

Lien: A debt secured by property, especially real property. A form of encumbrance that makes a specific property the security for a debt, especially mortgages, trust deeds, taxes, and judgments. It gives specified creditors the right to be paid through the sale of the property should the creditor default.

Lis Pendens: Literally, "suit pending." A notice of *lis pendens* is a legal warning placed on public record advising all who may be interested that legal action is pending in regard to the recorded document. In real estate, the notice of *lis pendens* is placed in the public record of title to a property when the title is in dispute or other legal action, such as foreclosure, has been initiated against the title or property. In most cases, you would not want to buy a mortgage on a piece of property with a notice of *lis pendens* on its title records.

Investment Analysis: See Cash-flow Analysis.

Loan-to-Value (LTV): The amount of a mortgage (or mortgages) on a property versus the current market value of the property. It is expressed as a percentage, as in: "70 percent loan-to-value (LTV)." The formula is:

$$\frac{Total\ of\ all\ Mortgages}{Current\ Market\ Value} \times 100\% = LTV$$

Lot and Block Description: A description of real property that identifies a parcel of land by reference to its lot and block numbers within a subdivision as specified on a plat of a subdivision recorded in the county recorder's office.

M

Market Value: The price at which a ready, willing, able, and informed buyer would purchase a property, where neither buyer nor seller is under pressure to act. The price a property would command in the normal market.

Marketable Title: A good and clear title, reasonably free from the risk of litigation and possible defects.

Mechanic's Lien: A lien created in favor of contractors, laborers, and materialmen who have performed work in the construction or repair of a property.

Mortgage: A conditional pledge or transfer of real estate as security for the payment of debt. Also, the document creating a mortgage lien.

Mortgage-backed Security (MBS): A security or pledge of money owed secured by a group or pool of mortgage obligations.

Mortgage Constant: A value used in conjunction with Cap Rate to determine whether there will be negative cash flow or not. It is expressed as a percentage:

$$Mortgage\ Constant\ (MC) = \frac{Annual\ Debt\ Service}{Total\ Loan\ Amount} \times 100\%$$

If the Mortgage Constant is greater than the Cap Rate, then you can expect negative cash flow. On the other hand, if it is lower than the Cap Rate, there should be a positive cash flow.

Mortgage Note: The legal and negotiable evidence of the debt created by the sale of a property on credit. A written promise to repay. It states the amount of the loan, rate of interest, repayment schedule, and other terms associated with the debt and its repayment.

Mortgage Purchase Agreement: An agreement to purchase a personally held mortgage or trust deed that can then be assigned to a buyer or purchased by the finder outright.

Mortgagee: The person or institution that lends money; the creditor. The owner (holder) of the mortgage.

Mortgagor: The borrower (or debtor, or payor); the owner of real estate purchased on credit. The person making payments on a loan.

N

Negative Cash Flow: When the expenses from real property exceed the income produced from rent(s) from that property.

Net Operating Income: The income after all fixed costs and operating expenses are deducted from the gross income.

Net Present Value: The technique of analyzing what future cash flows are worth today. It is used as a comparative method to determine which investment is more lucrative. The formula is:

Net Present Value (NPV) = Total Present Value − Initial Investment

Note: A written promise to pay a specified amount to a certain entity or person, on demand, over a specified period of time, in a specified manner.

O

Open-end Loan: A loan in which the borrower is given the right to incremental loan advances on an existing mortgage up to, but not exceeding, the original amount of the loan.

Option: The right given, for a consideration (payment), normally non-refundable, to purchase or lease a property for certain specified terms within a certain specified time. The person purchasing the option is not obligated to exercise the option, but normally will forfeit all option consideration if the option is not exercised.

P

Package: A loan on real estate that also includes personal property. Also, a group of loans considered as one unit for investment collateral purposes.

Paper: Generic term for mortgages and trust deeds when recorded, held, bought, or sold. Personally held mortgage notes and trust deeds. A purchase money mortgage.

Parcel: A specific portion of a large tract of real estate; a lot.

Plat: A map of a town, section, or subdivision indicating the location and boundaries of individual properties.

Power of Attorney: A written instrument authorizing a person to act as agent on behalf of another person to the extent indicated in the instrument.

Payback Analysis: The technique of assessing how long an investment will take to pay back the initial cash outlay.

Payback Period: The time it takes to pay back the original cash investment. This is inversely proportional to Cash-on-cash value. The formula is:

$$Payback\ Period = \frac{1}{Cash\text{-}on\text{-}cash}$$

Prepayment Penalty: A cash penalty for repayment of a debt before it comes due. If you are taking out a loan, avoid those with prepayment penalties, or negotiate a waiver of the prepayment penalty. When evaluating notes for purchase, always ask whether there is a prepayment penalty.

Prime Rate: The base rate on corporate loans posted by at least 75 percent of the nation's thirty largest banks.

Principal: The original amount (as in a loan) of the total due and payable at a certain date. In a fully amortized loan, this is the portion of the payment that is not interest. Also, a person who acts in his or her direct interest in a real estate or paper deal or other legal proceeding. In our example deal, Bill and Mary were principals when Bill bought Mary's house and she gave him the mortgage. The attorney or title company that handled the deal was not; both would be agents of the principals. In the paper deal, Bill was not a principal, but Mary, David, and John were principals.

Principal Rate Method: A method of analyzing an investment that takes into account the reduction in principal as the debt is paid off. Reduction of principal leads to equity buildup.

Private Mortgage Insurance (PMI): Private insurance on a loan made by an institutional lender that partially protects the lender in case of default by the borrower. Most banks, S&Ls, and commercial lenders require PMI on low down payment loans that are not insured by the government.

Probate: A legal process by which a court determines who will inherit a decedent's property and what the estate's assets are.

Property Manager: Someone who manages real estate for compensation for another individual.

Purchase Money Mortgage: The note and mortgage created at the time of purchase to facilitate the sale. It is usually given to the purchaser (mortgagor; borrower) by the seller (mortgagee; lender) to finance the property.

Q

Quitclaim Deed: A conveyance by which the grantor transfers whatever interest he or she has in the real estate without warranties or obligations.

R

Rate of Return: The measure of payback against the initial capital outlay for an investment.

Real Estate Contract: A contract for the purchase or sale of real property (real estate), that may or may not include certain items of personal property. The Statute of Frauds dictates that, to be enforceable, any contract for the purchase or sale of real estate must be in writing.

Recording: The placing in the public record of the county in which the property is located of any legal instrument (including mortgages) that affect the title to that property.

Recourse: The right of the holder of a mortgage or trust deed to seek compensation from the mortgagor or trustor personally, not just from the sale of the property, should the sale fail to produce enough money to satisfy the debt.

Redemption: The buying back of real estate sold at a tax sale. The defaulted owner is said to have the right of redemption to that real estate.

S

Satisfaction: The discharge of an obligation by paying a party that which is due him or her, as in paying off the full principal balance and interest of a mortgage.

Second Mortgage: A mortgage recorded after the first mortgage. A mortgage that is, because of its later recording date, subordinate or junior to the first mortgage.

Self-liquidating: A loan that is amortized over a specific period of time; at the end of that time period the loan is paid in full (assuming all payments have been made as scheduled; it does *not* mean that the loan somehow pays itself off!).

Setup: A listing of a property that shows all pertinent information, including but not limited to: rent roll, all operating expenses (broken down), and any outstanding violations or improvements.

Shared Appreciation Mortgage (SAM): A loan in which the lender, in exchange for the loan, participates in the profits the mortgagor receives when the property is sold.

Sheriff's Sale: A sale of property, conducted by a sheriff or sheriff's deputy, by virtue of the sheriff's authority to do so under the law. Usually used in reference to real estate sold as a result of a foreclosure judgment, in mortgage states. In trust deed states the equivalent action is called the *Trustee's Sale,* because the deed of trust gives the trustee authority to sell the property in default.

Simple Interest: Interest charged on a principal sum as a percentage of that principal sum. It is not compounded upon itself for further money owed, but is just paid once at the stated interest rate on the loan.

Single-payment Return: In a specific period of time, one payment is received for the total initial cash outlay. This is one type of cash flow calculated for the internal rate of return analysis.

"Subject to" Clause: A clause in the deed specifying exceptions and reservations affecting the title of the property. Also, a clause used in both real estate and paper purchase contracts stating that the agreement is "subject to" various conditions.

Subordination: Relegation to a lesser position. For example, a second mortgage is subordinate to a first mortgage.

Straight Line Cost Recovery: A method of calculating depreciation for tax purposes. It is computed by dividing the adjusted basis of the property by the estimated number of remaining years of useful life of the property. This number of years is set by the IRS. Your accountant or tax professional will make this calculation.

T

Take-out Loan: A permanent long-term mortgage loan commitment from a lender to "take out" (pay off) a short-term construction loan made by that lender or another lender when construction of a project is completed.

Term: The duration of a loan. In conventional loans, the term is usually between fifteen and thirty years.

Time Is of the Essence: A clause in a contract that requires the performance of a certain act within a specific period of time.

Title Insurance: Title insurance can benefit either the mortgagor or mortgagee, or both. Should the beneficiary suffer damages due to a clouded or false title to real estate, title insurance will compensate the damaged party to the extent of the covered damages, usually to the extent of money already paid or owed.

Torrens System: A method of evidencing title by registration with the proper public authority, usually called the *registrar*. This system began in England and was adapted by Canada and Australia. It was once used in California, but has been superceded.

Trust: A fiduciary arrangement whereby property is conveyed to a person or institution called a *trustee* to be held and administered on behalf of another person, the *beneficiary*. The one who conveys the trust is the *trustor*.

Trust Deed: An instrument used to create a mortgage lien by which the mortgagor conveys his or her title to a trustee, who holds it as security for the benefit of the promissory note holder (the lender). Also called a *deed of trust*.

Trustee: The neutral third party, in a trust deed state, which is the person or entity holding title to property in trust for the benefit of a lending institution or person, as security for repayment of the debt by the trustor (borrower), in order to purchase the real estate in question.

Trustor: In a trust deed state, the purchaser of real property; the borrower. The title to the property is placed in trust until the debt is satisfied.

Trust Deed: In many states and in the District of Columbia, a trust deed or deed of trust is the legal document by which a borrower pledges certain real estate as a guarantee for the repayment of a loan. It is a recordable instrument, like a mortgage. It serves a function similar to that of a mortgage in a mortgage state, but differs in a number of respects, including the use of a neutral third party, the trustee, to hold the note. In a mortgage state, when the borrower fails to pay, foreclosure is a legal proceeding in the courts, and a court judgment is issued for the sale of the property. In a trust deed state, the trustee has the power of sale.

Tax Bracket: The percentage of ordinary income taxed by the government.

U

Usury: Charging interest on a loan at higher rate than the maximum established by law.

V

VA (VA Loans): The Veterans' Administration, the federal agency that guarantees VA loans—loans made to people who have served in the U.S. armed forces, and certain dependents or survivors, to enable them to purchase homes for little or no money down, with relatively easy qualification terms and a comparatively low rate of interest. VA loans are similar in principle to FHA financing, but the details are different.

Variable Rate of Return: In a specific period of time, the cash flow from an investment that is not a constant value but varies over time. This is one type of income stream that the internal rate of return calculates for.

Variable Rate Mortgage: A mortgage loan in which the interest rate may increase or decrease at specified intervals. It is usually based on an outside index, such as U.S. Treasury bills or the cost of funds in the local Federal Reserve District. Also called an ARM (Adjusta-ble-rate Mortgage). There are other variations on this basic idea, each with their own name.

Variance: Permission obtained from zoning authorities to build a structure or conduct a use that is prohibited by the current zoning laws.

Vendee: A buyer (in Canada).

Vendor: A seller (in Canada).

W

Warranty Deed: A deed in which the grantor fully warrants good, clear title to the premises. The warranty deed offers the greatest protection of any deed.

Wraparound: A loan in which a lender places a new loan on a parcel of real estate that already has an existing first mortgage. The lender's new mortgage is in a secondary or subordinate position to the ex-isting first mortgage. The new mortgage wraps around the unpaid principal balance of the first mortgage and whatever amount the lender advances to the borrower as part of the wraparound mort-gage.

Y

Yield: Return on investment. The actual percentage (interest rate) earned on an investment. The term "discount to yield" is used in paper investments.

Yield-to-Maturity (YTM): The return on investment expressed as a percentage per year seen over the life of the loan.

Appendices 1 and 2 Amortization Schedules

Appendix 1 is the full amortization schedule for Bill's mortgage from Mary. The amount borrowed is $80,000 over 30 years with monthly payments of $775.00. The interest rate charged is 11.22%. The schedule is of the amount of interest and principal paid each month. The remaining principal is the balance on the loan at that point in time. For example, if a sale of the property took place on the 91st payment, the balance owing would be $76,152.81.

Appendix 2 is between David and Mary, whereby David bought a partial from Mary. David bought the next 36 payments of $775.00 from Mary and recorded a partial assignment of mortgage. This amortization schedule is an entire schedule for all payments, where the starting balance is $23,597.11, which self-amortizes down to zero principal remaining after the 36th payment has been made.

As an example of early payoff, let's say Bill sells the property in June of 1989. Who owes what to whom? Bill pays Mary $79,070.07 (as per Bill and Mary's amortization schedule) of which Mary pays David $12,784.49 (as per David and Mary's amortization schedule).

Appendix 1

	Mortgage Amount	=	80,000.00	BUYER: Bill
	Monthly payment	=	775.00	SELLER: Mary
	# of Months	=	360	ADDRESS: Any Street
	% Interest	=	11.220	CITY: Any City ZIP:_____

Payment Number	Date	Remaining Principal	Monthly Payment	Principal Payment	Interest Payment
1	01/87	79,973.00	775.00	27.00	748.00
2	02/87	79,945.79	775.00	27.25	747.75
3	03/87	79,918.24	775.00	27.51	747.49
4	04/87	79,890.49	775.00	27.76	747.24
5	05/87	79,862.47	775.00	28.02	746.98
6	06/87	79,834.18	775.00	28.29	746.71
7	07/87	79,805.64	775.00	28.55	746.45
8	08/87	79,776.82	775.00	28.82	746.18
9	09/87	79,747.73	775.00	29.09	745.91
10	10/87	79,718.37	775.00	29.36	745.64
11	11/87	79,688.74	775.00	29.63	745.37
12	12/87	79,658.84	775.00	29.91	745.09
Totals For 1987			9,300.00	341.19	8,958.81
13	01/88	79,628.66	775.00	30.19	744.81
14	02/88	79,598.19	775.00	30.47	744.53
15	03/88	79,567.43	775.00	30.76	744.24
16	04/88	79,536.39	775.00	31.04	743.96
17	05/88	79,505.06	775.00	31.33	743.67
18	06/88	79,473.43	775.00	31.63	743.37
19	07/88	79,441.51	775.00	31.92	743.08
20	08/88	79,409.29	775.00	32.22	742.78
21	09/88	79,376.77	775.00	32.52	742.48
22	10/88	79,343.95	775.00	32.83	742.17
23	11/88	79,310.82	775.00	33.13	741.87
24	12/88	79,277.39	775.00	33.44	741.56
Totals for 1988			9,300.00	381.48	8,918.52
25	01/89	79,243.64	775.00	33.76	741.24
26	02/89	79,209.57	775.00	34.07	740.93
27	03/89	79,175.18	775.00	34.39	740.61
28	04/89	79,140.47	775.00	34.71	740.29
29	05/89	79,105.43	775.00	35.04	739.96
30	06/89	79,070.07	775.00	35.36	739.64
31	07/89	79,034.39	775.00	35.69	739.31
32	08/89	78,998.36	775.00	36.03	738.97
33	09/89	78,961.99	775.00	36.37	738.63
34	10/89	78,925.28	775.00	36.71	738.29
35	11/89	78,888.24	775.00	37.05	737.95
36	12/89	78,850.85	775.00	37.39	737.61
Totals for 1989			9,300.00	426.57	8,873.43
37	01/90	78,813.11	775.00	37.74	737.26
38	02/90	78,775.01	775.00	38.10	736.90

39	03/90	78,736.56	775.00	38.45	736.50
40	04/90	78,697.75	775.00	38.81	736.19
41	05/90	78,658.57	775.00	39.18	735.82
42	06/90	78,619.03	775.00	39.54	735.46
43	07/90	78,579.13	775.00	39.91	735.09
44	08/90	78,538.85	775.00	40.29	734.71
45	09/90	78,498.20	775.00	40.66	734.34
46	10/90	78,457.17	775.00	41.04	733.96
47	11/90	78,415.74	775.00	41.43	733.57
48	12/90	78,373.93	775.00	41.81	733.19
Totals For 1990			9,300.00	476.96	8,823.04
49	01/91	77,331.73	775.00	42.20	732.80
50	02/91	77,289.13	775.00	42.60	732.40
51	03/91	77,246.14	775.00	43.00	732.00
52	04/91	77,202.74	775.00	43.40	731.60
53	05/91	77,158.95	775.00	43.80	731.20
54	06/91	77,114.74	775.00	44.21	730.79
55	07/91	77,070.11	775.00	44.63	730.37
56	08/91	77,025.07	775.00	45.04	729.96
57	09/91	77,979.60	775.00	45.47	729.53
58	10/91	77,933.71	775.00	45.89	729.11
59	11/91	77,887.39	775.00	46.32	728.68
60	12/91	77,840.64	775.00	46.75	728.25
Totals for 1991			9,300.00	533.31	8,766.69
61	01/92	77,793.46	775.00	47.19	727.81
62	02/92	77,745.83	775.00	47.63	727.37
63	03/92	77,697.75	775.00	48.08	726.92
64	04/92	77,649.22	775.00	48.53	726.47
65	05/92	77,600.24	775.00	48.98	726.02
66	06/92	77,550.81	775.00	49.44	725.56
67	07/92	77,500.92	775.00	49.90	725.10
68	08/92	77,450.56	775.00	50.37	724.63
69	09/92	77,399.72	775.00	50.84	724.16
70	10/92	77,348.41	775.00	51.31	723.69
71	11/92	77,296.62	775.00	51.79	723.21
72	12/92	77,244.34	775.00	52.28	722.72
Totals for 1992			9,300.00	596.34	8,703.66
73	01/93	77,191.57	775.00	52.77	722.23
74	02/93	77,138.31	775.00	53.26	721.74
75	03/93	77,084.56	775.00	53.76	721.24
76	04/93	77,030.31	775.00	54.26	720.74
77	05/93	76,975.54	775.00	54.77	720.23
78	06/93	76,920.26	775.00	55.28	719.72
79	07/93	76,864.46	775.00	55.80	719.20
80	08/93	76,808.14	775.00	56.32	718.68
81	09/93	76,751.30	775.00	56.84	718.16
82	10/93	76,693.92	775.00	57.38	717.62
83	11/93	76,636.02	775.00	57.91	717.09
84	12/93	76,577.57	775.00	58.45	716.55
Totals For 1993			9,300.00	666.80	8,633.20
85	01/94	76,518.57	775.00	59.00	716.00
86	02/94	76,459.03	775.00	59.55	715.45
87	03/94	76,398.92	775.00	60.11	714.89
88	04/94	76,338.25	775.00	60.67	714.33
89	05/94	76,277.01	775.00	61.24	713.76
90	06/94	76,215.20	775.00	61.81	713.19
91	07/94	76,152.81	775.00	62.39	712.61
92	08/94	76,089.85	775.00	62.97	712.03
93	09/94	76,026.29	775.00	63.56	711.44
94	10/94	75,962.14	775.00	64.15	710.85
95	11/94	75,897.39	775.00	64.75	710.25

96	12/94	75,832.03	775.00	65.36	709.64
Totals For 1994			9,300.00	745.56	8,554.44
97	01/95	75,766.06	775.00	65.97	709.03
98	02/95	75,699.47	775.00	66.59	708.41
99	03/95	75,632.26	775.00	67.21	707.79
100	04/95	75,564.42	775.00	67.84	707.16
101	05/95	75,495.96	775.00	68.47	706.53
102	06/55	75,426.85	775.00	69.11	705.89
103	07/95	75,357.10	775.00	69.76	705.24
104	08/95	75,286.70	775.00	70.41	704.59
105	09/95	75,215.64	775.00	71.07	703.93
106	10/95	75,143.92	775.00	71.73	703.27
107	11/95	75,071.53	775.00	72.40	702.60
108	12/95	74,998.46	775.00	73.08	701.92
Totals for 1995			9,300.00	833.64	8,466.36
109	01/96	74,924.71	775.00	73.76	701.24
110	02/96	74,850.26	775.00	74.45	700.55
111	03/96	74,775.11	775.00	75.15	699.85
112	04/96	74,699.26	775.00	75.85	699.15
113	05/96	74,622.70	775.00	76.56	698.44
114	06/96	74,545.42	775.00	77.28	697.72
115	07/96	74,467.42	775.00	78.00	697.00
116	08/96	74,388.70	775.00	78.73	696.27
117	09/96	74,309.24	775.00	79.47	695.53
118	10/96	74,229.03	775.00	80.21	694.79
119	11/96	74,148.07	775.00	80.96	694.04
120	12/96	74,066.35	775.00	81.72	693.28
Totals for 1996			9,300.00	932.14	8,367.86
121	01/97	73,983.88	775.00	82.48	692.52
122	09/97	73,900.64	775.00	83.25	691.75
123	03/97	73,816.61	775.00	84.03	690.97
124	04/97	73,731.80	775.00	84.81	690.19
125	05/97	73,646.19	775.00	85.61	689.39
126	06/97	73,559.78	775.00	86.41	688.59
127	07/97	73,472.56	775.00	87.22	687.78
128	08/97	73,384.53	775.00	88.03	686.97
129	09/97	73,295.68	775.00	88.85	686.15
130	10/97	73,205.99	775.00	89.69	685.31
131	11/97	73,115.47	775.00	90.52	684.48
132	12/97	73,024.10	775.00	91.37	683.63
Totals For 1997			9,300.00	1,042.27	8,257.73
133	01/98	72,931.89	775.00	92.22	682.78
134	02/98	72,838.80	775.00	93.09	681.91
135	03/98	72,744.84	775.00	93.96	681.04
136	04/98	72,650.00	775.00	94.84	680.16
137	05/98	72,554.28	775.00	95.72	679.28
138	06/98	72,457.67	775.00	96.62	678.38
139	07/98	72,360.15	775.00	97.52	677.48
140	08/98	72,261.72	775.00	98.43	676.57
141	09/98	72,162.37	775.00	99.35	675.65
142	10/98	72,062.09	775.00	100.28	674.72
143	11/98	72,960.88	775.00	101.22	673.78
144	12/98	71,858.71	775.00	102.17	672.83
Totals for 1998			9,300.00	1,165.42	8,134.58
145	01/99	71,755.60	775.00	103.12	671.88
146	02/99	71,651.51	775.00	104.09	670.91
147	03/99	71,546.45	775.00	105.06	669.94
148	04/99	71,440.42	775.00	106.04	668.96
149	05/99	71,333.39	775.00	107.03	667.97
150	06/99	71,225.36	775.00	108.03	666.97

151	07/99	71,116.32	775.00	109.04	665.96
152	08/99	71,006.26	775.00	110.06	664.94
153	09/99	70,895.17	775.00	111.09	663.91
154	10/99	70,783.04	775.00	112.13	662.87
155	11/99	70,669.86	775.00	113.18	661.82
156	12/99	70,555.62	775.00	114.24	660.76
Totals for 1999			9,300.00	1,303.11	7,996.89
157	01/00	70,440.32	775.00	115.30	659.70
158	02/00	70,323.94	775.00	116.38	658.62
159	03/00	70,206.47	775.00	117.47	657.53
160	04/00	70,087.90	775.00	118.57	656.43
161	05/00	69,968.22	775.00	119.68	655.32
162	06/00	69,847.42	775.00	120.80	654.20
163	07/00	69,725.49	775.00	121.93	653.07
164	08/00	69,602.42	775.00	123.07	651.93
165	09/00	69,478.21	775.00	124.22	650.78
166	10/00	69,352.83	775.00	125.38	649.62
167	11/00	69,226.28	775.00	126.55	648.45
168	12/00	69,098.56	775.00	127.73	647.27
Totals for 2000			9,300.00	1,457.08	7,842.92
169	01/01	68,969.64	775.00	128.93	646.07
170	02/01	68,839.51	775.00	130.13	644.87
171	03/01	68,708.16	775.00	131.35	643.65
172	04/01	68,575.58	775.00	132.58	642.42
173	05/01	68,441.76	775.00	133.82	641.18
174	06/01	68,306.69	775.00	135.07	639.93
175	07/01	68,170.36	775.00	136.33	638.67
176	08/01	68,032.75	775.00	137.61	637.39
177	09/01	67,893.86	775.00	138.89	636.11
178	10/01	67,753.67	775.00	140.19	634.81
179	11/01	67,612.17	775.00	141.50	633.50
180	12/01	67,469.35	775.00	142.83	632.17
Totals for 2001			9,300.00	1,629.23	7,670.77
181	01/02	67,325.20	775.00	144.16	630.84
182	02/02	67,179.70	775.00	145.51	629.49
183	03/02	67,032.84	775.00	146.87	628.13
184	04/02	66,884.60	775.00	148.24	626.76
185	05/02	66,734.97	775.00	149.63	625.37
186	06/02	66,583.94	775.00	151.03	623.97
187	07/02	66,431.50	775.00	152.44	622.56
188	08/02	66,277.64	775.00	153.87	621.13
189	09/02	66,122.35	775.00	155.30	619.70
190	10/02	65,965.60	775.00	156.76	618.24
191	11/02	65,807.39	775.00	158.22	616.78
192	12/02	65,647.69	775.00	159.70	615.30
Totals for 2002			9,300.00	1,821.73	7,478.27
193	01/03	65,486.50	775.00	161.19	613.81
194	02/03	65,323.80	775.00	162.70	612.30
195	03/03	65,159.58	775.00	164.22	610.78
196	04/03	64,993.82	775.00	165.76	609.24
197	05/03	64,826.51	775.00	167.31	607.69
198	06/03	64,657.64	775.00	168.87	606.13
199	07/03	64,487.19	775.00	170.45	604.55
200	08/03	64,315.15	775.00	172.04	602.96
201	09/03	64,141.50	775.00	173.65	601.35
202	10/03	63,966.22	775.00	175.28	599.72
203	11/03	63,789.30	775.00	176.92	598.08
204	12/03	63,610.73	775.00	178.57	596.43
Totals for 2003			9,300.00	2,036.96	7,263.04
205	01/04	63,430.49	775.00	180.24	594.76

206	02/04	63,248.57	775.00	181.92	593.08
207	03/04	63,064.94	775.00	183.92	591.37
208	04/04	62,879.60	775.00	185.34	589.66
209	05/04	62,692.53	775.00	187.08	587.92
210	06/04	62,503.71	775.00	188.82	586.18
211	07/04	62,313.12	775.00	190.59	584.41
212	08/04	62,120.75	775.00	192.37	582.63
213	09/04	61,926.58	775.00	194.17	580.83
214	10/04	61,730.59	775.00	195.99	579.01
215	11/04	61,532.77	775.00	197.82	577.18
216	12/04	61,333.10	775.00	199.67	575.33
Totals for 2004			9,300.00	2,277.64	7,022.36
217	01/05	61,131.56	775.00	201.54	573.46
218	02/05	60,928.14	775.00	203.42	571.58
219	03/05	60,722.82	775.00	205.32	569.68
220	04/05	60,515.58	775.00	207.24	567.76
221	05/05	60,306.40	775.00	209.18	565.82
222	06/05	60,095.26	775.00	211.14	563.86
223	07/05	59,882.15	775.00	213.11	561.89
224	08/05	59,667.05	775.00	215.10	559.90
225	09/05	59,449.94	775.00	217.11	557.89
226	10/05	59,230.80	775.00	219.14	555.86
227	11/05	59,009.61	775.00	221.19	553.81
228	12/05	58,786.35	775.00	223.26	551.74
Totals for 2005			9,300.00	2,546.76	6,753.25
229	01/06	58,561.00	775.00	225.35	549.65
230	02/06	58,333.55	775.00	227.45	547.55
231	03/06	58,103.98	775.00	229.58	545.42
232	04/06	57,872.25	775.00	231.73	543.27
233	05/06	57,638.36	775.00	233.89	541.11
234	06/06	57,402.28	775.00	236.08	538.92
235	07/06	57,163.99	775.00	238.29	536.71
236	08/06	56,923.47	775.00	240.52	534.48
237	09/06	56,680.70	775.00	242.77	532.23
238	10/06	56,435.66	775.00	245.04	529.96
239	11/06	56,188.33	775.00	247.33	527.67
240	12/06	55,938.69	775.00	249.64	525.36
Totals for 2006			9,300.00	2,847.67	6,452.33
241	01/07	55,686.73	775.00	251.97	523.03
242	02/07	55,432.40	775.00	254.33	520.67
243	03/07	55,175.69	775.00	256.71	518.29
244	04/07	54,916.58	775.00	259.11	515.89
245	05/07	54,655.05	775.00	261.53	513.47
246	06/07	54,391.07	775.00	263.98	511.02
247	07/07	54,124.63	775.00	266.44	508.56
248	08/07	53,855.70	775.00	268.93	506.07
249	09/07	53,584.25	775.00	271.45	503.55
250	10/07	53,310.26	775.00	273.99	501.01
251	11/07	53,033.71	775.00	276.55	498.45
252	12/07	52,754.58	775.00	279.13	495.87
Totals for 2007			9,300.00	3,184.12	6,115.88
253	01/08	52,472.84	775.00	281.74	493.26
254	02/08	52,188.46	775.00	284.38	490.62
255	03/08	51,901.42	775.00	287.04	487.96
256	04/08	51,611.71	775.00	289.72	485.28
257	05/08	51,319.28	775.00	292.43	482.57
258	06/08	51,024.12	775.00	295.16	479.84
259	07/08	50,726.20	775.00	297.92	477.08
260	08/08	50,425.49	775.00	300.71	474.29
261	09/08	50,121.97	775.00	303.52	471.48
262	10/08	49,815.61	775.00	306.36	468.64
263	11/08	49,506.39	775.00	309.22	465.78

264	12/08	49,194.27	775.00	312.12	462.88
Totals for 2008			9,300.00	3,560.32	5,739.68
265	01/09	48,879.24	775.00	315.03	459.97
266	02/09	48,561.26	775.00	317.98	457.02
267	03/09	48,240.31	775.00	320.95	454.05
268	04/09	47,916.36	775.00	323.95	451.05
269	05/09	47,589.38	775.00	326.98	448.02
270	06/09	47,259.34	775.00	330.08	444.96
271	07/09	46,926.21	775.00	333.13	441.87
272	08/09	46,589.08	775.00	336.24	438.76
273	09/09	46,250.60	775.00	339.38	435.62
274	10/09	45,908.05	775.00	342.56	432.44
275	11/09	45,562.29	775.00	345.76	429.24
276	12/09	45,213.30	775.00	348.99	426.01
Totals for 2009			9,300.00	2,980.99	5,319.01
277	01/10	44,861.04	775.00	352.26	422.74
278	02/10	44,505.49	775.00	355.55	419.45
279	03/10	44,146.62	775.00	358.87	416.13
280	04/10	43,784.39	775.00	362.23	412.77
281	05/10	43,418.77	775.00	365.62	409.38
282	06/10	43,049.74	775.00	369.03	405.97
283	07/10	42,677.26	775.00	372.48	402.52
284	08/10	42,301.30	775.00	375.97	399.03
285	09/10	41,921.82	775.00	379.48	395.52
286	10/10	41,538.79	775.00	383.03	391.97
287	11/10	41,152.18	775.00	386.61	388.39
288	12/10	40,761.95	775.00	390.23	384.77
Totals for 2010			9,300.00	4,451.36	4,848.64
289	01/11	40,368.07	775.00	393.88	381.12
290	02/11	39,970.51	775.00	397.56	377.44
291	03/11	39,569.23	775.00	401.28	373.72
292	04/11	39,164.20	775.00	405.03	369.97
293	05/11	38,755.39	775.00	408.81	366.19
294	06/11	38,342.75	775.00	412.64	362.36
295	07/11	37,926.25	775.00	416.50	358.50
296	08/11	37,505.86	775.00	420.39	354.61
297	09/11	37,081.54	775.00	424.32	350.68
298	10/11	36,653.25	775.00	428.29	346.71
299	11/11	36,220.96	775.00	432.29	342.71
300	12/11	35,784.63	775.00	436.33	338.67
Totals for 2011			9,300.00	4,977.32	4,322.68
301	01/12	35,344.22	775.00	440.41	334.59
302	02/12	34,899.69	775.00	444.53	330.47
303	03/12	34,451.00	775.00	448.69	326.31
304	04/12	33,998.12	775.00	452.88	322.12
305	05/12	33,541.00	775.00	457.12	317.88
306	06/12	33,079.61	775.00	461.39	313.61
307	07/12	32,613.90	775.00	465.71	309.29
308	08/12	32,143.84	775.00	470.06	304.94
309	09/12	31,669.38	775.00	474.46	300.54
310	10/12	31,190.49	775.00	478.89	296.11
311	11/12	30,707.12	775.00	483.37	291.63
312	12/12	30,219.23	775.00	487.89	287.11
Totals for 2012			9,300.00	5,565.40	3,734.60
313	01/13	29,726.78	775.00	492.45	282.55
314	02/13	29,229.73	775.00	497.05	277.95
315	03/13	28,728.03	775.00	501.70	273.30
316	04/13	28,221.64	775.00	506.39	268.61
317	05/13	27,710.51	775.00	511.13	263.87
318	06/13	27,194.60	775.00	515.91	259.09

319	07/13	26,673.87	775.00	520.73	254.27
320	08/13	26,148.27	775.00	525.60	249.40
321	09/13	25,617.76	775.00	530.51	244.49
322	10/13	25,082.29	775.00	535.47	239.53
323	11/13	24,541.81	775.00	540.48	234.52
324	12/13	23,996.28	775.00	545.53	229.47
Totals for 2013			9,300.00	6,222.95	3,077.09
325	01/14	23,445.65	775.00	550.63	224.37
326	02/14	22,889.87	775.00	555.78	219.22
327	03/14	22,328.89	775.00	560.98	214.02
328	04/14	21,762.67	775.00	566.22	208.78
329	05/14	21,191.15	775.00	571.22	203.48
330	06/14	20,614.29	775.00	576.86	198.14
331	07/14	20,032.03	775.00	582.26	192.74
332	08/14	19,444.33	775.00	587.70	187.30
333	09/14	18,851.13	775.00	593.20	181.80
334	10/14	18,252.39	775.00	598.74	176.26
335	11/14	17,648.05	775.00	604.34	170.66
336	12/14	17,038.06	775.00	609.99	165.01
Totals for 2014			9,300.00	6,958.22	2,341.78
337	01/15	16,422.37	775.00	615.69	159.11
338	02/15	15,800.92	775.00	621.45	153.55
339	03/15	15,173.66	775.00	627.46	147.74
340	04/15	14,540.53	775.00	633.13	141.87
341	05/15	13,901.48	775.00	639.05	135.95
342	06/15	13,256.46	775.00	645.02	129.98
343	07/15	12,605.41	775.00	651.05	123.95
344	08/15	11,948.27	775.00	657.14	117.86
345	09/15	11,284.99	775.00	663.28	111.72
346	10/15	10,615.50	775.00	669.49	105.51
347	11/15	9,939.75	775.00	675.75	99.25
348	12/15	9,257.69	775.00	682.06	92.94
Totals for 2015			9,300.00	7,780.37	1,519.63
349	01/16	8,569.25	775.00	615.69	159.11
350	02/16	7,874.37	775.00	621.45	153.55
351	03/16	7,173.00	775.00	627.46	147.74
352	04/16	6,465.07	775.00	633.13	141.87
353	05/16	5,750.52	775.00	639.05	135.95
354	06/16	5,029.29	775.00	645.02	129.98
355	07/16	4,301.31	775.00	651.05	123.95
356	08/16	3,566.53	775.00	657.14	117.86
357	09/16	2,824.88	775.00	663.28	111.72
358	10/16	2,076.29	775.00	669.49	105.51
359	11/16	1,320.70	775.00	675.75	99.25
360	12/16	0.00	775.00	682.06	92.94
Totals for 2016			9,858.05	9,257.69	600.36
Grand Totals			279,558.06	80,000.00	199,557.39

Appendix 2

Mortgage Amount	=	23,597.11	BUYER: David
Monthly payment	=	775.00	SELLER: Mary
# of Months	=	36	ADDRESS: Any Street
% Interest	=	11.220	CITY: Any City
			STATE; USA: ZIP:_____

Payment Number	Date	Remaining Principal	Monthly Payment	Principal Payment	Interest Payment
1	01/88	23,042.74	775.00	554.37	748.00
2	02/88	23,042.74	775.00	559.55	747.75
3	03/88	21,918.41	775.00	564.78	747.49
4	04/88	21,348.35	775.00	570.06	747.24
5	05/88	20,772.96	775.00	575.39	746.98
6	06/88	20,192.19	775.00	580.77	746.71
7	07/88	19,605.99	775.00	586.20	746.45
8	08/88	19,014.31	775.00	591.68	746.18
9	09/88	18,417.09	775.00	597.22	745.91
10	10/88	17,814.29	775.00	602.80	745.64
11	11/88	17,205.85	775.00	608.44	745.37
12	12/88	16,591.72	775.00	614.13	745.09
Totals For 1988			9,300.00	7,005.39	2,294.61
13	01/89	15,971.85	775.00	619.87	155.13
14	02/89	15,346.19	775.00	625.66	149.34
15	03/89	14,714.68	775.00	631.51	143.49
16	04/89	14,077.26	775.00	637.42	137.58
17	05/89	13,433.88	775.00	643.38	131.62
18	06/89	12,784.49	775.00	649.39	125.61
19	07/89	12,129.02	775.00	655.47	119.53
20	08/89	11,467.43	775.00	661.59	113.41
21	09/89	10,799.65	775.00	667.78	107.22
22	10/89	10,125.63	775.00	674.02	100.98
23	11/89	9,445.30	775.00	680.33	94.67
24	12/89	8,758.61	775.00	686.69	88.31
Totals for 1989			9,300.00	7,833.11	1,466.89
25	01/90	8,065.50	775.00	693.11	81.89
26	02/90	7,365.91	775.00	699.59	75.41
27	03/90	6,659.78	775.00	706.13	68.87
28	04/90	5,947.05	775.00	712.73	62.27
29	05/90	5,227.65	775.00	719.40	55.60
30	06/90	4,501.53	775.00	726.12	48.88
31	07/90	3,768.62	775.00	732.91	42.09
32	08/90	3,028.86	775.00	739.76	35.24
33	09/90	2,282.18	775.00	746.68	28.32
34	10/90	1,528.52	775.00	753.66	21.34
35	11/90	767.81	775.00	760.71	14.29
36	12/90	0.00	774.99	767.81	7.18
Totals For 1990			9,299.99	8,758.61	541.38
Grand Totals			27,899.99	23,597.11	4,302.88

Appendix 3
Mortgage Worksheet

Date _____ Name _____ Phone # ___

Property Information

Property Location:_____

Property Type:_____

Owner Occupied _____ Rental _____ Commercial _____

Sales Date: _____

Sales Price: $_____

Down Payment: $_____

First Mtg.: $_____

Second Mtg.: $_____

Mortgage Information

Date of Mtg.:   _____

Position: 1st_____ 2nd_____ other_____

Amount: $_____

Term in Months: _____

Payment Amount: $_____

Balloon Date: _____

Balloon Amount: $_____

Interest Rate: _____

Date 1st Pmt: _____

No. Pmt Made: _____

No. Pmt. Remain: _____

Next Pmt Due: _____

Current Balance: $_____

Full $_____

_____Pmts $_____   Balance $_____

_____Pmts $_____   Balance $_____

_____Pmts $_____   Balance $_____

Appendix 4
Canadian Interest
Conversion Chart

Most mortgages in Canada have their interest payments calculated with compounding half-yearly, not in advance. The U.S. calculations are based upon monthly compounding. Therefore, the effective interest rates will be different.

John Stefanchik uses, in his book, monthly compounding. Using Canadian amortization tables to check calculations will produce different results.

The following table converts interest rates between Canada and U.S. (to nearest three decimal places):

Canada	U.S.A.
10.000	9.798
10.211	10.000
11.000	10.756
11.255	11.000
12.000	11.711
12.304	12.000
13.000	12.661
13.357	13.000
14.000	13.608
14.415	14.000
15.000	14.552
15.477	15.000
16.000	15.491
16.543	16.000
17.000	16.427
17.614	17.000

18.000	17.360
18.689	18.000
19.000	18.289
19.768	19.000
20.000	19.214
20.852	20.000

If your calculator is not preset for Canadian mortgage calculations, you will find the technique for converting your financial calculator to Canadian compounding is easily and quickly learned through repetition and practice.

Index